Islamic Ethics

Islamic Ethics

Fundamental Aspects of Human Conduct

ABDULAZIZ SACHEDINA

OXFORD
UNIVERSITY PRESS

OXFORD
UNIVERSITY PRESS

Oxford University Press is a department of the University of Oxford. It furthers the University's objective of excellence in research, scholarship, and education by publishing worldwide. Oxford is a registered trade mark of Oxford University Press in the UK and certain other countries.

Published in the United States of America by Oxford University Press
198 Madison Avenue, New York, NY 10016, United States of America.

Library of Congress Control Number: 2021941267

ISBN 978–0–19–758181–0

DOI: 10.1093/oso/9780197581810.001.0001

1 3 5 7 9 8 6 4 2

Printed by LSC communications, United States of America

To
my teachers
and
my students
over the
past sixty years

This book was commissioned as part of the Contending Modernities Initiative at the University of Notre Dame, and supported by a grant to Contending Modernities and its Science and the Human Person working group by the Henry Luce Foundation.

Contents

Acknowledgments ix

1. Introduction 1
2. In Search of a Comprehensive Definition of Ethics 17
3. The Genesis of Moral Reasoning in Religious Ethics 50
4. Scriptural Sources of Ethical Methodology 89
5. Natural Law and Ethical Necessity 120
6. The Ethics of Interpretive Jurisprudence 153

Epilogue 180

Notes 185
Select Bibliography 203
Index 209

Acknowledgments

This inquiry in Islamic ethics is the result of years of study in Islamic philosophical theology (*kalām*), jurisprudence (*fiqh*), and applied ethics (*akhlāq*). My published studies have so far treated disparate indicators of ethical consideration and application in Islamic religious thought and practice.[1] My earliest education in the academic study of Islam, which mainly constituted the evolution of historiography and religious-social institutions that indicated religious and legal practice in the early community, inspired me to discover the ethical discourse in Islam about which there was hardly any reference in the Orientalist scholarship focused on philological and literary examination of religious lore preserved in the Qur'an and the tradition. While Western scholarship concentrated on discussing the legal aspects of Islamic sources to guide everyday human activity, there was hardly any reference to the Qur'anic stance on morality or ethics as an important resource to guide human conduct in the highly religious and spiritual milieu of Islamic revelation. Islamic tradition was frequently described as legalistic in its approach to determine the licit from illicit aspects of human acts. My own readings of religious sources suggested a far more intricate relationship between legal and ethical components of Islamic orthopraxy. In view of that, all my published studies have discussed Islamic ethics in different contexts. I have identified this academic project as "ethicization"[2] of strictly theological and juridical discourses in Islam. The arguments developed in the present work refer to all my earlier publications that led me to call attention to the moral nature of religious thought in Islam. Additionally, the present study embarks on synthesizing my studies in theology and jurisprudence, which, in turn, will bring juridical theology and Islamic ethics into conversation.

My academic interest in ethics has been in working for many years. I was determined to present well-researched and well-thought-out theses about locating the possibility of Islamic ethics in Islamic interpretive jurisprudence—the "ethicization" enterprise. A major inspiration for this project of relating ethical reasoning to jurisprudence was provided by Richard M. Frank's indicative observation about moral obligation in Sunni theology. In that book he underscores the importance of expounding ethics in interpretive jurisprudence that undertakes to elaborate Islamic scriptural sources as they connect to fundamental aspects of comprehensive human conduct.[3] At different times during this intellectual journey I have engaged my colleagues in the West and in many parts of the Muslim world, more particularly in Najaf, Iraq, and Mashhad, Iran. My engagement with the latter group of scholars was to explore and expound a number of questions that are now relatively competently answered to support the main thesis of the book, namely, that Islamic ethics is not only integral to the development of juridical methodology and extrapolation of vast numbers of judicial opinions related to social ethics; it is also a critical component of the entire religious worldview presented by the Qur'an. Any shortcoming in my appraisal of ethical issues related to human relations is mine.

I have dedicated this book to all my teachers and a number of my students who during these six decades have directed my research interests and critiqued my published works, assisting me to sharpen my thought regarding Islamic ethics. Obviously, without intellectually stimulating conversations with my colleagues, among them James Childress, David Novak, David Little, and Charles Mathewes, all experts in ethics at the University of Virginia, I would have been deprived of the fundamental comprehension of the extent of moral reasoning and the ways in which it has shaped secular modernity and its ethical backdrop.

My commitment to work on the relationship between law and ethics emerged in my intellectual interactions with colleagues working on the Contending Modernities Initiative at the University of Notre Dame. Scott Appleby and Ebrahim Moosa supported the project by becoming the critical interlocutors for stimulating and adjusting the rough edges of this research. Under Scott Appleby's direction this book was commissioned as part of this initiative and supported by a grant to Contending Modernities and its Science and the Human Person working group by the Henry Luce Foundation. There are a number of colleagues in Iraq and Iran who provided highly appreciated hospitality during my sojourn in 2014–15. Without their support this research would not have achieved its goal. I need to acknowledge at least three colleagues in Najaf: Dr. Hassan Nadhem, director of UNESCO Chair in Interreligious Studies; Professor Dr. Aqeel A. Mubdir Alkhaqani, dean of the Faculty of Arts; and Professor Dr. Akeel Abed Yasseen, president of the University of Kufa, Najaf. In Iran, Dr. Mohammedreza Hashemi, vice president for academic affairs, and Dr. Ali Yousofi, vice president for sociocultural affairs, at Ferdowsi University of Mashhad, provided valuable help in locating research assistants and accessing the resourceful libraries connected with the shrine in Mashhad and Qom.

At my home institution, the College of Social Sciences and Humanities and the provost's office at George Mason University supported the project in comparative ethics by granting me research leave. Becky Hartley's team from the Office of Research Integrity and Assurance provided the critical guidance and paperwork that took care of the compliance requirements for traveling to Iraq and Iran.

At Oxford University Press, Cynthia Read, with whom I have worked on all my OUP publications since 1988, gave enormous support to enable smooth publication of this volume.

1
Introduction

The present study on Islamic ethics comes at almost the end of my career in academia. Since my days of undergraduate studies in India, Iran, and Iraq, the question of the relation between religion and ethics—revelation and reason—has been on my list of "things to do." From all that I had studied in my history, philosophy, and Islamic studies courses I was confident that there existed a far-reaching relation between religion and ethics in Islamic tradition. My graduate work in Islamic studies further confirmed the contours of the debate among Muslim scholars who often deliberated about the priority of locating ethics as a fundamental source for deriving epistemic guidelines about human conduct. Historically, the critical question for Muslim religious thought has been to establish a logical epistemological relation between the two fields of law and ethics to demonstrate a cognitively undeniable correlation between reason and revelation in derivation of authoritative orthopraxy. The controversial aspect of this attempt to affiliate law and ethics was whether such a relationship could be shown to be solely the product of a religious worldview firmly founded upon scriptural authority, or whether it was possible to guide human moral conduct without reference to any revelatory sources. In other words, was the emerging idea about the correlation between reason and revelation a result of the logical necessity to provide continuous guidance for the developing and culturally diverse Muslim societies, or was it a byproduct of historical circumstances that determined the contemporary social and political practice? The main thrust of the classical Muslim intellectual development was to anchor moral epistemology reliably within the primarily religious sources to underscore its inseparable and logical relationship to interpretive jurisprudence that provided time-specific responsa in general to resolve pressing issues related to religious practice. The independence of self-subsisting and universal moral values that did not require religious affiliation or justificatory reasoning was in the making. The more immediate religious inquiry was not to explore the sources of human conduct; rather, it was to comprehend divine will as it related to human life in this and the next world. God's will, as declared by the revelation, was embodied in the divinely ordained system that would define and formulate the boundaries of orthopraxy. This was the scope of the emerging field of interpretive jurisprudence (*al-fiqh*) in the classical period.[1]

Islamic Ethics. Abdulaziz Sachedina, Oxford University Press. © Oxford University Press 2022.
DOI: 10.1093/oso/9780197581810.003.0001

The Qur'an laid the moral foundation of Islam on a universal idiom that sought to apply moral values to all human beings, regardless of their religious affiliation. It was an a priori endorsement of intuitive reason's ability to autonomously pursue happiness. This was the core of Islamic secularity, which held all of humanity accountable for their conduct irrespective of their membership in a faith community. The relationship between religiously and non-religiously informed moral conduct was emphasized in the Qur'an so that, despite their religious differences, human beings were guided to learn to live in peace and harmony with one another. The emphasis on human coexistence and cooperation as civic virtues was founded upon the idea of justice and fairness as the essential principles needed to regulate interhuman relations. Islamic revelation provided the moral-cum-religious idiom to initiate the notion of inclusive political society that, in addition to the legal-ethical responsibilities of all people living under Muslim political order established by the Prophet, afforded human nature a critical role in extracting universal values to organize a multifaith society. Human nature was conceived as a central doctrine of the revelation that regarded human beings as totalities that manifest all the attributes of the macrocosm (*al-ʿālam al-akbar*), of which other creatures are simply parts of a whole (*al-ʿālam al-asghar*). This latter objective was proposed in the historical document known as the Constitution of Medina.[2] The document shows the contexts of potential threat to the well-being of the tribes that resided in Medina, where close social interaction between Arabs and Jews revealed relations of dependency and interdependency that had become precarious for Arabs with the coming of the Prophet. The framework of the Prophet's experiment on building a civil society under that constitution was based on the divinely endowed infused[3] morality (Q. 91-7-10) that shaped human character through natural and social relationships. In order to be perfected, human beings had to undergo a process whereby they became what they were to be. Unlike any other being, human beings were endowed with the capability to be more or less than human. More important, this infused morality was available to all humans regardless of connection to a confessional community. Technically, morality founded upon naturally endowed human constitution was regarded as capable of creating processes to guide relationships within and outside other communities.

Based on this possible relationship between the early history of Islam and emerging moral discourse as the community settled in various regions of the empire, my long-standing research question has remained consistent: Is it possible for a document like the Qur'an, which initiated its emphasis on common moral constitution (*fiṭra*) upon which humanity was created and expected to become one community, to ignore ethics as the main constituent of its collective emphasis on justice and unity, and to insist upon absolute homogeneity based on religious creed? For the Qur'an to ignore variations in the choice of spiritual path and relativity in human cultures and traditions would have meant the demise of its notion of morally cohesive humanity, potentially united in its emphasis on fairness and empathy in dealing with one another.

From my readings in scriptural interpretation among Muslims I always found hesitation among the prominent exegetes to genuinely explore the possibility that infused morality should be expounded as having no relation with confessional doctrine that limited salvation to the believers only. The Qur'an, based on its account of the previous monotheistic communities that discredited one another in their claim of exclusive salvation, was desirous of overcoming the same kind of exclusivist preunderstanding about the soteriological claim regarding the singularity of Islam. Obviously, such an exclusivist preunderstanding would have hampered Islam's ability to demonstrate the universal moral values that overshadowed religious differences to forge coexistence based on common emphasis on morality as a source of unity among human beings ("compete with one another in doing good": message of Q. 5:48). The core of the Qur'an was and remains spiritual equality founded upon common morality—social ethical sensibilities generated by one's faith in God. It is very clear from the importance the Qur'an attaches to the innate moral nature (*al-akhlāqī al-fiṭrī*) as a divine gift to humanity that rules out any doubt about the self-subsisting moral law that is appropriate for all people, whether believers or not. Accordingly, moral norms do not stem only from divine legislation (*tashrī*ʿ) founded upon revelation (*shar*ʿ = *naql* = textual); rather, in keeping with scriptural justification, rationally derived (ʿ*aql* = rational) moral values undergird religious obligations and prohibitions, rendering an inevitable integration of religious and ethical in derivation of orthopraxy. In other words, ethics in general, and social ethics in particular, was incorporated in interpretive jurisprudence (*al-fiqh*). It was in this sense that Abū Ḥāmid al-Ghazālī regarded jurisprudence as everyday discipline committed to exploring the external aspects of religious practice as it related to a believer's mundane life, whereas ethics was the inner dimension of interpretive jurisprudence that afforded deeper meaning to orthopraxy—both being connected to interpersonal social transactions. His criticism of jurisprudence being a worldly enterprise suggests that the scope of ethics was undermined by the formalism attached to interpretive jurisprudence.[4]

In my studies in Islamic jurisprudence, at various points I have engaged in initiating discussions about the profound relation between theology, law, and ethics, based on a key question: How integral is the subject of morality to the study of Islamic religious law? Whether dealing with the legality and morality of engaging in offensive militancy in the name of *jihād* or the constitutionality of highest juridical authority in matters of the Sharīʿa rulings, how does ethics become integrated in jurisprudence? At what stage of their legal-moral evaluation of historical paradigms are the jurists actively engaged in introducing these rational maxims as part of their search for universal moral law or ethics? Contemporary research has demonstrated that juridical methodology (*uṣūl al-fiqh*) from the classical age was based on the strictures provided by the revelation and extrapolated with the aid of reason.[5] One of the most striking features of this methodology is the critical sifting and authenticating of the textual repository by revealing the incongruency of the traditions ascribed to the early community. Both linguistic and lexicographical investigation was based on comprehending the ordinary language as spoken by Arabs in the classical age—the Qur'anic Arabic. It is not far-fetched to suggest that rational inquiry (*al-ijtihād al-ʿaqlī*) in ordinary language provided legal scholars with analytical tools to direct human relations resolutely based on moral principles resulting from scriptural values. This rational inquiry undertook to resolve the inconsistencies and disagreements between revelation and reason in determining the cognitively valid orthopraxy. The latter resolution indicated the development of legal theory that, on the one hand, provided thoroughly text-based orthopraxy to the community and, on the other, provided it with rationally extricated ethics of relationship for interpersonal and intercommunal harmony.

My interest in religious ethics was sparked by my substantial interest in juridical studies. I wanted to investigate the relationship between juridical theology and ethics: How does ethics interrogate the cognitive validity of judicial decisions? Is it by extracting moral principles from moral and factual elements secured by rational analysis of moral experiences and judgments or by evaluating and comprehending the types of moral reasoning that revelatory sources like the Qur'an and the Sunna employ to infer the right course of action? In other words, my research was based on clarifying the intimate, and almost inevitable, relationship between law and ethics in Islam. The major obstacle to achieving this objective, as I discovered in my readings in interpretive jurisprudence, was the way Muslim jurists conceived the project of deriving valid orthopraxy without formally taking up ethics as an organically related field to analyze and acquire authentic orthopraxy.

Ethics, as a systematic exploration of the ontology and epistemology of human social behavior, was regarded disapprovingly by Muslim traditionalists since, as they argued, in view of the divinely ordained text-based morality, ethics as derived on the basis of morally infused human nature and intuitive reason was superfluous. For these jurists, religion preserved in juridical sources and practice was sufficient to guide humanity to life in both this world and the hereafter. In principle, the classical curriculum for religious education in Muslim seminaries (*madrasa*) primarily included subjects that critically evaluated transmitted sources (*al-naql*) and developed an adequate methodology for the derivation of orthopraxy (*aḥkām*) based on linguistic and lexical analysis of classical heritage. Nevertheless, linguistic and lexicographical studies continued to encounter rationally derived scriptural moral principles integral to religious law. Revelatory sources attained authoritative status in epistemological hierarchy as the principal source of both the orthodoxy and the orthopraxy, with the caveat that its epistemology relied heavily upon the divinely inspired textual repository. Such a narrow view of Sharīʿa-oriented orthopraxy has unwittingly led to total disregard for taking up ethics as a distinct rational source for social and political reform in the context of modernity.[6]

As long as the founder of Islam was alive, questions about the role of divinely endowed intuitive reason (*al-ʿaql*) in relation to the absolute authority of the revelation (*al-naql*) defined the parameters of interaction between reason and revelation. And although the orthopraxy depended consistently on the paradigmatic authority of the Prophet and the early community to derive the Sunna (Tradition) as part of the scriptural basis, the role of reason remained disputed by those who emphasized traditionalism (*ahl al-ḥadīth*) as its primary source for solving the expansive problems generated by social and political transformation of Muslim society. In my many years in Iran and Iraq (between 1966 and 1979) the epistemology that prevailed and dominated the seminarian educational culture was, strictly speaking, text-bound and avoided entanglement with rationalist universalism that characterized moral philosophy in the modern world. Consequently, investigation of the nuances and theories of moral philosophy was shunned for fear of the relativity of ethical opinions and plans of action under the impact of modernity. To put it differently, religious law was regarded as sufficiently equipped with moral philosophy and was actually integrated with the religion of Islam. Religion, according to this understanding, was one and the same with ethics. There was no need to separate the two fields that dealt with the teleology—ends or goals pursued by human minds—that transcended the divinely decreed deontic nature requiring humans to obey the divinely commanded praxis. I did not gauge the fear of universalism or secularity in the 1960s since religious authorities everywhere in the Muslim world were retreating from their claim to speak authoritatively for the orthodoxy and orthopraxy. Modernization had been introduced through mass education and intellectual development external to the seminaries.

There was another fear about admitting ethics as a separate discipline that seemed to challenge and outstrip the monopoly of religious authority as the sole representative of authoritative orthopraxy and substitute that for modernly educated men and women, modern in outlook and secular in their approach to everyday problems faced by men and women. Ironically the moral foundation of the Qurʾanic guidance to lead humanity to accomplish moral excellence in social transactions was overtaken by the overemphasis on deontic normative concepts and normative reasoning. Revelatory notions of obligation (*ilzām*, *wujūb*), permission (*jawāz*), prohibition (*taḥrīm*), and related concepts were part of these deontic commandments that undertook the project to reveal the necessity of bringing back the revelatory goal of creating a moral order in which all humanity was guided and required to follow the ethical impulse infused in human nature in addition to the guidance embedded in the revelation.

In view of the epistemological and ontological objectives of this research, the study of Islamic ethics has a limited objective of indicating an extensive itinerary pursued by Muslim scriptural as well as juridical sources to show, however implicitly, historical and theological-juridical notions and/or conceptions related to religious praxis that epistemically and ontologically pursued the path that led to prosperity in this and the next world.

In Chapter 2, I trace the classical development of the scriptural worldview that was firmly founded upon the moral language of Islamic revelation. I have endeavored to outline the ethical-legal terminology that was developed by Muslim legal thinkers to point toward a gradual exploration of the texts in the context of Arabic linguistic and lexical nuances to underscore the inner dimensions of religious praxis.[7] Chapter 2 functions as a historical backdrop for other chapters engaged in exploring the doctrinal, theological, and juridical foundations of Islamic ethics.

Chapter 3 takes up the legal-moral reasoning that became an indispensable part of formulating the deontological ethics of Islamic juridical tradition. The scriptural guidance in Islam connected the ultimate salvation to adherence to orthopraxy. Muslims were obligated to discover God's will in acts of obedience that guaranteed salvation to those who performed righteous actions. The scope of interpretive jurisprudence was to provide methodological procedures to ascertain the reliability of orthopraxy derived from revelatory sources like the Qur'an and the Tradition. The chapter traces the evolution of legal-ethical reasoning that has provided the conceptualization and compliance of reason with the standards and precepts provided in the revelation to advance human endeavors to identify processes that lead to meaningful existence. Moreover, the chapter advances the major question in interpretive jurisprudence, namely: how to adhere to deontological ethics of the Sharīʿa to seek what is advantageous and beneficial by performing all those acts that are prescribed as morally obligatory while avoiding those that are disapproved by the divine lawgiver. Muslim jurists had to grapple with a fundamental uncertainty about the ramifications of rational methodology (*al-ijtihād al-ʿaqlī*) that questioned cognitive validity of textuality promoted as unadulterated evidence without ascertaining their judicious reliability. Reliability of textual evidence depended upon its sound transmission, which in turn depended upon investigation of transmitted information and its congruity with the overall objectives of the Sharīʿa. The traditions were meticulously scrutinized for their admission as documentation prior to the formulation of a moral-religious action-guide (*taklīf*). The rational derivation of a moral-religious action-guide (*al-taklīf al-ʿaqlī*) based upon the concepts of value, their meanings, and their relation to each other without textual corroboration was always suspect in the eyes of Muslim jurists committed to uphold the inviolability of scriptural precepts.

Chapter 4 undertakes to investigate scriptural sources to expound the ethical foundation of Islamic orthopraxy. Scholarly analysis of the scriptural materials, including theological and juridical formulations from its inception in the classical period, was founded upon the logical necessity of discovering the underlying moral connotation of divine commandments to determine whether these prescriptions could be used as precedents to extrapolate other, related ordinances. To verify the reliability of the judicial decisions thus arrived at, justificatory reasoning had to make plain the correlation (*talāzum*) between scripturally and rationally derived moral values that formed an integral part of orthopraxy in the two major fields of Islamic jurisprudence: human-God relationships (duties of worship) and human-human relationships (duties accruing from natural and contractual familial or societal relations) as manifestations of divinely approved religious-moral action-guides (*taklīf*). The Sharīʿa repeatedly emphasizes performance of righteous action (*ʿamal ṣāliḥ*) as the sole guarantor of human prosperity in this life and as an efficacious criterion for salvation in the hereafter. As long as human existence is distinctively geared toward a life in the hereafter with compliance and extensive power over adaptation in this life, then the first obligation that humans have to themselves is to get accustomed to living a morally upright life so that they can personify virtues. The legal-ethical action-guides provided by the Sharīʿa profoundly capture the characteristic of a desired moral paradigm when they affirm the essential responsibility of rationally endowed human moral agency to work toward utilizing a divinely endowed constitution (*fiṭra*) by remaining committed to moral self-advancement in order to attain prosperity in this and the next world.

Chapter 5 undertakes to further establish a legitimate connection between juridical methodology and Islamic ethics in interpretive jurisprudence. The chapter elaborates juridical theology based on humanity's equality in decoding the basic moral law infused in human nature through reason. Islamic political theology, with its goal of establishing a just public order, laid the doctrinal groundwork for the Muslim community to work toward reaching a consensus about the need for a peaceful and just relationship with other faith communities on the basis of a common human nature under a universal divine law of justice. For the Qur'an it was a given that different communities and groups ought to come to terms with the fact of cultural and religious diversity and regulate interhuman relationships on the Qur'anic command about every community having its own law and ritual (Q. 5:48) that functioned as a toleration-generating principle among various claims of exclusionary religious truth. Nonetheless, even though coercion in the matter of one's choice of spiritual path was ruled out, the Qur'an did not overlook the necessity of providing some workable principle like universal human nature (*fiṭra*) to serve as a foundation for what is good and what we ought to do to manage just interhuman relations.

The thrust of Islamic revelation, more specifically the Qur'an, was to guide humanity toward good character and decent conduct founded upon justice. In order to achieve that end, the Qur'an paid attention to the ways in which it could provide decrees and models for developing a Muslim personality of excellence. Nevertheless, to avoid any dispute about whose religion is superior, the principle of bringing peoples of diverse religious and cultural backgrounds to respect and treat one another as equals had to be based on some extrarevelatory notion. Providing such an extrarevelatory principle that could be acceptable to all faith communities and groups was a challenge for the Qur'an that included both universal and particular aspects in its message. In the modern period, more particularly in the 20th century, Muslim jurisprudence was faced with the challenge of redefining the relationship between the normative standards ("ought") required by the revealed texts and mundane forces ("is") that activate society. The role of religion, as it emerged in modern times, could only influence the social and political order indirectly, and that also through individuals. Communities were human inventions, and often to gauge the level of moral development within community it was the individual who revealed the impact of religious guidance. The basic assumption in Islamic ethics is that it is the conscience of an individual—the innate nature—that is the recipient of rationally knowable values of things. This naturally infused moral knowledge is interlocked with the purpose and function determined by the revelatory framework that regards God as the provider of purposive directives. Chapter 5 undertakes to explore the theistic source of natural morality to avoid secularization of its juridical ethics with an unavoidable adoption of secular values, which could not correlate reason with the comprehensive spirit of religious "ought."

Chapter 6 relates law and ethics to highlight the ethical presuppositions of legal methodology. The legal theory derives its epistemology from philosophical theology and critical study of traditional materials used to provide reliable textual information to formulate judicial decisions. Philosophical theology (*kalām*)[8] and juridical methodology have undertaken to relate ethics to divinely ordained orthopraxy as a major part of justificatory reasoning for the derivation of rulings dealing with social ethics. However, traditional revelation-based jurisprudence (*al-ijtihād al-shar'ī*) has adamantly resisted any suggestion that it needs to strike a partnership with and be guided by the secularity of interpretive ethics (*al-ijtihad al-'aqlī*) to infer morally sound and universally applicable ethical and religious opinions. If modernity is understood as a period that challenged traditionalism by questioning the authority of tradition in providing the sole criteria of judging an act's cognitive validity, then one should reckon with a crisis of epistemology in contemporary traditional interpretive jurisprudence (*'ulum shar'īya*). Chapter 6 investigates a major source of contention between tradition and modernity that is related to the determination of the source of human moral behavior, whether it originates in revelation or reason. Modernity is ostensibly nurtured by modern secular ethics that rejects supernatural sources for justificatory moral reasoning. The prioritization of secular public reason over the claims of supernatural religious reason rooted in its metaphysical foundation in revelation has created the debate over the role of religious tradition in determining the social and political standards in the development of nation-states. Whereas traditional jurisprudence continues to discuss the absolute rights of God (*ḥaqq allāh*) and the relative, not natural, rights of humans (*ḥaqq ādamī*), modernity, with its firm belief in social change and individualism, has moved toward total emancipation of individuals from community, and ethics from tradition, leading to thorough secularization of public space and equality of all human beings. By submerging ethics into religion, Muslim jurists insisted on the text-based logic and methodology that guaranteed the absolute status of the revelation as the only source for future ethical decisions. Instead of asserting the moral foundation of interpretive jurisprudence to deduce practical decisions for a changing community, the traditionalists emphasized absolute obedience to the Tradition. For them, it was the interpretive jurisprudence that defined the parameters of God's absolute rights and the contours of limited rights of human beings. The ethical presuppositions of religious practice were totally disregarded in order to maintain the absolute authority of the traditional interpretive approach that determined the validity of contemporary social practice regulated by the revelatory texts.

The Innovative Title of *Islamic Ethics: Fundamental Aspects of Human Conduct*

The challenging feature of this research was its scope and title. Needless to say, when one speaks about "Islamic ethics" in the context of Western studies of Islamic thought and practice, one is pushed to deal with Muslim philosophical ethics—a hybrid of Hellenism and Persian-Semitic cultures. From the outset, following my preliminary research in religious practice, the scope of the book was shaped by my studies in Islamic theology and jurisprudence—the two fundamental sources to understand the manner in which divine and human will interacted. Hence, I was in search of a title that would indicate the shift to essentially ethical discourse in the context of Muslim interpretive jurisprudence before the classical juridical corpus was composed. I wanted to delve into orthopraxy that defined Muslim social-religious identity. Historically, orthopraxy was the most important source of Muslim identification. Orthopraxy put forward by various schools of religious practice—*madhāhib*—defined the boundaries of religious duties. Creedal affiliation (*ʿaqida*), once formulated and formalized as part of one's faith (orthodoxy) in Islam, took a back seat. The subsequent and sociologically and psychologically enduring identification began with the practice performed individually and in congregation. My academic interest was to understand and expound the constituent elements of this objectified faith in practice. My entry into this exploration was marked by the role revelation and reason played in providing the fundamental aspects of human conduct as envisioned by Islam.

After much consultation and deliberations with colleagues working in the fields of interpretive jurisprudence, religious ethics, and moral philosophy, I adopted the following title for the present study: *Islamic Ethics: Fundamental Aspects of Human Conduct*. There was a suggestion to title it *Juridical Ethics and Modernity*, but that title would have restricted me to devote the entire study to contemporary Islamic interpretive jurisprudence. Although I am interested in exploring the way juridical heritage continues to determine the scope of applied ethics in Islam, my research interest was to investigate juridical ethics as an integral part of Islamic ethics in order to argue in support of rational inquiry (*al-ijtihād al-ʿaqlī*) in formulating relevant orthopraxy in the context of modernity. I am interested in understanding the reasons why Islamic reforms in the area of orthopraxy have, because of their total emphasis on textual inquiry (*al-ijtihād al-naqlī*), fallen short of upholding the promise of the traditionalist slogan "Islam is the solution!"[9] Can a traditionalist approach to problem-solving in Islamic religious law deliver the critically needed response to modernity by limiting itself to textual hermeneutics without fully expounding the moral foundation of the revelation? This study essentially explores the feasibility of undertaking to expound Islamic ethics as an integrated methodology of Islamic jurisprudence. In jurisprudence ethics was firmly established as a major source of the interpretive enterprise that led to investigate and propose fundamental aspects of human conduct based on scriptural and rational methodology. These scriptural sources include not only what Muslims regard as revelatory texts, like the Qur'an and the Tradition; they also reserve a substantial function for human deliberations based on substantive use of reason in a variety of its indicators and conclusions in order to articulate relevant orthopraxy for individual or group action.

There are two aspects of Islam that determine its doctrinal and practical teachings. The former, usually termed *uṣūl al-dīn* (= orthodoxy), deals with creedal facets of religion; the latter, termed *furu*ʿ *al-dīn* (= orthopraxy), deals with the practical branch of religion. Human conduct is related to orthopraxy, which expounds practical obligations in two general categories: the duties that are commended (*irshādī*) to be performed and those that ought to be (*mawlawī*) accomplished. The function of interpretive jurisprudence is to identify the duties that ought to be performed on the basis of textual evidence, collectively identified as "revelation." Hence, the revelation—the Qur'an and the Tradition—function as the main repository of the divine commandments requiring the faithful, both collectively and individually, to abide by the rulings deduced from them. In contrast, the optional duties are customarily derived from experience and rational analysis of the practical aspects of social and political life. On the whole, optional duties are derived on the basis of moral analysis, sometimes in the light of the revelation, at other times through rational analysis that generally conforms to the spirit rather than the letter of revelatory text. Historically, both the obligatory as well as optional aspects of orthopraxy were part of the religious guidance to establish an ideal public order. The extratextual, rationally extrapolated moral guidance was integrated in the juridical methodology in such a way that later generations of Muslim jurists working on expansive practical principles like "the public good" (*maṣlaḥa*) took the undergirding moral law for granted and declared in no uncertain terms that the sole guarantor of obedience to God was religious guidance without any reference to rationally inferred moral principle. More pertinently, the doctrinal basis for human moral conduct and moral agency—the two indispensable parts of rational ethics—could not be treated as a threat to the total well-being of humanity. Neither could secular ethics be dismissed as incompatible with Islamic ethics founded upon attainment of moral excellence in all human beings.

Accordingly, the main objective of this study is to search for and identify ethical norms and values in judicial decisions (*fatāwā*) to excavate an underlying moral ideal in the methodology (*uṣūl al-fiqh*) intended to be utilized in all similar cases to deduce authoritative orthopraxy. The ideal component in the Shar'ī action-guides makes it possible for the jurists to claim concurrence (*ijmā'*) among scholars to assert consistency in their judicial decision to bind the believers in the community to act accordingly. Correspondingly, the search in juridical literature is undertaken to understand the kinds of moral judgments Muslims make regarding what is right or wrong, good or bad, praiseworthy or blameworthy in the relations within and between individuals or groups in applied juridical practice. An operational presumption here, as elsewhere in this volume, is that the investigation into the rightness or wrongness of a judicial quandary (*masa 'ala must aḥdatha*)[10] dealing with personal, interpersonal, and social acts has always, whether directly or indirectly, depended upon an inquiry about the public good ideals that demonstrate how to avoid negative impacts that a certain decision can have on others affected by them. Since in interhuman situations a person is never merely centered on herself but always stands in relationships with others, meticulous moral assessment of the case must precede its declaration as licit or illicit. Detailed investigation to assess moral aspects enables the jurist to envision the person in her attitudes about rightness/wrongness toward others and indicate the way she associates with others whom she meets in individual or one-to-one encounter. In the final analysis, in order to deduce a viable practical ruling, the Muslim jurist undertakes to analyze the natural and moral consequences of human acts. Deontological juridical ethics founded upon principles and rules, when derived from the revelatory and rational indicators, take into consideration a person's moral behavior in the context of the community in which she is imbedded and by the common cultural and religious heritage that influences her relationships and attitudes.

Islamic jurisprudence serves as a critical matrix for extracting and applying ethical theories and their governing principles and rules to formulate a predictable and reliable outcome for a case under review. As a matter of fact, ethical considerations serve as the inextricable foundation of legal deliberations to arrive at a judicial decision. In other words, from a religious point of view, the precedence of ethics over religion is analogous to the decision deduced from just, wise, and compassionate moral authority over a decision deduced from absolute, obedience-exacting legal authority. For instance, based on one of the most commonly applied moral principles by the jurists, namely, "averting probable harm" (*nafy al-ḍarar al-muḥtamal*), ethics takes precedence in deducing the rule about the inviolability of human dignity in juridical deliberations. Hence, in a similar case involving human dignity, the dignity of a terminally ill patient has to be considered when healthcare providers have to decide the end-of-life care. The same moral principle can be expanded to deduce another important objective about "preservation of life" that can be applied to various social and medical cases. To be precise, this study builds its practical ethics upon the theoretical foundation of a legal-ethical framework of Islamic jurisprudence. The ethical discourse in this study will be governed by the classical juridical tradition in Islam, in particular its methodology, to elicit major principles and rules that have been applied continuously by Muslim jurists to formulate fresh decisions in the area of interhuman relations. An additional functional postulation, in light of a growing literature on the intimate and almost identical objectives in ethics and law in Islamic tradition, makes it possible to regard religious action-guides serving the same objective of naturally endowed moral law. Fundamental juridical sources like the Qur'an and the Tradition essentially remain morally oriented religious principles since they concentrate upon the individual moral agent (*mukallaf*) who lies behind and participates in legally and ethically provided structures and arrangements.

A question that is related to the scope of this study is: Why not concentrate on Islamic philosophical ethics modeled after Aristotelian ethics of virtue? As mentioned earlier in this chapter, a number of Muslim ethicists in the classical period authored major influential studies on Islamic virtue ethics. Let us consider a few points in this regard. To begin with, it is true that books on Islamic ethics have been written by Muslim scholars working in Islamic philosophy. These works, from time to time, point out the debt Muslims owe to Aristotelian and neo-Pythagorean sources of Hellenistic discourses on ethics. Moreover, these historians of Greek-into-Arabic heritage have also discredited any originality in Islamic tradition when it comes to the study of ethics. After all, the argument goes, a number of Muslim ethicists who worked on Muslim philosophical ethics mostly appeared in the 9th and 10th centuries during the ʿAbbasid period, and only after the Greek heritage was made available in Arabic translations. Hence, unlike Christianity, which was imbued with Greek thought from the outset, Islam awaited the age of translation of Greek philosophical works under the ʿAbbasid patronage to benefit from, for instance, Aristotle's *Nicomachean Ethics*.[11] That the translation of the latter heritage was instrumental in the development of philosophical ethics in Islamic civilization is indisputable. However, Qur'anic themes dealing with individual moral agents for whom the ethical guidance was provided in the revelation were not devoid of what we identify as religion-based moral questions. Islamic religious sources provided criteria to evaluate human progression on the spiritual path through the development within human beings of habits, postures, attitudes, and traits which characterized them as decent individuals (*ṣāliḥīn*). Clearly, the Qur'an saw human virtues as an important source of ultimate salvation promised by one's faith in God. The Qur'an was concerned to state the sources of moral law unambiguously to endow all human beings in general, and Muslims in particular, with the responsibility of their conduct. Moreover, in view of the brevity of religious guidance through revelation, the scope of human intuitive reason (*al-ʿaql*) and its role in the development of moral law was asserted unmistakably in its earlier message. The Meccan sections of the Qur'an spoke about the evil that existed as a result of humans' choices in their interpersonal dealings with one another. Human culpability for wrongdoing was at the center of debates that treated questions about the overpowering divine will and its influence in character formation. Rudimentary theological inquiries about divine justice were already being formulated to understand the reasons behind the existence of economic and social imbalances and inequalities. At the heart of the Qur'anic message was whether disbelief could lead to heightened immoral behavior or whether human agency could, independent of revelation, exercise free will in humans' choice of course of action that enabled them to cultivate and develop those virtues which acted as auxiliary for the discharge of religious and moral duties. The literary production in this area was varied and included both religious and worldly dimensions of the juridical discipline.

Muslim scholarly production in the area of interpretive jurisprudence and speculative theology began to articulate divine purposes for humanity as well as deontological and teleological ethics that held human beings responsible for furthering the creation of a just and equitable social order. Contrary to Christianity, which began its earthly career as a persecuted minority with no public dimension to its ascetic inclinations in faith, from its inception Islam revealed its earthly mission by speaking about the public order that was dependent upon the good will in the form of religious faith in God and God's emissaries, who worked diligently with self-discipline and character formation to execute social responsibilities in order to create the moral order on earth. Since the Qur'an recognized the naturally endowed intrinsic human need to stand in relationships, ethics, which contemplates an individual in her attitudes and actions toward others whom she meets in individual encounters, was simply formulated in a straightforward sense of individual and collective duties in the divine command ethics of the revelation.

It is important to point out that the age of translation from Greek into Arabic in the 9th and 10th centuries sparked interest in rational religious thought leading to sophisticated defense of Islamic doctrines in newly emerging theological debates about human moral agency and the purpose of human creation. Divine attributes like the "Seeing" (*baṣīr*) and "Hearing" (*samīʿ*) God, who was also a moral God, led to controversies about God's knowledge of universals and particulars. Does God know all the particulars of the events that occur every moment, or does God know only the generalities? The battleground of ideas was dominated by the monotheistic experience of a living God accessible to human faith in the Qur'an, and the philosophical and abstract notion of a metaphysical concept of God to be rationally expounded. Nonetheless, Muslim belief in an omniscient and omnipotent God, if pushed to its logical conclusion, tended to reduce human agency to some form of predeterminism that denied human beings the most basic experience of choice. Furthermore, determined human behavior advanced a morally complacent society. Human initiative to combat social inequalities and to take responsibility to redress wrongs was curbed under the pretext of God's overpowering will. The query about moral accountability was a theological issue which needed both textual and rational proofs to establish the substantial role that reason plays in formulating ethical responses to everyday moral predicaments. The stage was set for the elaboration of ethical epistemology that, on the one hand, endeavored to decipher God's actions expressed through God's omnipotence and, on the other, dealt with the controversial question about ingrained human knowledge about the moral law. Is this knowledge available through revelation at the exclusion of reason, or is it infused in human nature, with revelation providing the details?

The pioneering and seminal study of Muslim theological ethics was undertaken by George F. Hourani. In his *Islamic Rationalism: The Ethics of ʿAbd al-Jabbār*[12] the author has shown the level of sophistication that existed about

Islamic ethics in theological work produced by one of the prominent rationalist theologians, Qāḍī ʿAbd al-Jabbār (d. 1024/5). Undoubtedly, Hourani's major contribution remains the emphasis he laid on theological works to explore Islamic ethical discourse. Philosophical ethics of virtue, as Hourani correctly pointed out, was secular and accommodated Islamic revelation to the philosophical framework, incorporating Aristotelian elements. However, it was in the area of theological studies that one could begin to explore the basic foundations of Islamic ethics.

A major contention of this study, then, is that Islamic juridical studies were never conceived independent of theological assumptions about the ontology of human acts and the status and extent of revelation, both the Qur'an and the Tradition, and their parameters in evolving a complete practical action-guide for human society. Islamic ethics is customarily related to interpretive jurisprudence. It is impossible to imagine juridical studies in Islam without excavating their foundation in the ethics of human conduct in relation to others. If moral deliberations take precedence in evaluating the lawfulness of human choices in the area of human interaction, then inevitably one needs to explore theological works in appraising the ontology, epistemology, and teleology of human moral conduct.

In view of this hypothesis I decided to scrutinize fundamentals of Islamic ethics as an inquiry connected with interpretive jurisprudence. My long-term research in Islamic theological and juridical primary sources has thus far brought to light not only the influence of Hellenistic thought in providing the conceptual framework to Muslim philosophical ethics; these classical sources also indicate that transmission of Aristotelian ethics was interactive. Translations of Greek works into Arabic demonstrated the malleability and capacity of Arabic language in adapting the debates and arguments within the different social-political and cultural contexts of Muslim society. Muslims, like all faith communities, were searching for ethical solutions that shaped their moral thought in unraveling responses to everyday moral dilemmas. These dilemmas, in which past, present, and future confuse human ability to comprehend unexpected moments to derive meaningful and realistic solutions, shaped value judgments to guide future choices. Spiritual and temporal were interconnected in an Islamic tradition that was closely aligned with public manifestation of the prophetic ethical foresight that insisted on justice and equality in interpersonal relations. Faith in God and God's revelatory guidance was inherent in the public realm. Consequently, religious devotion manifested itself in the formation of an ethical society that cherished the notion of divinely inspired human capacity to lead the life of an individual toward some cosmic and social vision of meaning and purpose. Obviously, to reach that goal people were required to acquire and reflect appropriate attitudes and actions toward one another and administer the power with justice. In this sense, from its inception Islam required the spiritual and temporal—religious and secular—to work together to create the ideal society. Even when the realm of personal faith remained private and inscrutable to anyone but God, the public manifestation of religious experience became the basis for the secular order founded upon the experience of living and practicing religion in public. The central function of Islamic creed and ritual, as elaborated in the Sharīʿa, when performed in public, became the indispensable source of interpersonal ethics that led to the exercise of just political power and its legitimation. Theoretically, morality was integral to the foundation of the Sharīʿa. The religious law sought to guide the Muslim individual and community into conformity with the morally delineated objectives for humanity. The Qur'an regarded faith in God as the compelling force for social integration and legitimation of the secular order.

2
In Search of a Comprehensive Definition of Ethics

This study in Islamic ethics is the culmination of a number of years in my studies in Islamic philosophical theology (*kalām*), jurisprudence (*fiqh*), and applied ethics (*akhlāq*). My interest in jurisprudence and ethics, in particular, was driven by my search for the application of the Qur'anic notion of personal moral purification (*zakā*). My major research hypothesis was to uncover the main instrument of divine guidance, namely, the Qur'an, for its moral worldview. Whatever the classical sources say about philosophical ethics or ethics connected with Islamic orthopraxy, for this research I wanted to "return" to the earliest source that preserves the revelatory ethos about human conduct on which the entire spiritual and moral foundation of the new message about *islām* ("submission" or "surrender") is erected. While I could have initiated my assessment of the primary sources by going directly to the detailed analysis of the traditional materials in the Sunna to learn about virtue ethics, the Qur'an provided me with a first-hand opportunity to reexamine its well-known and oft-repeated message: "This book is a guidance to the morally-spiritually aware (lit. god-fearing = *muttaqīn*) who believe in the unseen (*al-ghayb*)" (Q. 2:3).[1] I knew the danger of entering my principal source with a prefabricated Muslim thesis about their holy book that it is a "comprehensive" repository of *all* human knowledge. With my juridical-theological approach to the study of Islamic ethics I was convinced that the challenge for my research would be to uncover the moral impulse of the scripture that ought to be evaluated and elaborated on its own terms, without taking the aid from the Tradition (Sunna). Hence, I began with the critical question addressed to my own person: What does the Qur'an expect from me as a "detached" (claiming "objectivity") researcher of the Muslim scripture? Can I avoid being subjective while maintaining my scholarly neutrality? I was already encumbered with my preunderstanding about the book and my personal identity with it. After more than sixty years of close contact with the Qur'an, was it possible to be detached and analyze its major theme about human spirituality and morality? As I turned the pages of a number of Orientalist works on the Qur'an and their well-entrenched thesis about its "not being" a divinely ordained scripture, I resorted to W. Montgomery Watt's monumental study *Introduction to Bell's Translation of the Qur'an* (1970). I greatly benefited from this technical study about the features

Islamic Ethics. Abdulaziz Sachedina, Oxford University Press. © Oxford University Press 2022.
DOI: 10.1093/oso/9780197581810.003.0002

and contents of the Qur'an, in addition to Bell's endeavors to determine the text's chronology. It struck me that Watt's discussions were still valuable and that his other related studies, particularly *Muhammad at Mecca* (1953), was pertinent in opening up with the rare opinion that the Prophet had introduced his religion as *tazakkī* (purification through moral behavior). Watt's insightful observation, based on classical primary sources, was accurate. Before *īmān* (faith), as the Qur'an stated (Q. 2:3), there had to be something potentially universal that would prepare an individual to "surrender" (*islām*). That was *tazakkī*. My journey in this book is, consequently, built upon that valuable insight about the Qur'an as the source of *tazakkī*.[2]

Zakā and its derivative "undertaking moral excellence" (*yuzakkī*) signify morality based on and informed by the purposes of revelations and commissioning of the prophets to become spiritual and moral guides to humanity in order to lead them to acquire morality[3] as part of the principal objective of existence. The revelation constitutes all that human reason cannot know except through the divinely transmitted message. The Prophet, according to the Qur'anic idea about God being perfect, steered Muslims to assert that God's emissary also enjoys immunity from making errors of judgment. Consequently, knowledge from God is trustworthy. Intuitive reason is capable of knowing the possibility and conditions when the revelation is transmitted. Moreover, it is capable of recognizing the evidence that establishes the veracity of the Prophet's claim to bear such a message from God. The Qur'an appears to suggest that the prophetic mission receives increase and blessings of God through enabling a prophet to guide human beings, one by one individually, by purifying them (*tuṭahhiruhum*) through the practice of sharing their possessions (Q. 9:104) in the form of almsgiving (*zakāt*). The performance of a moral act of sharing one's possessions (*māl*), according to the Qur'an, purifies the performer (*nafsahu*) and occasions an increase in the rest of the assets. More pertinently, in view of the emphasis upon purification of wealth through charity for developing a Muslim personality of excellence, the Qur'an makes it abundantly clear that in principle self-purification (*ṣafwat nafs*) leads the person to perform goodness (*zakkaytuhu*) or righteousness (*al-ʿamal al-ṣāliḥ*) to attain higher level of piety.[4]

From the very early days of the Prophet's mission in the 7th century, the ethical goal of the divine revelation, based on the intimate connection between almsgiving (*zakāt*) and the act of worship (*ṣalāt*) in the Qur'an, was to underscore that *zakā*, in the meaning of righteousness, is a divine endowment to further moral ideals of the revelation. The Qur'an provided decrees and models to influence the social and political indirectly and to shape every private individual within the faith community directly. The integration of personal moral excellence with caring for the downtrodden sums up the spiritual-moral worldview of Islam that incorporates morality with the objectives (*maqāṣid*) of orthopraxy—the blueprint for the community that includes "preservation of human life, the faculty of reason, chastity and material possessions," that would define one's faith and practice in the context of the community.[5]

My major argument to be elaborated in this study is that while it is plausible to write an alternative account of philosophical, scriptural, or theological ethics based on the classical sources that have already been utilized by major contributions in the field of ethics by George Hourani and Majid Fakhry,[6] my limited research goal has been influenced by some studies on Islamic ethics in Arabic and Persian. These studies have followed either the main thesis of Aristotelian virtue and happiness ethics or have presented the Islamic sources, especially the Qur'an and the Tradition, to extract moral virtues and discuss moral development of human personality by adopting the revealed ethical values in various passages of the Qur'an. The Qur'an emphasizes both the objective morality infused in human nature and the divine-command ethics embedded in God's decrees in the revelation.[7] Islamic juridical studies have regarded normative ethics that defends a particular moral position integrated in the divine law, the Sharīʿa, which needs to be discovered through text-based legal-ethical hermeneutics and by way of linguistic and lexicographical analysis of revelatory sources, including the Qur'an and the Tradition. The juridical studies in Islamic tradition have completely ignored the field of moral philosophy as a separate domain of inquiry about the ontological status of value in ethics or about the epistemological position of human knowledge of such value.

The hypothesis of this research in Islamic ethics is built upon epistemological study of moral values and their application in interpretive jurisprudence to derive reliable orthopraxy. The epistemic objective is to demonstrate that, in large measure, Sharīʿa-related reforms in Muslim societies, whether dealing with human rights of minorities or protection of women's legal or moral equality, cannot obtain desired objectives without instituting an interpretive jurisprudential methodology (*uṣūl al-fiqh*) firmly based on a rationalist ethical theory. Since morality has something to do with practical matters and is supposed to make a qualitative difference in human life and relationships, it functions as an indispensable safeguard to evaluate moral claims and judgments about the equal dignity of all humans, regardless of race, gender, or creed. This study investigates the Qur'anic notion of infused or innate morality and, closely related to it, natural law ethics to uncover the pivotal concern of Islamic revelation, namely, to uphold justice and moral excellence as the practical outcome of the juridical ethics of the Sharīʿa founded upon *zakā* (the moral purification) that leads to righteousness. The research is essentially guided by the incentive of the Qur'anic ethics founded upon its conviction that good character and good conduct are founded upon justice. The hypothetical observation about the Qur'an is that without expounding the moral worldview of the revelation, which lies in the circumstances in which humanity lives, its emphasis on living a moral life as absolutely necessary objectification of any claim of faith in God, Islamic jurisprudence cannot establish its suitability or relevance to promulgate newly defined interpersonal justice under the impact of the social and cultural changes in the modern world. Secular modernity is staunchly bestowing the dominant place that must be occupied by rationalist ethics as the sole custodian of brokering civility and equal rights for the political salvation of contemporary societies. Accordingly, religion cannot influence the social and political order directly. Needless to say, secular ethics is extremely intolerant of any input by religious communities engaged in making sense of meaningful existence in modern times. As I shall expound in this study, the absence of any epistemological rethinking about the sources of moral knowledge among Muslim jurists, and their absolute rejection of integrating ethical theory to strengthen their scripture-based reasoning (*al-ijtihād al-sharʿī*), has led to their inability to fully participate in the impending discourse of modernity facing all Muslim societies—not only in the field of education but also in the appropriation of the right kind of religiosity that is relevant today. After all, religion has to do with conscience, the divinely ordained sense of right and wrong, whereas society has no conscience to function as its criterion of praiseworthy and blameworthy except for its reliance on universal rationality. This research is engaged in rediscovering the moral origins of the juridical methodology (*uṣūl al-fiqh*) by focusing on juridical theology and ethics connected with the conscience of every private believer within a community.

Interpretive jurisprudence depended upon those doctrines that evolved to guide the early community to understand the need to overcome the evil of disbelief that afflicted humanity and hampered its progression toward reliable practice to establish ideal public order. The revelation emphatically asserted the source of this evil that derives this condition largely by ignoring the dictates of conscience and failing to engage reason to understand everyday living experience. Since the Qur'an projected its direct moral guidance first at the individual level and then at the community, understanding individual encounter with one's conscience became an indispensable inquiry for extracting principles that could be applied to extrapolate further judicial decisions as part of the authoritative sources of legislation (*tashrīʿīya*). Obviously, the juridical tradition appropriated hermeneutically derived pertinent textuality preserved in the revelation. Islamic ethics, whether rationally or textually derived, evaluates the goodness or wrongness of human acts—both individual and collective. The intellectual objective of interpretive jurisprudence is to appraise the epistemic engagement between the human understandings of the divine will expressed in the divine command ethics and its application to obtain orthopraxy that finds solutions to everyday problems faced by humanity. The thrust of this study is to go back to the tradition, more specifically in the Qur'an and the Tradition. This revisiting is undertaken to investigate the moral foundation of the scriptural sources that have continued to influence the fresh rulings derived by methodically exploring the feasibility of preserving human beings' interests (*maṣāliḥ*) in this life and the life to come (*ākhira*).

This research will show that early sources on religious practice have substantially leaned on the ethical dimensions of the revelation to provide authoritative orthopraxy. As a matter of fact, just going through the juridical sources of the classical age (9th–11th centuries), it is clear that preservation of human interests was inductively used to claim that the sole justification of the interpretive jurisprudence was to derive occasion-based interpretations of the divine decrees to infer further rulings from the well-established moral objectives in the revelation. The revelatory texts were rationally scrutinized to infer both general and specific interpretations of some of the rulings that required the people to exercise moral awareness in order to treat one another with justice or kindness and to forbid that which is shameful and against common sense. In other words, the textual hermeneutics, in large measure, relied on reason and consideration for human good. In particular, emphasis was laid on ascertaining social obligations toward one another by determining how human beings ought to avoid corruption and to endeavor to rid oneself of one's defects that lead to neglect of the moral duties laid upon all members of society. More often than not, Muslims were reminded about the pursuit of morality in fulfilling religious obligations and refraining from forbidden acts, as required by the Qur'an, and to bear the responsibility of accounting for their behavior, both individually and collectively, at all times.[8]

Before I continue my narrative, a digression about the most essential usage in this study is required. In the history of Islamic jurisprudence, the legal categories of "permissible" and "nonpermissible" are customarily employed to express the ethical categories of "moral" and "immoral." The underlying assumption in this deontic characterization is that divine command that allows for a duty to be performed (*al-jawāz*) carries within its terms grounds that can be categorized as "good" and "praiseworthy," and the prohibition (*al-taḥrīm*) in the divine decree carries in its terms grounds that can be categorized as "evil" and "blameworthy." In this study I have used "morality" and "ethics" interchangeably to identify religiously promulgated orthopraxy, sometimes distinguishing between an individual moral stance and the community's or group's take on a specific moral issue as ethical. I realize that the distinction between two concepts, from time to time, can be useful when an individual stance contradicts the collective or group interests in the community. The Muslim community often stifles the conscience of an individual believer, requiring conformity to the collective will of the faith community. It is for this reason that the Qur'an regards the private individual within the faith community a better clue to gauge the level of faith than the collective will. Thus, for instance, changing one's religion is that kind of religious-moral issue which is collectively regarded as unethical (for one's abandoning the community), whereas individually changing one's communal affiliation is often silently approved as a better choice than the evil of hypocrisy. By expressing one's personal choice of spiritual path, the difference between individual endorsement of freedom of choice and collective requirement to declare one's loyalty to the faith community points to the possibility of one's personal morality to trump the group ethics of collective identity. Nevertheless, in everyday conversation Muslims tend to use terms like "moral"(*ḥasan*) and "immoral" (*qabīḥ*) when discussing juridical issues related to changing one's religion, regardless of whether it assumes an "unethical" categorization in a personal or communal situation.

In the following pages I will discuss the historical development of the concept of *akhlāq* in the context of Islamic ethics exploring the meaning of "morality" as well as "ethics" as far as jurisprudential methodology and applications are concerned. I will have opportunities to clarify the use of ethics when it serves as a personal code of conduct for people working professionally in medical or business fields that are highly debated and contentious. Muslims, whether scholars or not, however, hardly use the term "ethics" when speaking about the permitting or forbidding *fatwā* (judicial decision) on any issue. This is expected, since the juridical authorities working on the religious action-guide, which includes both the religious and the moral, as a matter of practical consideration do not mention ethical grounds or moral reasoning as justification for cognitive validity of their rulings. In general, moral obligations and duties (*al-taklīf al-ʿaqlī*) imposed upon humankind have two interrelated ontological references in two categories: (1) the common obligations known and required by reason (*al-ʿaql*) and (2) the common obligations known and required in the revelation (*al-naql*). Both categories are promulgated as moral-religious duties, although secularly educated modern Muslim physicians, who might be religiously inclined, seek to differentiate between "moral" and "ethical" when reading or writing English articles, for instance, in bioethics. As far as Islamic rulings are concerned, the dominant idiom in deductions of moral-religious action-guides is one of the revelation (the Sharīʿa) and not ethics per se.

The Concept of *akhlāq* in Islamic Sources

In Arabic, the words *akhlāq* (plural form of *khulq* or *khuluq* = morality) and *adab* (manners) are used to signify the inner dimension of human personality, whereas *khalq* (creation) signifies its external aspects. *Khulq* essentially refers to ethics or morals. Both *khulq* and *adab* appear in the classical Islamic texts that deal with personal character and proper etiquette, respectively. Muslim philosophers like

Ibn Miskawayh (d. 1030) and Naṣīr al-Dīn Ṭūsī (d. 1274) speak about "refinement" of character (*tahdhīb al-akhlāq*) as part of the total formation of moral and spiritual personality. Certainly, among Muslim philosophers the focal point in ethics was what constitutes the excellence of the human person in relational contexts. Evaluation of human conduct was actually evaluation of human attitudes, habits, motives, dispositions, and traits by assigning value founded upon the human ability to live in harmony with others. Here reference to virtue was actually reference to the traits observed in good people who set the example to do that which is right and praiseworthy. Performance of the right acts was inextricably connected to their acquisition by means of developing a sense of duty, a will to do something fitting.

In modern classification of ethics, ethicists speak about three schools: virtue ethics, consequentialist ethics, and deontological or duty-based ethics. The three schools propound specific ways to understand ethics. Each approach is pivotal in guiding human acts to their desirable moral objectives. However, in making ethical decisions all three approaches function together. It is important to keep in mind that Islamic ethics does not restrict itself simply to determine the good and bad aspects of human conduct; rather, it maintains and advocates a particular moral school of thought by investigating the religious sources to account for a person's specific moral choice to pass moral judgment on its cognitive validity. In Islamic philosophical ethics, virtue ethics emphasizes the virtues, or moral character, in order to undertake the performance of right acts. In contrast to the approach adopted by Islamic ethics as part of Islamic jurisprudence (*al-fiqh*), Islamic philosophical theology (*'ilm al-kalām*) (depending upon a traditionalist or rationalist take in its discussion about the Muslim creed) undertakes to introduce the notion of innate cognition and volition given to human beings by God. God has created the human being as a living corporeal being having sensations, perceptions, needs and desires. In addition, God has endowed her with intelligence (*'aql*) and the power (*qudra*) of autonomous action. Since she naturally has physical and mental needs, she is capable of experiencing pleasure and pain and of receiving benefit and suffering detriment. Having such a capability she can consider the pros and cons of doing something and be held morally accountable for her action. She is actually endowed with knowledge and understanding of good and bad and the ability to infer moral principles and act accordingly. In view of this human ability, the juridical project endeavors to methodically understand and deduce regulations and principles to formulate subsidiary rulings that emphasize duties or rules (deontology), whereas theology strives to characterize the objective nature of good and evil and to assert human beings as free moral agents to fulfill their ends—telos (teleology).

Theoretically, classical religious texts ground the experience of the divine in piety-cum-morality (*taqwā*) by promoting awareness of the spiritual aspect of one's moral decisions. *Taqwā* in its primary signification of "piety, reverential fear of God" is not simply individual spiritual and moral responsiveness; it is primarily the essential source of ethical conduct at both the individual and societal levels. Ethics, then, is inherently regarded as providing standards that emphasize virtues, rules, and telos. Indeed, Islamic normative ethical theory, as I shall expound in this study, has something to say about all three dimensions of human acts as it relates to the formulation of moral guidance to advance ideal human personality.

Certainly, what distinguishes virtue ethics from teleology or deontology in Islam is the fundamental and foundational importance of virtue because it presupposes an ethics of conduct within its ethical theory. The revelatory sources, both the Qur'an and the Sunna (the Tradition in the form of divine guidance through the prophetic paradigm),[9] provide the essential parameters of ethical life that is oriented toward a comprehensive system, which nurtures the sacred and the profane as two inseparable features of human religiosity. Religious commitment (*diyāna*) seeks to understand this complex connection between spiritual and secular (*dunyā*) in order to figure out the right course of action that has deliberated over the natural and social necessities of life broached through revelation and intuitive reason divinely implanted in nature (*tabīʿa, fiṭra*). In other words, from its inception as a normative source of guidance for human conduct, Islamic ethics took the bidimensional form of natural and religious guidance needed to build an ideal public order. Morality, in this political-social context, was assigned the task of encouraging individuals and directing social-political systems to strive toward creating a divinely ordained moral order—an ethical society.

Moving on from the fundamental practical signification of ethics in Islamic thought, it is possible to speak about prescriptive ethics that deals with empirical and analytical accounts of human action. To clarify, moral prescriptions depend upon the way Muslim jurisprudence has conceived the scope and function of legal-religious terms. Most of the differences among the jurists relate to the substance and nature of ethical terminology and the ways in which it is applied to human personality traits in social and political contexts. These traits reveal the way mental processes dealing with thought, emotion, instincts, and volition influence the ordering and directing of moral considerations in human conduct. Moral obligations are imposed in large measure because of the given disposition in human beings. Because of their needs and desires humans know that performance of their duties entails hardship and difficulty. However, they deserve reward for having undertaken to fulfill onerous duties imposed by God. God, in fact, created human beings to benefit by offering them a reward that is the greatest of compensations.

If we now turn our attention to the primary sense of the term in Arabic lexicons, we find that "ethics" (*al-khulq*) has various, closely related meanings: moral character, innate disposition, the nature with which the human is created, determination, and even religion. As a matter of fact, "ethics" describes the inner face of human being, which is human personality that can be recognized by exploring its description and understanding its nature (*fiṭra*). Islamic revelatory sources refer to this subject in both the Qur'an and the Tradition. It is significant that the language of the revelation is replete with guidance to develop virtuous conduct as an objective indicator of one's faith in the divine. The revelation describes the best people (*khayr al-barīya*), time and again, as those "who have believed and who act righteously" (Q. 97:7)—evidently underscoring the inherent connection between faith (*īmān*) and moral conduct (*'amal ṣāliḥ*), between spiritual and moral, as we saw earlier in the term *taqwā*. Actually, Abū Ḥāmid al-Ghazālī (d. 1111), in his book *al-Iqtiṣād fī al-I'tiqād* on Muslim creed, makes it quite clear that no one can claim to be religious who regards shameful deeds like adultery as permissible.[10] In other words, morality is intrinsically connected with religiosity (*diyāna*). The prophetic mission is a comprehensive one requiring the Prophet not only to purify (*zakaya*) human souls by purging disbelief, but also to create a moral system that would institutionalize the spiritual and moral (*taqwā*) through a prophetic paradigm founded upon teaching and exemplifying a perfect ethical life, like the verse that sums up Muḥammad's calling: "Surely thou art upon a mighty morality (*khuluq*)" (Q. 58:4). Most Muslim commentators have interpreted the word "morality" in this verse to signify "religion." In fact, the synonyms of *khulq* include "religion" (*al-dīn*), "moral character" (*al-sajīya*), and "innate disposition" (*al-ṭab'*). In a tradition ascribed to 'Ā'isha, the Prophet's wife, she described the Prophet's moral character (*al-khulq*) as "being [founded upon teachings of] the Qur'an."[11] In other words, just as the Qur'an, with its rules of discipline and its commands and prohibitions and the excellences and beauties comprised in its verses, provided a sacred foundation of morality, the Prophet stood out as the exemplar of righteousness for humanity (Q. 6:90). The Qur'an firmly asserts the teaching of morality through self-purification (*tazakkī*) and emulation of the exemplary conduct of the prophets, who are sent with the message (*kitāb*) and inspired ability to judge right from wrong (*al-ḥukm*). Muḥammad's mission is in line with the teachings of all the previous prophets, who brought forth God's message (*kitāb*) and noble character (*khuluq*) and who came to enlighten their communities to a spiritual and moral life. In this sense, "Mighty in morality (*khuluq 'aẓīm*)" (Q. 58:4) is a stature attained through being created with the inherent capacity to acquire moral character, with its peculiar qualities and attributes. It is in this sense of being endowed with greatness in morality that Muḥammad is "the compassion to all humanity" (*raḥmatan li'l-'ālamīn*) (Q. 21:107). This stature is further proclaimed in the tradition that declares the purpose of his prophethood as being the perfection of the noble virtues (*makārim*). Accordingly, Muslim thinkers have emphatically affirmed that there is nothing heavier in the balance in which good and evil will be weighed than goodness of the moral character with the divinely endowed ability to engage in moral evaluation of one's behavior through introspection.

Muslim philosophers in their treatment of the ideal state of human existence spoke about ethics in terms of predisposition or propensity toward one of the two tendencies, the good or the evil, although the preponderant tendency, in their view, is toward the latter, because to do evil is effortless and easy. However, this pessimistic opinion does not align well with the one that maintains that morality is natural. Obviously, just as it is not suitable to speak about natural skills one observes in some people who actually invest lots of effort in learning crafts like calligraphy or commerce, one can also maintain that simply having a predisposition does not make a person skillful in that art. It is important to emphasize that having an inclination does not necessarily make a person ethical. Muslim philosophers have time and again stated the obvious fact that being endowed with a disposition to acquire a praiseworthy trait does not make a person virtuous until she has observed self-discipline through habituation and has become moral. To be precise, having a predisposition or a propensity does not make a person virtuous or skillful in that art. Furthermore, having been bestowed with both good and bad tendencies does not make people virtuous or vicious, respectively, until they have trained themselves in those dispositions.

The Muslim ethicist Ibn Miskawayh (d. 1030), in his book *Refinement of Character* (*tahdhīb al-akhlāq*), identified morality as a "condition in the soul that calls individuals toward action [spontaneously] without thinking or deliberation. This condition is divided into two kinds: one stems naturally as part of one's disposition; the other is the result of habituation and practice."[12] Accordingly, morality is of two kinds: natural and acquired. The latter kind of morality scrutinizes character formation that leads a person to adopt socially a desirable character and behaviors. Theoretically, acquired character reveals the processes involved in order to garner natural potentials that facilitate a pursuit of praiseworthy conduct that is acquired through habituation and practice until it becomes a character trait for its possessor, just like natural disposition. The social-political consequence of philosophical ethics retained its natural connection with human religiosity. Faith in supernatural being provided the original impulse for discovering the divinely ordained innate connection of human personality to moral law. It would seem that Ibn Miskawayh's secular philosophical ethics disclosed the practical role of spiritual commitment in furthering relational aspects of the social order in an ideal Muslim political state. The relationship between reason and revelation in philosophical ethics would continue to develop the status of humanly acquired virtue in the context of religiously ordained ethical conduct.

As a religious thinker and unbending appraiser of Muslim philosophical discourse, Ghazālīhad a multifaceted interest in ethics. Since Islam had not denigrated the useful secular aspects of social practice, Ghazālī's aim in providing a profound application of ethics in all aspects of human activity was founded upon a realistic understanding of social-political order. This comprehension of the worldly order advanced sophisticated natural morality in transforming the everyday deontological ethics of the Sharīʿa to a code of virtue as a form of devotion to the common good (*maṣlaḥa*) of all humanity. Accordingly, Ghazālī endeavored to interpret and demonstrate the ways in which the Sharīʿa ordinances covering the broad range of personal and social obligations became the essential sources for forming human character. Interpretive jurisprudence—*al-fiqh*—was construed as a major foundation of ethical processes connected with the salvation promised to the faithful in the community. To be exact, for jurists like Ghazālī, who had developed a profound appreciation for juridical methodology, it was not theoretically possible to separate the two disciplines of law and ethics. According to these thinkers, jurisprudence dealt with external aspects of the Sharīʿa, whereas ethics was concerned to show the spiritual-moral aspects of external performance of religiously prescribed duties.

Of course, not all Muslim jurists explored the inner dimensions of orthopraxy. Most of them were interested in providing the rules that dealt with preservation of the social and political order. In contrast, some jurists, like Ghazālī, explored the ethical dimensions of religious practice as these impacted human interaction and cooperation with one another. The difference in emphasis on moral dimension of human acts between these scholars did not mean that ethics was not within the juridical purview of orthopraxy. As a matter of fact, juridical ethics, which guided the formulation of all judicial decisions in interpretive jurisprudence, remained an indispensable component of all legal-ethical analysis of humans' conduct toward one another. The reason was that ethics dealt with providing the moral reasoning behind the divine commandments that could not be easily understood by the generality of believers in the community. On examining the narratives that provide the detailed information on legal norms reflecting evaluation of judgments related to the expressions of personal inclinations, attitudes or even expressions of approval or disapproval rather than the ethical standards directly, one can appreciate the overall difficulty of expecting the generality of believers to fathom the juridical deliberation engaged in understanding deeper moral meanings and inner aspects of the Sharʿī rulings that were appraising human character.

Consequently, Ghazālī laid down several characterizations of the term "ethics" dealing with moral and factual elements in a given judicial ruling by pointing out that one needs to pay attention to the actual signification of moral judgments in the context of personal and social processes connected with human endeavors in bringing about religious ideals of virtuous existence. The process, according to him, was to analyze expressions of attitudes and feelings in ordinary language that undertook to articulate morality (*khuluq*) that expressed a state of orderly existence. More important, his analysis of moral narrative preserved in historical accounts functioned as a paradigm in identifying the consequence of moral life. Accordingly, one needs to pay attention to the overall effect of ethics in the context of an ideal for human behavior. Significantly, it seems that Ghazālī is proposing to take into consideration the outcome, step by step, as it impacts the approach of the agent in a given cultural and social milieu in understanding and articulating God's role in effecting the virtuous life.

In theory, Ghazālī cites several definitions to demonstrate that the richness of the term "ethics" does not allow reducing it to one or another aspect of its manifestations in a person's life. The term signifies its true meaning by underscoring its comprehensiveness in bringing about wide-ranging effects that need exploration and understanding. It is in this sense that the famous ascetic Ḥasan al-Baṣri's description of good morals as "clear in delineation, generous in giving, and refraining from harming [anyone or anything]" is cited by him. On the other hand, Ghazālī cites 'Alī b. Abi Ṭālib's identification of three characteristics of good morals: refraining from committing forbidden acts, seeking legitimate sources of sustenance, and showing compassion toward one's dependents.[13] Most of these descriptions deal with some of the effects of good morals without treating the signification of the term "ethics" itself. Hence, Ghazālī next undertakes to deal with the term itself.

According to Ghazālī, *khulq* or *khuluq* are the two terms interchangeably used to describe a person well created (*khalq*) with good morals (*khulq*). This description includes external and internal goodness since human beings are created with a body that has eyes to perceive and a spirit and soul capable of seeing and perceiving with discernment. Each of these two aspects has a character and manifestation, either beautiful or ugly.[14] Ghazālī points out clearly that the soul, with its capability of discernment, is far superior to the body, with the organ of sight. It is for this reason that the Qur'an explains its greater station in the following verse: "See I am creating a mortal of clay. When I have shaped him, and breathed my spirit in him, fall you down, bowing before him!" (Q. 38:71). The passage reminds humanity that the body is attributed to clay, and the spirit to God, the Lord of Creation. The words "spirit" (*rūh*) and "soul" (*nafs*) are synonymous in this verse. Accordingly, Ghazālī defines *khuluq* (ethics) as "an unwavering state in the soul (*nafs*) from which action flows effortlessly without any need to ponder about or to plan its performance."[15]

In most cases, Ghazālī takes the term "ethics" to mean good moral cultivation of the three basic aptitudes of the soul: rational (*tafakkur*), irascible (*ghaḍab*), and appetitive (*shahwa*). Knowing very well the human condition that inclines toward immorality more readily, he defines the concept as something that a person performs unwillingly. He cites a tradition to support this latter definition: "Paradise will be surrounded with loathsome things and hell will be surrounded with appetites." He then cites the Qur'an: "Yet it may happen that you will hate a thing which is better for you; and it may happen that you love a thing which is worse for you" (Q. 2:216). In a third place he defines the term by saying, "It is something that eliminates all the bad habits that have been explained in detail in the revealed law (*al-shar'*), in such a manner that the bad habits make the person loathsome and, consequently, he avoids them just as he avoids a bad command in order to resume good habits, while longing for these good habits since these have an impact on him and he enjoys them."[16] To be sure, these definitions are limited to one aspect of morality, which is good morals, although the actual signification of the term includes both the good and the bad together. It appears that these definitions are divided according to their rhetorical usage rather than meticulous analysis of their technical sense.

In his major work written under Sufi inspiration, *Revival of Religious Sciences* (*iḥyā' 'ulūm al-dīn*) Ghazālī offers a comprehensive definition of morality. This book undertakes to interpret every Shar'ī rule ethically and is given a devotional dimension such that it can become the starting point for inner purification. The intended audience is a private person concerned for his own life or charged with the spiritual direction of others. In general, as a theologian-jurist-mystic, Ghazālī regards virtue as a divinely infused attribute (*hay'a rāsikha*) of the soul that emanates from an individual without difficulty and deliberation and without requiring habituation that endeavors to reach an ideal. Hence, when this infused trait results from the performance of good and praiseworthy acts that can be derived from both reason and revelation, it is called good disposition. Conversely, if this trait results from bad acts, it is called bad disposition. No distinction is made between acquired and infused virtues except that a good act done only occasionally (e.g., being charitable only when encountering a needy person) does not qualify as stemming from infused disposition. Only those virtues that emanate effortlessly and without deliberation as part of one's habitual conduct qualify as infused and form part of human personality.[17]

Accordingly, Ghazālī defines morality as a "firmly established condition in the soul from which actions originate with ease and effortlessly without any need to think or deliberate about them. If the condition is the originator of rationally and religiously good actions then it is called good ethics; however, if the condition motivates bad actions then it is identified as bad ethics."[18] In principle, Ghazālī is a mystic-theologian closely allied to the Qur'anic doctrine that spoke of humanity that had originally experienced a primordial state of perfection. This blessed power was taken away by an act of disobedience provoked by the devil in paradise. However, it was part of the divine mercy that prescribed ritual practices such as fasting and prayer to restore an individual to an original state of proximity to God. Personal piety was treated as conducive to initiating or maintaining one's original status with God to obtain sacred power.[19]

Several Muslim scholars have quoted this definition and refuted its terms. For instance, Fakhr al-Dīn al-Rāzī (d. 1209) in his exegesis of the Qur'an mentions that *al-khulq* is the natural disposition that makes it easy for an individual to accomplish good conduct through habituation.[20] In general, when Rāzī speaks of *al-khulq* he restricts the term to good actions without applying it to the bad ones, which he introduces with the modifier "bad." However, Ghazālī offers an even more accurate signification of the term *al-khulq* when he says that the everyday sense of the term refers to the hidden aspect of an individual's personality (his soul, with its qualities and ascriptions), similar in status to his external physical form and its qualities and meaning applied to it. Hence, when we describe someone as good in form and in character, we mean that person is good outwardly (*ẓāhiran*) and inwardly (*bāṭinan*). Indeed, human personality has the good and bad qualities that stem from infused nature. Ritual preparation and habituation lead one to be in touch with the divine at important times in one's life. The objective of the rituals, according to these scholars, is to guide the human spirit to something or someone greater. Hence, for instance, regular fasting is treated as a means of ridding the body of its attachment to material possession and pleasures, thus freeing the person for attaining a higher state of piety and morality. Abstinence (*zuhd*) was particularly effective in regulating the balance between body and spirit. Divine reward and punishment for one's conduct applied more to the inner aspect of the personality than to the outer.[21]

These definitions indicate that morality includes good and bad. However, they do not consider the acquisition part in morality. It is human agency through human action that renders ethics ethical. A common feature in these definitions is that they treat morality as a disposition or condition that can be originated in nature through God's gift. God's endowment infuses the human agent with the capacity to acquire moral conduct with training and practical experience. It is practice and experience that enable an agent to achieve moral conduct through repeated actions whose validity is infused in one's nature. The reason human agency is emphasized in acquired morality is that attainment of good actions loses its integrity if human capacity is undermined by overemphasis on infused morality, whose attainment is easier because it is a divine gift to humanity. To acquire the condition that actually enables a person to attain the level of inherent moral sense, with its ability to develop the necessary aptitude in the performance of moral acts effortlessly, one needs to engage in habituation. This is the signification of *al-khulq* (morality). The distinction between infused and acquired morality is preserved in *al-khulq*—morality—that affords acknowledgment of God's guidance in attaining the ideal without putting at risk human agency.

Obviously, the acquired behavior or the act is not moral until it attains morality through habituation, or a compelling inclination in the person. God's guidance provides an ideal with an explicit command to approximate it through personal striving (*jihād bi-nafs*). In other words, it is watchfulness (*al-murāqaba*) over one's progress in the acquisition of moral conduct through repeated action that renders human struggle ethical. The major qualification of such an ethical act is that it is done habitually and willingly in such a way that agents perform it as part of their disposition with ease to attain the moral end. This is identified as moral character, *khulq*. However, such a distinction between a habitual and willingly done act and the requirement for attainment of moral conduct gives rise to false claims of being virtuous. Muslim scholars were aware of the negative implications of habituation and the constant watchfulness over one's acts. Hence, *khulq* had to be rescued from *takhalluq* (feigning morality). Indeed, in Arabic usage there is a subtle distinction between *al-khulq* and *al-takhalluq*. To be sure, ethics (*al-akhlāq*) in Arabic conveys moral characteristics and natural dispositions. In contrast, the term *takhalluq* (from the same root verb, KHLQ) is the opposite of *akhlāq*, which signifies feigning something that is not in one's natural disposition. *Takhalluq* threatens the integrity of ethics by predisposing a person to act as if in an effective way of achieving a good end.

It is pertinent to note that Islamic tradition, as it evolved in its legalistic environment, regards religion as an essential source for understanding what constitutes the realization of the human person. Consequently, the terms "religion" (*dīn*) and "ethics" appear as two sides of the same coin. In fact, Islam equates noble morals with religion, and religion with noble character. According to Ibn 'Abbās (d. 687), a prominent exegete of the revelation, when the Qur'an speaks about the Prophet as being "great in morality (*khuluq*)" the description in reality applies to being "great in religion (*dīn*)." However, Rāzī has disputed this tradition narrated on the authority of Ibn 'Abbās by pointing out that human beings are actually endowed with two faculties: theoretical and practical. Religion reverts to the theoretical aptitude; whereas morality reverts to the practical aptitude. As such, it is not possible to regard them as one and the same.[22] It is, however, important to point out that the implications of the tradition and Rāzī's comment on it do not negate what Ibn 'Abbās had in mind. After all, religion obtains all the admirable and praiseworthy moral conduct, just as morality acquires deeply religious aspects like the inclination to become an exemplar for good people. The difference between the two comments reverts to religion leading to theoretical propensity, whereas ethics leads to practical capacity. In this context, Ibn Qayyim al-Jawzīya (d. 1350) points out that, according to the first chapter of the Qur'an, namely, al-Fātiḥa (The Opening), which lays down essential beliefs and the human desire to attain moral excellence through righteous acts, religion is all ethics.[23] Whoever attains a high level of morality also attains a high level of religious faith. However, this convergence of the high attainment to the traits that make up excellence of character does not collapse the difference between the two terms. It simply suggests that they are closer in their objective based on their intended good ends. We will revisit the relationship between religion and ethics in detail in Chapter 5.

Islamic Ethics Is Essentially Deontological Ethics of the Sharīʿa

The Sharʿī norms provide a legal-moral action-guide[24] in the form of virtues and the ends that must be acquired by obeying the prescribed duties in religion that are good and must be perceived as such and performed in an efficient and effective way. The acquisition of the divinely prescribed excellence has depended on God's specific natural endowment that enables reason to perceive the purpose of life and to strive for it tirelessly. The Sharʿī obligations are deontological in the sense that they appraise the rightness (or wrongness) of actions without regard to the consequences of such actions. Natural reason is capable of grasping the inherent correlation between rationally derived knowledge about good and bad and the guidance provided in revelation about the ultimate objective of religion. As a divinely ordained system its norms are mainly concerned with instilling obedience to God's commandments. By contrast, teleological norms determine the rightness (or wrongness) of actions on the basis of the consequences of those actions. Additionally, a teleological justification must deal with the theological issue of capacity (*istiṭāʿa*) or capability (*qudra*) that enables the agent to produce good or evil. Obviously, without the willful ability to attend to one's duties, there does not seem to be any other ground to assess the good or bad consequences of one's acts. In the context of revelatory promise of rewards and punishments, it is important to note references to desert that follow compliance with God's decrees. Since God imposes (*kallafa*) duties upon human beings, who also go through hardship and difficulty in fulfilling them freely and deliberately, they deserve high praise and reward in the form of compensation. As part of God's benevolence (*luṭf*) toward human beings God is obliged to benefit them by offering them a reward (*thawāb*). Nevertheless, repeated appeals to divine sanctions as a motivating reason become irrelevant when the sole emphasis in the Sharīʿa rulings is moral-religious obligation.

In Islamic ethics, as I shall discuss later, moral norms are subdivided into objectivist and subjectivist standards: objectivist because the ethical value is intrinsic to the action independently of anyone's decision or opinion; subjectivist because the action derives value in relation to the view of a judge who decides its rightness (or wrongness). In Islamic religious law it is God's judgment that renders an act obligatory, and from that perspective the deontological norms are subjectivist. The study of juridical deontological ethics is important for this research, since one of the major issues that we need to tackle in this study is the intricate and inherent relationship Islamic ethics has with juridical theology and interpretive revisions. Traditional juridical theology, based on scriptural sources, affirms that every agent acts by virtue of an ability (*qudra*) created by God to act. Action by definition is the act or performance of the one to whose ability to act it is related as object. Whatever God wills comes to be, and whatever God does not will does not come to be. God creates whatever comes to exist in the world, as it exists in itself and in its attributes. God's will is, in an absolute sense, the originator of whatever occurs in the world. Human agents are the agents of their voluntary actions in a secondary sense, because if God does not create the act and the ability to act, there is no human action. The determination of occurrences, both praiseworthy and blameworthy, good and bad, belongs to God. God is the author of deliberate human actions. There is no autonomy on the part of human agents. The agent simply performs an act and acquires the responsibility for its performance, not for its creation.

Could God impose a duty that the agent is incapable of doing? This question is valid if the ontological reference to "ability" is grounded in a specific instance of the ability to act which has the given action as its object. For example, God commands us to be charitable. God's commands must be performed voluntarily, especially if the agent knows that she is required to do so based on God's explicit command. However, when the agent omits the act, she intuitively knows that if she had wished to perform it, she could have done so simply because she had a genuine ability to perform it. Why would God require the act without creating the ability? In this particular instance omission of a commanded duty because of any disability on the part of the agent has no ethical value. The failure to do what one is required to do, that which one cannot choose to avoid, is not subject to ethical valuation, since the agent, in possession of genuine ability, is unable to avoid it. There can be neither obedience nor disobedience where the agent cannot choose voluntarily to do or to avoid what is enjoined.[25]

The difficulty of gauging the intricate relationship between theological ethics and interpretive jurisprudence has discouraged many a scholar of philosophical theology and the history of the development of orthopraxy in studies related to the Islamic juridical heritage. Let me point out that until recently such a relationship between law, theology, and ethics in Islam has been noted without any sustained elaboration about the exact nature of their relationship. Quite often scholars have spoken about ethics being integral to Islamic juridical studies. And yet, it is only recently that some Muslim jurists have paid attention to this essential connection, expounding the scope of legal studies to include ethics. To begin with, some Muslim jurists have differentiated the two technical terms in

Muslim ethics, namely, *al-khulq* and *al-sulūk* . Among these jurists some are of the opinion that whereas *khulq* (ethics) deals with theoretical issues connected with evaluating human conduct, *sulūk* (behavior) deals with practical aspects of human behavior. Furthermore, this group maintains that these two terms are also distinguished by their two well-defined scopes (theoretical and practical), one for the study of Islamic jurisprudence and the other for ethics. As a matter of fact, they contend that Islamic jurisprudence or any secular study of law, as a distinct discipline from ethics, depends upon its peculiar juristic methodology (*uṣūl*) to discover the principles and rules for deducing practical action-guides in various fields of religious-moral-legal acts (*furūʿ*) and, more important, to provide legitimate textual and rational sources for regarding it as authoritative. Furthermore, based on the juridical methodology that is applied in inferring juristic practice, the system deals with human acts, whereas ethics, which has as its subject matter human personhood, deals with prescribing *al-sulūk*—behavior to guide human external comportment. To be exact, *al-sulūk* is an indicator of one's moral attitude as manifested outwardly in one's comportment. However, the difference between jurisprudence and ethics is the result of the two distinct areas of inquiry: the scope of jurisprudence is determined by authoritative religious-moral action-guides (*fatwā*), whereas ethics is concerned with deriving a practical solution for distinguishing moral from immoral.[26]

Muslim jurists who maintain that the study of law and ethics is intertwined contend that their methodology and the expected outcome of their investigation in both fields are not that different. In fact, the legal ruling and ethical solution converge in developing a moral sense of what is right distinct from what is wrong by clarifying an action-guide that achieves the well-being of a person and secures the social order. Consequently, the jurist is not only committed to discovering an authoritative ruling that would guarantee one's salvation in the hereafter; he is also committed to discovering the correlation between purely religious and ethical decisions to generate confidence in distinctive legal norms that provide grounds for overlap between religious and moral action-guides.

Both jurisprudence and ethics are geared toward solving the practical problems encountered by people in their everyday life. Undoubtedly, Muslim jurists, having been trained in evaluating textual hermeneutics, concentrate on juridical theology that functions as the foundation of juridical ethics by postulating creedal sources to expound issues of deontic importance to generate faith in obedience and against disobedience to God's will expressed in the Sharīʿa. This search in theological issues leads them to discover those doctrines that have relevance to orthopraxy that could be applied to infer comprehensive action-guides. Although their investigation takes them on a distinctive path that extrapolates the permissibility or impermissibility of a certain act from the Sacred Lawgiver's point of view, the intrinsically moral nature of the juridical inquiry directs them to understand the rationally derived knowledge about the good and bad aspects of the act in order to distinguish praiseworthy from blameworthy human behavior. Technically, the entire investigation is based on the object of providing an ideal and justifiable action-guide.

The Distinct Discipline of Ethics

Muslim scholars differentiate between the concept of ethics, *al-akhlāq* (a plural form of *khulq*), and the discipline of ethics, *'ilm al-akhlāq*. I have, more or less, explained the concept of ethics among these scholars. As for the discipline of ethics, according to some, it deals with the discernible human conduct from the point of its sources, motives, and objectives. Moreover, it defines values and practical rules needed to be observed in one's conduct. This intellectual undertaking determines different aspects of attitude or its form, just as one deals with the instruments that influence a sense of duty to do right and to avoid bad behavior.

It is significant to affirm that, according to Muslim scholars, the discipline of ethics does not simply deal with the values that apply to human conduct or the enactment of the standards or criteria that apply to its foundation; rather, if human behavior becomes distorted, ethics can transform and restore it to its healthy state. Most Muslim thinkers agree that vices must be treated as psychological disorders that require therapy. In this sense, the discipline of ethics (*'ilm al-akhlāq*) resembles medicine because ethics treats the spiritual ailments of human dispositions. Accordingly, ethics is regarded as a technique of treating psychological disorders and maintaining sound mental health. Indeed, the ultimate goal of ethics is the attainment of happiness (*al-sa'āda*).[27]

The major source of the discipline of ethics among Muslims is the Prophet Muḥammad, who is retrospectively regarded as the embodiment of Qur'anic morality. This belief about the prophetic moral paradigm is based upon highly authenticated tradition reported on the authority of 'Ā'isha, the Prophet's wife. According to this tradition Sa'īd b. Hishām asked her to describe the Prophet's personality. In response she said, "Haven't you read the Qur'an?" Sa'īd said, "Yes, I have." She went on to say, "[The Qur'an] is the Prophet's disposition." Sa'īd asked again, and she replied, "His personality was the Qur'an." She went on to recite the first ten verses of the chapter *al-Mu'minūn* (The Believers): "Prosperous are the believers, who in their prayers are humble and from idle talk turn away, and at almsgiving are active, and guard their private parts . . ." (Q. 23:1–10).[28] The tradition underscores the centrality of the prophetic paradigm in disciplining the soul to attain moral excellence. More important, the tradition has served as the foundation of the Islamic ethics that depended upon the prophetic paradigmatic precedent to underscore the justificatory reasoning to deduce fresh rulings in the Sharīʿa based on the natural order of things.

In theological works, both the traditionalists and the rationalists have acknowledged the element of supernatural commissioning of moral-religious obligation (*taklīf*). More appropriately, they have considered social custom (*al-ʿurf*) and intuitive reasoning (*al-ʿaql*) as the major sources of moral cognition.[29] In fact, the Qur'an regards intuitive reason as a divinely endowed faculty with the infused capacity to know what is right and wrong. God's guidance to humanity includes revelation as well as intuitive reason as the sources of moral judgment. Significantly, although social custom is variable in its moral directive, the Qur'an considers it an important component of human ethical reflection. Undeniably, Islamic revelation treats human cultures as intricate bodies of factual information about human existence in specific historical contexts. Moral wisdom (*ḥikma*) is a cumulative expression of attitudes and feelings secured by the knowledge of factual elements related to human existence and rational method.

Muslim jurisprudents were divided on the issue of the availability of universal morality, clashing on whether it is totally conditioned by social and cultural conventions, and hence relative, or derived from a universal standard of rationality ontologically grounded in human nature.[30] The relativity of moral norms, as I shall discuss later, will pop up time and again in order to scale the level of interaction between divine will and human will, to determine the absolute requirement to obey the commandments. As discussed earlier, the traditionalists, who laid emphasis on the absolute nature of divine will, ignored the intricate relationship that God's commands have with the intuitively known human ability to perform good and avoid bad, since they regarded God to be good and obedience to God's commandments to be beneficial for humanity. In contrast, those who called attention to justice as God's essential attribute insisted that the performance of obedience was rationally tied to freedom of the human will that could, individually and collectively, based on experience in an extended process of trial and error, determine whether to obey or not to obey. It is important to underscore that Islamic revelation provides a complex language for deontic orthopraxy that posits the Divine Will as absolute and that takes for granted that humans must categorically abide by the commandments. On the other hand, based on the doctrine of human accountability on the Day of Judgment and human ability to affirm free will, it is reasonable to take as fact human being under divinely ordained moral obligation, with the ability to act freely and deliberately and face divine judgment. More to the point is the doctrine of divine justice, as maintained by the Muʿtazilites and the Shīʿites, which empowers human beings to explore the meaning and value of moral good to affirm God as just and moral in an objective sense as understood by humans. As a matter of religious principles, the just and moral God is expected to treat humanity with the most commonly apprehended sense, which decrees reward for good and punishment for evil deeds, both in this and the next world. At the same time, the revelation proclaims that in the realm of ethics, social and political life, and religious faith, God does not impose any duties that are beyond human capacity to carry out (Q. 2:286). Based on these doctrines, it is plausible to maintain that, even within the contextual language of moral responsibility and accountability that characterizes the community of the faithful, the revelation seems to be speaking about a universal criterion for "common morality" that lays down a set of rules or directives—categorically obligatory for all in thought, word, and deed—as a projection of human faith in God.[31]

As part of their morally infused nature, all humans are endowed with an innate scale with which they can think about the rightness and wrongness of their act. The Qur'anic paradigm of ethical knowledge is based on the belief that the Creator God does not leave human beings without intrinsic guidance in the nature God imparts to humanity:

> So, set thy purpose for religion (*dīn*), a human by nature upright (*ḥanīfa*)—God's original [nature] (*fiṭratallāh*) upon which God created humankind. There is no altering [the laws of] God's creation. That is the right religion (*dīn al-ḥaqq*); but most humans know it not—[that they should] turn to God [only]. (Q. 30:30–31)[32]

The convergence between the divine command that human beings must treat each other justly and the rational cognition of justice being good underscores the importance of formulating specific judgments first, and then searching for and extricating principles that can be generalized and, subsequently, when needed, applied to new cases. The Qur'an uses the word *al-ma'rūf* (the "known" paradigms) for these generalizable principles, which must be inferred from the concrete ethical practice of everyday life. There is a correlation between "known" moral convictions and God's purposes as mentioned in the revelation. General moral beliefs that are guided by the revelation seek their application in specific situations, thereby furthering the authenticity as well as the relevance of the religious belief system.

In the verse just cited (Q. 30:30–31), the major objective is inviting humanity to understand the purpose of creation and to work on their moral purification (*tazakkī*)—the "original nature of God." Moreover, the verse commands humankind that is already fortified with the divinely infused morality in an "upright nature" to achieve a "reflective equilibrium"[33] between the "known" (the moral convictions determined through the process of reflection) and the "unknown" (*al-maṭlūb*, the desired objectives of moral life)[34] moral judgments by placing the "known" in the contexts of history and culture, simultaneously. In Islamic ethics that aims to establish authoritative orthopraxy, human beings are treated as those endowed with willpower (*irāda*) and capacity (*istiṭāʿa*) to grasp intuitively as well as through pondering about the revelatory prescriptions the consequences and the general principles that can be extrapolated from a particular command. The moral categories of good and evil are thought of as attributes—that is to say, byproducts of one's ethical position as intuitively grasped through reflection. It is for this reason that Islamic ethics anchors moral principles in the insightful process that involves evaluation about the consequences of human acts (teleological context) and their generalizability in other analogous situations (deontological contexts).[35] The Qur'an captures this dual aspect of authoritative orthopraxy to underscore reflection over the telos and the deontic nature of the divine ordainments:

> How many a city we have destroyed in its evildoing, and now it is fallen down upon its turrets! How many a ruined well, a tall place! What, have they not journeyed in the land so that they have hearts to understand with or ears to hear with? It is not the eyes that are blind, but blind are the hearts within the breasts. (Q. 22:45–46)

The passage, while acknowledging the capacity of a sound "heart" (= mind) to understand the consequences of evildoing, appeals to the human capacity for learning from past destructiveness in order to avoid it in the future. There is something tangible about human conditions that cannot be denied by any reasonable person (with "hearts to understand"). But moral reasoning could become blurred if not fortified by belief in transcendence, in obedience to the ultimate authority to whom "shall you return, all together" (Q. 5:48).

Accordingly, the concept of a "known" moral language in Islam does not fail to acknowledge the concrete historical and social conditioning of moral concepts. But it insists that different cultures must seek to elicit the universal ideal out of the diversity of concrete human conditions—a common foundation upon which to construct an ethical language that can be shared cross-culturally in the project of creating a just society. Both the "known" (*al-maʿrūf*) and the "unknown" (*al-gha'ib*, desired *al-maṭlūb*) moral principles in the Qur'an point to concrete ways of life constructed in different cultural idioms ("races and tribes") that must be understood in order to elicit the universals and apply them in their specific context. The moral-spiritual consciousness (*taqwā*) that ennobles human existence and leads it to carry out duties to God and other humans functions as a torch of the divinely created innate human nature (*fiṭra*), enabling it to discover the universals that can build bridges of understanding and share divine gifts across cultures.

However, this relativism anchored in the contextual dimension of human action is a major source of tension and differentiation in the absoluteness of Qur'anic divine command ethics and the considerations due to the need to accommodate cultural variations in appropriating and applying these timeless norms in orthopraxy. Accordingly, Islamic ethics needs to be treated as a multilayered tradition-based moral evaluation with divergent views about the nature and grounds of moral action-guides. The original principles in Islamic moral decision-making are not always discernible on the first inspection. As a matter of fact, conflicting opinions in resolving a moral dilemma in jurisprudence are an indication of various contradictory principles and rules that are evoked as grounds for deducing the ultimate ruling.

The Foundational Sources of Ethical Predisposition in Islam

Meticulous examination of the early Meccan sections of the Qur'an reveals that the Prophet sought the transformation of *jāhilīya* (pre-Islamic) tribal culture by balancing the naturally infused human ability to know right from wrong (one of the recurring usages in the Qur'an to indicate moral acts is *al-ma'rūf* = known just conduct) within a well-articulated Qur'anic notion of human moral agency in the context of individual and collective human responsibility to uphold moral uprightness (*qisṭ* and *'adl*) in interactions with one another. In other words, without negating the pre-Islamic virtues (known as *muruwwa* = loosely translated as "qualities that befit a human being") as pagan and unworthy of emulation, the Qur'an connected the entire edifice of faith in one merciful and just God to the timeless human moral responsibility of upholding justice and compassion in all interhuman relationships. The moral transformation that the Qur'an envisioned was built upon critical evaluation of the limits of the experience of living in a tribal culture, which prided itself upon its achievement in upholding *muruwwa* and which attributed and defended the place of kinship and blood relationship in its accomplishment. Seemingly inspired by natural bonds of kinship, there was a conspicuous absence of the supernatural to render the pre-Islamic ethical system the authoritative and universal source of moral life.

The objective nature of the concept of justice in the Qur'an is summarized by Ibn Manẓūr, the author of a classical Arabic lexicon, *Lisān al-'Arab* (11:430ff.), in his detailed entry on the meaning of "justice" ('ADL). He cites a letter written by an early jurist-theologian of Medina, Sa'īd b. Jubayr (d. 714), in reply to an inquiry about the meaning of the term "justice" by the Umayyad Caliph 'Abd al-Malik b. Marwān (d. 705). According to his explanation, the Qur'anic passages demonstrate that "justice" in revelation should be understood as a universally objective value that denotes moral virtues like "fairness," "balance," "temperance," and "straightforwardness." The term "justice," the theologian points out, has a real, concrete, physical signification first, and an extended, abstract signification second. As such, the scriptural concept of justice becomes comprehensible by logically appealing to the universally self-subsistent value of justice.

In another place, the Qur'an recognizes the universality and objective nature of moral virtue, for example "goodness" (*khayrāt*), which transcends different religions and religious communities, admonishes human beings "to be forward in good work (*khayrāt*)," and holds them accountable for their deeds regardless of their religious differences (Q. 5:48). This passage reveals the assumption that certain basic moral requirements, like "being just" or being "forward in good work," are self-subsistent and apply to all human beings, regardless of differences in their religious beliefs. The ideal human being, then, combines moral virtue with complete religious submission (Q. 2:12). Nonetheless, it seems that there is a basis for distinguishing between religion and morality in the Qur'an, where moral virtues are further strengthened by the religious act of "submission" (*islām*) to sacred authority. Religion necessarily advances human-God relations, whereas morality undergirds interpersonal justice. As stated earlier, all human beings are held accountable when they fail to uphold justice in their social relations. The ultimate aim of religion and morality converge in their directives to foster harmony and orderliness in society regardless of one's religious affiliation. In spite of the fact that faith is emphasized as a critical ingredient in developing an ideal moral personhood (*nafs al-mutma'inna*, Q. 89:27), the role of religion is constrained to testifying the empirical history preserved in the moral narratives of revelation that capture everyday human experience to uphold morality.

It is in the cognition of universal moral truth that human beings are treated equally and held equally responsible for responding to the ethical duty of being "forward in good work." Furthermore, it is this fundamental equality of all humanity at the level of moral responsibility that directs humankind to create an ethical order on earth and makes it plausible that the Qur'an manifests some kind of natural law accessible to all irrespective of a particular revelation. Certainly, the concepts of divine command, wisdom, and guidance all point in the direction of natural and supernatural sources of ethics. God infuses human beings with the necessary cognition and volition to further their comprehension of the purpose for which they are created and to realize it by using their naturally infused knowledge of right and wrong. However, the Qur'an also speaks about basic human weaknesses: "Surely human being was created fretful, when evil visits him, impatient, when good visits him, grudging" (Q. 70:19–20). This weakness reveals a basic tension in the scripture-based ethics that must be resolved by further acts of guidance by God. The prophetic and scriptural guidance is revealed to show human beings how to change their character and bring themselves into conformity with the divine plan for human conduct. In this way, the Prophet's paradigm, the Sunna (the Tradition), is included in the revelatory guidance. Guidance from God signifies the direction God provides to procure the desirable ethical society, first by creating in the soul a disposition that can guard against spiritual and moral peril, if a person harkens to its warnings, then by further strengthening this natural guidance through the revelation and the Prophet. "Guidance" meaning "showing the path" is a fundamental feature of the Qur'an and is reiterated throughout to emphasize the fact that this form of infused guidance is not only part of normative human nature but is also universal and available to all those who aspire to become "god-fearing" (morally and spiritually sound) and "prosperous" (in this and the next world).

The Overlap between Religious and Secular in Islamic Ethics

In many societies that foster secular values and a clear demarcation between public and private spheres of human activity, religiously inspired moral values are excluded as being incompatible to the development of a universal moral action-guide institution. In general, modernity tolerates religious values without affording them a clear voice in the public arena. In most instances religion is clearly seen as a threat to secular modernity when it challenges the secular values that increasingly promote self-gratification as the primary human imperative. Abrahamic religions include, among their theological doctrines of divine justice and human moral agency, concepts of individual and collective responsibility to further a divinely ordained ethical order on earth. Judaism, Christianity, and Islam identify and articulate precepts of responsible individual living under answerable political authority—an indispensable feature of ideal governance. Human beings endowed with innate disposition and fortified with the upright system of belief and practices that constructs individual responsibility through communal bonds are morally and spiritually required to fulfill God's purposes requiring the establishment of justice and equity on earth.

However, historically all three traditions, when in control of political power, have stumbled in fulfilling their moral ideals in acknowledging the dignity of all humans regardless of their race, gender, or creed. The traditionalist scholarship on the Jewish, Christian, and Muslim scriptures has refused to grant individuals freedom of conscience in negotiating their spiritual destiny. The doctrine of individual responsibility to God, instead of conferring validity on the reality of the autonomous infused moral nature of individuals capable of appropriating the divine message of accommodation and toleration, has given rise to a community of individualized moral agents pursuing the social program of excluding the "other" at God's behest. The political society is then driven to adopt the idea of intertwined private and public domains without requiring individual rational consent to legitimize the theology of systematic exclusion of the "other."

Thus arises the concentration of comprehensive religious-secular power in the hands of an exclusivist leadership whose views of private morality are divorced from the communalistic vision of society, with the attendant mistreatment of those within and outside the community who reject that community's religious exclusivist claims. Monotheistic communities have from time to time denied their individual members a right to dissent from or to reject the communalistic interpretation of their respective traditions out of fear that such internal dissension (usually labeled "apostasy") is potentially fatal to the collective identity of the faith community and its social cohesiveness.

The extent of human agency and its intrinsic relation to the supernatural divine agency had ramifications for determining the jurisdictions of revelation and reason in guiding human moral choices: Do humans have the freedom to choose to obey and carry out the stipulated duties in accordance with the aims of serving the divine interests as elaborated in the revelation? What is the role of nature (*fiṭra*) infused with moral disposition in deciphering the details of revelatory guidance about fulfilling divine commandments (*aḥkām sharʿīya*) to build an ethical society?

Undeniably, the disagreements and endless debates among Muslim thinkers, both the traditionalists and the rationalists, are about the fundamental function of tradition under changed circumstances. The discourse on ethics touches upon a debate regarding normativity of the sources of the inherited legal tradition as compared with the norms in secular ethics. These norms are derived from a continuous stream of events in which past, present, and future obscure the paradox of habits that impact and entail making indispensable decisions about a vivid and meaningful experience in deciding morally charged issues. Theoretically, the debate revolves around ethics beyond religion: Is it possible to be moral without being religious? Can revelation continue to serve as the sole custodian and expounder of orthopraxy? Most traditionalist jurisprudents, who regarded revelation to be the only dependable and legitimate source of deriving orthopraxy and who engaged in text-based hermeneutics to infer fresh rulings, remained committed to downplaying the role of human reason to provide validity to judicial rulings. Hence, the question that remains to be resolved is whether scriptural sources can suffice in providing justificatory reasoning to uphold the cultural legitimacy of, for instance, modern institutions of governance for which, as all engaged in this debate acknowledge, there exists no precedent in the classical juridical formulations. This tension in the public arena can be observed in the two major areas of interpretive jurisprudence. At the theoretical level, the critical task for Muslim jurists remains to define two separate jurisdictions in implementation of the Sharʿī values.

Let us consider the two jurisdictions. That which falls directly under the divine jurisdiction in the Sharīʿa is the human-God relationship. The acts of devotion (*ʿibādāt*) are done as part of one's faith commitment to God as the sole Sacred Lawgiver and Blessed Creator. These acts are prescribed in the form of divine commandments (the legislative part of the Divine Will) that maintain the human-God relationship. They provide a social as well as religious framework for organizing the community on the basis of common belief and orthopraxy. More important, they emphasize the religious necessity of observing and maintaining not only the performance of individual and communal acts of piety but also moral excellence to advance social discipline in maintaining the integrated spiritual-moral aspects of devotional acts. This latter characteristic of personal piety in Islam was the foundation of a heightened consciousness of intertwined private and public—spiritual and secular—domains in community's religious ethics. Whereas the authority and validity of moral law were derived from the belief that God's legislative (*tashrīʿī*) will in the form of religious law—the Sharīʿa—embodies the entire way of life, primarily for individuals and secondarily for the community, the motive behind conforming to its sanctions was founded on religious devotion that is aware of the consequences of disobeying these laws. From this consequential perspective, fulfillment of divine commandments presupposed developing the divinely gifted moral disposition (*fiṭra*) with the purpose of attaining self-regulating moral perfection (*tazkīya*) as part of one's total faith commitment (*īmān*).

In working on the religious justification for obeying the fulfillment of the acts of devotion as part of one's duty, the main task confronting the traditionalist Muslim jurisprudents, for whom all human behavior is determined and free will is nothing but an illusion, was the problematic of responding to the rationally asserted doctrine of self-regulating human moral agency (= *fāʿil al-mukhtār*). In contrast, for the rationalist, affirming free will was rooted in human nature that asserted deliberate acts of freedom. The most vexing aspect of the traditionalists' doctrine about determined human behavior was that the revelation had asserted in no uncertain terms that moral law was an integral part of the divinely ordained human nature. According to the Qur'an, the autonomous moral agency (Q. 91:6–7) was not circumvented by God's legislative will to force people to observe the devotional acts. Just as acceptance of faith was independent of any compulsion, the revelation guaranteed people freedom from coercion in acts of devotion (Q. 2:256). Hence, the traditionalists' resolve to uphold God's absolute will that left little or no room for including even a restricted role for human freedom made moral accountability at all levels of missing the performance of devotional acts inconsequential and socially ineffective in building an ideal public order. This was the jurisdiction entirely under God's power.

The second area of separate jurisdiction in the Sharīʿa was invested in interpersonal relations (*muʿāmalāt*). This domain of interhuman relationships was dependent upon human institutions that oversaw the smooth functioning of society. Because of the critical importance of regulating and managing human interactions and relations in everyday situations, the scholastic debates over the status of and relationship between natural and supernatural agency and how to reconcile the role of reason and revelation in Muslim ethical and legal studies have constituted a serious and ongoing part of religious ethical discourse. The Qur'an called attention to regulating human relations with due consideration to the principle of cooperation (*taʿāwun*) and the necessity to observe factors in human interaction that impact claims and responsibilities in all social transactions (Q. 5:2). The main source for the ethics of human relationships was divinely inspired intuitive reasoning that undergirded the divine revelation transmitted through a prophet—the human embodiment of spiritual-moral perfection. According to the Qur'an, a true submission to God was conditional upon believing in the divine providence that regulated human existence to create all human institutions to reflect God's all-comprehensive will and that provided the perfect embodiment of God's will in the Prophet in his role as the guide and teacher for all human beings.

The role played by temporal or mundane circumstances in Muslim ethics of relationship was meticulously justified and legitimized under the latter jurisdiction, dealing with interpersonal relations, as part of social experience and as part of true submission to God. Practical ethics affecting one another remained a critical part of problem resolution for fundamental institutions of society, such as marriage, kinship, inheritance, economic activity, and statecraft. Since the Qur'anic guidelines on certain social and political topics were brief and required elaboration by equally authoritative source of religious ethics in Islam, Muslim scholars compiled religious action-guides afforded in the *ḥadīth*-reports ascribed to the Prophet to interpret the religious sources as they began to be applied to concrete conditions. The classification of the *ḥadīth*-reports to form the Tradition (Sunna) as part of the revelation provided credible and detailed sources to discover the effective reason or the morale (*dalīl*, *ʿilla*) in God's commandments affecting the public life of an individual believer in the context of the faith community. The latter movement became the foundation of interpretive jurisprudence (*al-fiqh*), affording the Sharīʿa a methodology to formulate judicial decisions (*aḥkām*) in all areas of human interaction in order to lay down ordainments with practical consequences in the way of obligatory acts that were decreed as duties (*farāʾiḍ*). Islamic jurisprudence was comprehensive in its scope: it ruled not only on strictly religious action-guides (e.g., duties toward God) with an explicitly separate jurisdiction and otherworldly consequences but also on moral and legal action-guides to manage interpersonal and social matters (e.g., duties toward fellow humans) with clearly this-worldly jurisdiction and consequences. The concrete obligations covered rules of conduct, public and private, assigning ethical categories in terms of the five-degree scale of ethical-religious values: required (*farḍ*), recommended (*mandūb*), permitted or neutral (*mubāḥ*), reprehensible (*makrūh*), and forbidden (*ḥarām*).

Philosophical Theology as the Prime Source of Islamic-Ethical Reflection

The scope of theology includes not merely elaboration or demonstration of the truthfulness of certain religious claims by a faith community. It also undertakes to expound the doctrines that have direct relevance in comprehending the practical guidance imbedded in the religious texts. Hence, for example, Muslim thinkers engaged in analyzing divine acts as they impacted human freedom of choice: Does God's decision to provide guidance determine human behavior? Does God compel humans to act in a certain way? Jurisprudential investigations are carried out to extrapolate the rulings by requiring acting upon them with faith in obedience and assessing the practical consequences. The jurists need to understand the manner in which divine will interacts with human capacity to undertake the performance of religious-moral duties. Can God impose a task beyond human capacity? Can human beings find a legitimate excuse to avoid certain obligations? At the practical level there are many theological questions that have been raised about God's decision to inflict human beings with unbearable suffering. Does suffering occur as a punishment for missed obligations? How about human sinful behavior? What is the role of penance to expiate for missed duties or sinful behavior?

As pointed out earlier, from its inception Islamic revelation was a world-embracing message that saw the earthly life of humanity as preparation for salvation in the hereafter. Public and private were intertwined to provide an integrated system of law and ethics. Islamic religious sources have a single goal in mind: the creation of an ideal public order that can accommodate diverse religious communities to enact an intercommunal political society founded upon universally comprehensible idioms of divinely ordained moral law. This moral law, according to the Qur'an, is ingrained in human nature (*fiṭra*) with which God created humanity. The passages that speak about this principle of innate nature are part of the early Meccan revelation that laid down the purpose of creation, namely, the attainment of moral and spiritual perfection to undertake divine deputyship (*khilāfa*) on earth. The Qur'an explicitly laid down that without God's inspiration (*ilhām*) at the time of creation and infusion of basic moral knowledge humanity was not capable of attaining moral awareness on its own. There were inborn weaknesses in human beings that would have defeated the fulfillment of divine objects of creation. Hence, God's infusion of morality in human nature is regarded as part of divine benevolence (*lutf*) to encourage humanity toward ethical conduct even though faith in God gradually becomes stable in human minds.

Islamic religious ethics, with its goal of establishing a just public order, laid the doctrinal groundwork for the Muslim community to work toward reaching a consensus about the need for just relationships with other faith communities on the basis of common humanity under divine guidance. For the Qur'an it was an actuality that different communities and groups ought to come to terms with the fact of cultural and religious diversity and regulate interhuman relationships on the dictum that functioned as a toleration-generating principle among various claims of exclusionary truth, namely, "To you your religion [*dīn*], and to me my religion [*dīn*]" (Q. 109:6). In God's wisdom, as the Qur'an asserted, humans were to be left alone to exercise their volition in the matter of religion (Q. 2:256). Nonetheless, even though coercion in the matter of one's choice of spiritual path was ruled out, the Qur'an did not overlook the necessity of providing some workable principle to serve as a foundation for interhuman relations. To avoid any dispute about whose religion is superior, the principle of bringing peoples of diverse religious and cultural backgrounds to respect and treat one another as equals had to be based on a common moral terrain. Providing such a universal ethical principle that could be acceptable to all faith communities and groups was a challenge for the Qur'an that included both universal and particular guidance to set up an ideal political society in its message. Generally, in most cases, the manner in which the Qur'an addressed humanity was clearly marked off by the universal address "O humankind!," as the following passage explicitly underscores: "O humankind, We have created you male and female, and appointed you races and tribes, that you may know one another. Surely the noblest among you in the sight of God is the most morally and spiritually (*atqā*) aware among you. God is All-knowing, All-aware" (Q. 49:13). The particular aspect of the Qur'anic message, specifically meant for the Muslim community, was addressed to "O believers!" The following passage underscores this particularity: "O believers, be aware of your spiritual and moral duty and fear God as He should be [reverentially] feared, and see that you do not die save in submission [to God's will]" (Q. 3:102). Hence, the Qur'an is engaged in guiding all humanity as well as its particular faith community, making sure that the latter group becomes exemplary by avoiding extremism of all sorts and following the path of moderation to earn the title of "median community" (*umma wasaṭa*) so that it can serve as God's witness to other people (Q. 2:143).

The universal and specific communications of the revelation point to the wide-ranging objective of the Qur'an to serve as the "reminder" (*dhikr*) to all human beings, regardless of their creedal differences. In view of their equally endowed innate nature—the *fiṭra*—human beings were rational beings capable of knowing the law of nature to choose their spiritual path individually and freely, without any compulsion. Consequently, the conception of moral perfection and autonomy of the natural sphere meant human beings could be held accountable for behaving appropriately to this knowledge of moral truth regardless of their refusing to accept religious claims of truth. The Qur'an required observance of the moral law as an infused source of ethical guidance which any person with common sense could adopt as a strategy to benefit from individually as well as collectively to advance toward justice. Such a universal dimension of the divine guidance, as a rule, materialized with God's creation of humanity—a humanity endowed with infused morality, a humanity that shares a common parentage to claim equality, a humanity that is endowed with nobility and dignity to assume God's work on earth as God's deputy (*khalīfa*). Even more in the nature of universal concern is the moral admonition that calls upon all human beings to work for the common good (*al-khayrāt*) of all regardless of their religious differences (Q. 5:48).

Undeniably, this Qur'anic universalism is thoroughly spiritual in the sense that it essentially responds to God's claim as the Creator. But this claim requires humanity to respond to its own nature in relation to others in the temporal order in order to actualize God's purposes. The divine purposes in religion are closely linked to the ethical perfection of the temporal order in which human beings, assuming moral agency, strive (the true sense of the term *jihād*) to become fully and authentically human by undertaking the duty to be virtuous: "God commands you to deliver trusts back to their owners; and when you judge between the people, that you judge with justice. Good is the admonition God gives you; God is All-hearing, All-seeing" (Q. 4:58–59). The substance of the divine command in this passage reflects social convention based on a rationally derived sense of duty, appropriate to naturally infused moral law, toward delivering trusts back to their owners and of justice in dealing with others. Simultaneously, the command appeals to the community of the faithful, whose claim to truth is based on revelatory sources that regulate the community's relations with other communities living under its governance. This inclusive characteristic of Islamic public order seeking to build a common ground between Muslims and non-Muslims is similar to the modern search for an overlapping consensus between religious and secular premises for a political order. In fact, Ghazālī underscored this overlap when he explicated the absolute necessity of secular order to manage human affairs in an Islamic order:

> Exercise of authority (*sulṭān*) is necessary in managing the religious public order (*niẓām al-dīn*); and secular public order (*niẓām al-dunyā*) is necessary in managing the religious public order (*niẓām al-dīn*). . . . Surely, religious public order cannot be achieved without secular public order. Moreover, secular public order cannot be achieved without the imam (leader) who is obeyed (*al-imām al-muṭāʿ*).[36]

In this statement Ghazālī indicates that while publicly maintained religious action-guides are essential for managing the success of ideal political order structured on the principles of secular requisition, religious reason on its own is insufficient to manage a religious public order built on political consensus; rather, it must look for public reason that functions as the justificatory rationale for the derivation of universal ethical principles to obey legitimate the power structure under an imam. Remarkably, the source for public reason in this ideal public order is by the same token derived from scripturally prescribed moral duty to exercise authority with justice. This latter command about justice is the most critical aspect of political ethics which requires the moral assessment of the rule that claims to be "Islamic." An Islamic government at that point opens itself to a two-pronged evaluation that combines the spiritual and the secular as the interlinked jurisdictions in evaluating its claim and performance as an ideal form of governance. In this sense, religious ethics underscores the interdependence of this- and the next worldly objectives of human existence. In addition, religious ethics takes a lead in providing functional legitimacy for the secular and religious reasons by showing the correlation between the good that was induced by secular and religious reasons. In Islamic political theology it was not implausible to demonstrate the overlapping consensus that revealed the agreement between the religiously and secularly derived sense of right and wrong. Ethical knowledge, whether delivered through revelation or human rationality, had a metaphysical grounding in divine will. In the final analysis, in general, it was the divine will that comprehensively directed the human will to be aligned with God's guidance for the creation of the best public order for humanity.

It is important to reemphasize that this repository of overlapping consensus in traditional communities was derived from scriptural sources, collectively labeled divine revelation, which, on the one hand, excluded other communities from its particular brand of salvation and, on the other, encouraged its own community to benefit from an innate sense of human moral worth to forge a practical consensus to treat other faith communities with respect and fairness. To be sure, religious debates about political ethics were shaped by the question of human moral agency and divine providence. These early debates had their genesis in the determination of the responsibility for the corruption of power structures and appropriate individual or collective responses. Like any exercise of authority that is plagued by the sinful behavior of those in power, Muslim rulers were no exception to this political reality. Did they act as God's free agents, or were their acts predetermined by God's overpowering will? The Qur'an proffered a complex view about God's will as it interacted with human will. There are verses that speak about God "sealing their hearts" or "When they swerved, God caused their hearts to swerve; and God guides never the people of ungodly" (Q. 61:5). These were taken to imply that God foreordains everything for good or bad. Other verses imputed to people the responsibility of being misguided, thereby making it possible to speak about human free will. Certainly, the Qur'an suggested a multifaceted correlation between divine predetermination and human responsibility.

To the extent that human beings are free agents, they can reject God's guidance, although, because of their innate disposition (*fiṭra*) prompting or even urging them subtly to believe in God, they cannot find any valid excuse for this rejection. Even then, their rejection pertains to the procuring of what is desirable, and not to the act of grasping the importance of what is desirable in the first place. However, when human beings choose to reject this guidance, God denies further guidance to them: "Those that believe not in the signs of God, God will not guide them" (Q. 16:104). This denial of guidance clearly pertains to the guidance that would lead to the procurement of the desirable end, not to the initial infused moral guidance that is engraved in the hearts of all human beings in the form of an innate disposition to guide them toward the good end.

3

The Genesis of Moral Reasoning in Religious Ethics

In Chapter 2, I asserted a need for an independent inquiry in the area of Islamic ethics related to interpretive jurisprudence (*al-fiqh*) and its legal-ethical methodology (*uṣūl*), which I identified as a major source for understanding Islamic ethics. The reason is that insofar as the objective structure of human acts is concerned, ethical deliberation regarding ethical rules and principles belongs to the field of interpretive jurisprudence and its methodology for derivation of judicial decisions. At this level of inquiry about the effective principles and rules that are operative in the religious action-guides (*aḥkām*) of the Sharīʿa and the way they are applied to rationalize God's command and prohibition, the academic scope becomes determining what one ought to do to fulfill one's obligations.

This approach is based on the change of perspective in the development of religious ethics in Islam, which is usually related to the Aristotelian ethics of virtue. The present study undertakes to identify ethical foundations of interpretive jurisprudence to demonstrate the need for a fresh line of investigation to extract sources of moral reasoning in Islam that shares its moral and spiritual genome with other Abrahamic traditions. Abrahamic traditions have given humanity the hope and the method of establishing justice that commenced its vocation objectively by implementing the idea that spiritual equality is to be realized on earth by implementing God's will as expressed by its law. The ultimate moral excellence can be attained by obeying God. The main objective in such obedience is to draw close to God (*qurbatan ila-allāh*). Hence, the purification of intention (*niyya*) is critical in Muslim piety.

Sufi writings have devoted much space to the acquisition of this habit by emphasizing purity of intention (*ikhlāṣ*). However, the scope of this research is to search for sources of moral reflection in jurisprudence. As long as that juridical vision remained part of the ideal, these traditions continued to evolve sophisticated methods to demonstrate the close alignment between spiritual and moral development in Muslim religious praxis. The heart of this evolution has remained the conceptualization and compliance of reason with the standards and precepts provided in the revelation to advance humanity toward beneficial articulation of human endeavors to identify processes that lead to meaningful existence. Although I will deal with the ethics of interpretive jurisprudence in

Islamic Ethics. Abdulaziz Sachedina, Oxford University Press. © Oxford University Press 2022.
DOI: 10.1093/oso/9780197581810.003.0003

Chapter 4, in this chapter I will raise the major question in interpretive jurisprudence, namely: how to adhere to deontological ethics of the Sharīʿa to seek what is advantageous and beneficial by performing all those acts that are prescribed as morally obligatory while avoiding those that are disapproved by the divine lawgiver to merit reward in the hereafter.

In determining the primary evidence used in moral-legal reasoning in the context of Islamic juridical tradition, Muslim legal scholars had to grapple with a fundamental uncertainty about the ramifications of rational methodology (*al-ijtihād al-ʿaqlī*) that questioned blind adherence to textual proofs as unadulterated evidence without ascertaining their judicious validity. Let us remind ourselves that if, as maintained by the traditionalists, doctrinally God determines each event and human action, directly and strictly, moral reflection would be redundant since good and evil would have been decided by obedience and avoidance of divinely ordained duties. There is no room for rational investigation, since God's command and prohibition cannot be rationalized. They simply need to be obeyed. However, reliability of transmitted textual proofs depended upon their sound transmission, which in turn depended upon investigation of transmitted information and its congruity with the overall objectives of divine legislation. Whereas the Qur'anic text remained, in general, immune from the critical assessment of its reliability in transmission, the traditions were meticulously scrutinized for their admission as documentation prior to the formulation of a moral-religious action-guide (*taklīf*). The rational derivation of moral-religious action-guides (*al-taklīf al-ʿaqlī*) based upon the concepts of value, their meanings, and their relation to each other, without textual corroboration, was always suspect in the eyes of traditionalist jurists committed to uphold the inviolability of scriptural[1] precepts.

The philosophy built upon the notion of flawlessness of divine legislation (*al-taklīf al-samʿī*) seemed to cast a long shadow of doubt over the reliability of reasoning as an independent or even an auxiliary source of legal-ethical decision-making. However, reason, as asserted by the Qur'an, was also part of the divine guidance to enable human beings to fathom natural and social activity and correlate it to the activity of the divine revelation. Accordingly, in order to become correlated to the revelation, reason had to anchor itself firmly upon religiously authenticated textual precedents. Moreover, moral reasoning could not afford to overlook the plurality of human lived experience, leading to a variety of and relatively formulated opinions about the religious-moral action plan as an ideal for human behavior. Nonetheless, in order to obtain text-based religious-moral action-guides (*al-taklīf al-samʿī*) in terms of their classification in interpretive jurisprudence into permissible or forbidden, good or bad, obligatory or recommended, and to determine the ways of knowing the presence, absence, or degree of these values, the jurists acknowledged the requirement to go beyond the authorized religious texts to garner the wisdom that was obtainable in vivid and meaningful human experience of living with others. Analytical questions about these value concepts form part of the toolkit that analyzes textually or rationally collected information, evidence, and advice for a specific action plan or activity. This methodological toolkit functions as the source of moral erudition and its applicability in the two related fields of ethics and law in Islamic jurisprudence. The ethical system that emerges from this deep-rooted relation between the moral and the legal leads me to assert with confidence that the essential nature of ethics in Islam systematically covers religious and secular, spiritual and temporal, as brought to light in juridical analysis.

As pointed out in Chapter 2, the secular and the religious in Islamic tradition are interwoven to assert the indispensable nature of Islamic public order with its noncompartmentalized private and public domains of human life. Islamic jurisprudence is concerned with public and private. From its inception Islam emerged as a comprehensive system in need of expanding its doctrinal formation to accommodate the practical needs of its political society as demanded by its Sharīʿa-oriented practice—the orthopraxy. The intimate partnership between spiritual and temporal could be construed as the bedrock of the intellectual rigor and vitality that established an unavoidable rationalistic approach to the ethical ideal presented by the revelation. Historical accounts show that the emphasis laid by Islamic revelation on the community's social-political and economic welfare was a major motivation for the development of rationalist methodology. Rationalism undergirded the legal-ethical system to evolve to respond to the growing demands of the expanding empire. The inevitable and indispensable collaboration between the affairs of the hereafter (spiritual) and the affairs of this world (temporal) was reflected in the legal methodology that went beyond the interpretation and appropriation of religious validations to and vindications of the reason-based indicators in order to extract fresh practical rulings in all areas of human processes and dealings. Nevertheless, Muslim scholars had some understandable concern in supplementing the absolute nature of the divine commandments with extrarevelatory, relative, and context-bound (*sabab taghȳr al-aḥwāl*)[2] sources like reason and human experience. It is pertinent to note that textual information was deemed concise, and yet its elaboration required jurists to equip and engage in its reason-based linguistic and lexical interpretation. Hence, part of the jurists' education included mastering of nonscriptural subjects like Arabic language and literature to aid them in deciphering the intent and application of the divine commandments preserved in the Arabic of the 7th century. For the rationalists, the critical question surrounded the extent and legitimacy of utilizing autonomous reason as a substantial source in deducing divine injunctions. In contrast, the traditionalists, who upheld divine commandments as the sole basis of practical ethics, denied the rationalist thinkers' emphasis on autonomous reason and human conscience as valid sources for the derivation of absolute moral decisions. For them the most reliable sources of ethical-legal rulings are set forth in the teachings of the Prophet in the Tradition and in the Qur'an—the two primary scriptural sources for interpretive jurisprudence.

Rationalist and Traditionalist Religious Ethics

When one considers the normative Islamic tradition for standards of conduct and character, it becomes apparent that besides scriptural sources like the Qur'an and the Tradition ascribed to the founder of Islam, which stipulate many rules of law and morality for the smooth functioning of society, Muslim scholars recognized the value of decisions derived from specific human conditions as equally valid resources for formulating responses to ethical problems in Muslim societies. Early on, the jurists, who also took a deep interest in theological questions, conceded that the scriptural sources could not easily cover every situation that might arise, especially when the Muslim political domain extended beyond the Arabian Peninsula and required rules for urban life, commerce, and government in relatively developed societies. But how exactly was human intellectual enterprise to be directed to determine the effective cause (*'illa*), the philosophy, and the objectives (*maqāṣid*) behind certain paradigm rulings (known as *aṣl*, plural *uṣūl*) provided in God's commandments? Apparently, ascertaining these principles as part of basic procedure was crucial for their application to formulate a consistent methodology for deducing future decisions.

Besides the problem of resolving a substantive role of reason in understanding the implicit effective cause of paradigm cases and elaborating the juridical-ethical dimensions of revelation as they relate to human conduct in public and private spheres, there was the problem of situating the credible religious authority empowered to provide validation to the ethical-legal reasoning associated with the rationale behind practical rulings. On the one hand, following the lead of Sunni jurists like Shāfi'ī (d. 820) and Aḥmad b. Ḥanbal (d. 855) in the 10th and 11th centuries, Sunni Islam located that authority in the interpreters of the Qur'an and the Tradition. These scholars represented the predominant schools of Sunni theology which held that in deciding questions of orthopraxy one could work out an entire system based on juridical-ethical elaboration of Islamic revelation and the Tradition. On the other hand, following the line of thought maintained by the Shī'ite leaders, Shī'ite Islam located that authority in the rightful successors of the Prophet. The Shī'ite imams maintained that there was ongoing revelatory guidance available in the expository competence of human reason in comprehending and correlating the divine revelation with reason, exemplified by the solutions offered by the Shī'ite leadership.

In general, Muslim theologian-jurists paid more attention to the nature of God's creation than God's nature per se. Any inquiry into the divine nature was ruled as reprehensible since human intelligence had no access to such information. In addition to creation, they discussed human beings' relation to God as the Creator, Lawgiver, and Judge. They were also interested in understanding the extent of God's power and human free will as these affected the search for the right prescription for human behavior. In the final analysis, in view of the absence of the institutionalized religious body (resembling the church in Christianity) that could provide the necessary validation of the legal-moral decisions on all matters pertaining to human life, the problem of determining the sacred lawgiver's objectives (*maqāṣid*) behind juridical-ethical rulings that had direct relevance to the social life of the community was not an easy task. It required individual as well as collective exertion of rational capability (*ijtihād*) to understand its basic procedures (*uṣūl*) and apply divine objectives expressed in the revelatory sources for an ideal society. The entire intellectual activity related to Islamic juridical-ethical tradition can be summed up as the jurist-theologians' attempt to engage in interpretation of the scriptural sources in order to indicate a relationship between moral-legal rulings (*aḥkām*, singular *ḥukm*) and the divine purposes expressed in the form of norms and rules in the Qur'an and the Tradition (not without ambiguities, necessitating rigorous rational analysis and defense). In view of the incomplete state of their familiarity with the existing circumstances and their understanding of the future contingencies of human circumstances, in most cases of ethical judgment the jurists proceeded with caution on the basis of what seemed most likely (*ẓann* = conjecture) to be the case. Such ethical judgments were normally appended with a clear, pious statement that the ruling lacked certainty (*'ilm* or *qaṭ'*) because it was only God, who, being aware about the circumstances and consequences affecting human beings, was the most knowledgeable about the true state of affairs.

In due course, the jurists were able to identify two forms of rational inquiry (*ijtihād*) for understanding the justificatory reasoning behind a legal-ethical decision. Sometimes the effective causes of the rulings were derived directly from the explicit statements of the Qur'an and the Tradition (*al-ijtihad al-shar'ī* or *al-sam'ī*) that stated the rationale of legislation, as in the case of retributive justice in the Qur'an.[3] At other times, human reason independently discovered the relationship between the ruling and the effective cause (*al-ijtihād al-'aqlī*), as in the case of, for instance, gratitude to the benefactor, in order to provide a sound theoretical foundation for interpretive jurisprudence. Under all circumstances, the jurists could not easily reject admitting and determining the substantive role rationalism played in providing intercommunal ethical sources for valid legal or moral decisions. More significant, autonomous reason's role in outlining the procedures depended upon the jurist's comprehension and endorsement of the moral epistemology, whether it was rationalist-objectivist or theistic-subjectivist, as maintained by the Muʿtazilite or Ashʿarite theologians, respectively. In other words, it depended upon the way the human act was defined in terms of the nature of derivation of moral knowledge about good and bad, and whether the responsibility for having obeyed or disobeyed God could be directly ascribed to human beings. In an important way, any advocacy of reason as a substantial rather than formal source for procuring moral-legal verdicts required authorization derived from religious sources like the Qur'an and the Tradition. The Qur'an advocated a teleological view of human being with the actual ability to use reason to discover ultimate causes of actions in relation to their ends or utility. God's will through evidence supplied in creation bestows a natural reasoning that may aid humans to acquire a natural knowledge of God's existence and God's commands and prohibitions, more particularly when the revelation itself endorsed reflection on the reasons for revealed commandments as well as obeying them. It is important to keep in mind that the majority of jurist-theologians, whether belonging to the Sunni or the Shīʿite school of thought, maintained that without the endorsement of revelation, reason-based investigation to figure out fresh rulings (*al-ijtihād al-ʿaqlī*) could not become an independent source of religious moral-legal (*al-takilīf al-samʿī*) decisions.

This cautious attitude toward reason has its roots in the belief that God's knowledge of the circumstances and of the consequences in any situation of ethical dilemma encountered by human existence is exhaustive and infallible. Whereas the Qur'an and the Tradition had provided in some cases the underlying effective cause for moral-legal rulings when declaring them obligatory or forbidden, on a number of issues the rulings were expressed simply as God's commands which had to be obeyed without knowing the reasons behind them. For instance, according to the universal moral principles known to all intelligent people, one ought to avoid what is harmful to one's own being (*dafʿ al-ḍarar*) and to seek what is beneficial (*istiṣlāḥ*). Thus, the effective cause for the duty of seeking medical treatment is to avoid grave and irremediable harm to one's well-being, whereas the reason for the prohibition against taking human life is firmly based on one of the objectives (*maqāṣid*) about protection of life as declared by the revelation. The commandments were simply part of God's prerogative as the Creator to demand unquestioning obedience to them. To act in a manner contrary to divine commands is to act both immorally and unlawfully. The major issue in deontological juridical ethics ("Do it, because God commands it!"), then, was related to defining the admissibility and parameters of human reasoning as a divinely enacted and substantive source for discovering or formulating religious-moral decisions (*aḥkām*). Can autonomous reason discover the divine will in confronting emerging contemporary legal-ethical issues without succumbing to human self-interest?

Evaluating Rational and Scriptural Obligations (*al-taklīf al-ʿaqlī wa al-samʿī*)

The fulfillment of obligations, that is, those actions that ought to be done simply because they are part of God's commandments, defines the scope of Islamic jurisprudence. Interpretive jurisprudence was, in large measure, concerned with understanding divine commandments in revelatory sources in order to discover, elaborate, and extrapolate the details of the moral and religious action-guides in orthopraxy. However, juridical inquiries were ontologically grounded in the metaphysical aspects of the divine directives which needed to be understood through theological speculation based on the doctrines provided in the revelation. The doctrines functioned as legitimating sources for comprehending the philosophy and intent of the essential commandments and provide supporting documentation to enable scholars to formulate detailed deontological rulings. Deontological rulings were determined by evaluating the rightness (or wrongness) of actions without regard to consequences produced by performing such actions. With the expansion of the Muslim empire through the conquest of different regions, the domain of applied Islamic ethics was expanding at an accelerated rate and was demanding authoritative rulings in all areas of human relationships. The common objective that combined the scholarly endeavors of the theologians-cum-jurisprudents was to identify tangible manifestations of the divine will throughout creation and in the divine legislation through meticulous application of reasoning processes to extract the desired moral instructions from the revelation. In this way, Muslim religious thought adopted a two-pronged approach to determine the objectives of divine creation and legislation. On the one hand, some rationalist theologians, particularly the Muʿtazilites and the Shīʿites, asked questions about the purpose of creation that led them to the doctrine of universal moral principles known to all intelligent individuals who ought to avoid what is harmful to their own being and to seek its good; on the other hand, the traditionalist theologians, like the Ashʿarites, asked how to obey God's commandments that were sent through the prophets who informed those under moral obligation (*al-mukallafūn*) of the rewards and punishments of the next life. Inevitably, reason and revelation had to maintain an integrated method to relate the compatibility or lack of it in the related fields of inquiry in the area of juridical studies under two related categories: *al-uṣūl* (principles) and *al-furūʿ* (application). The substance of this inquiry was provided by the epistemological question about the knowledge of right and wrong, whether its sources were rational or traditional, or both. In spite of everything, reason and tradition were united in the common task of establishing a public order that was respectful of the omnipotent God and that was for total conformity with divine purposes, as extrapolated from the scriptural sources, in preserving human equality and dignity in creation.

The use of "rationalist" and "traditionalist" in this chapter, as discussed earlier, conforms to the general identification of the two major trends in Islamic ethics. Let me reiterate that the rationalist and traditionalist theses about moral conduct can be summed up by taking into consideration the relationship between religion and ethics in Islamic religious thought. As a matter of fact, it was essentially a theological dispute that sought to reconcile God's omnipotence and omniscience and the ramifications for the human freedom to act under the divinely ordained system of the Sharīʿa. If the Sharīʿa was the source of all human acts, then their attribution to human beings meant advancing the traditionalist thesis regarding predeterminism. The problem was reconciling God's absolute discretion over human will that promulgated the idea that God can command the impossible and hold humans responsible for failing to do it. Such a doctrine was contrary to what the Qur'an taught about human initiative and responsibility (Q. 2:286). The latter doctrine was compatible with God's justice, as maintained by the rationalists, that necessitated autonomous moral agency to deserve praise for having performed good deeds and having avoided particular sins. As for the traditionalists, justice for God is thus to be God, to will what God wills and command what God commands; for God's creatures it is to obey God at all times. Interestingly, though God wills that sin and unbelief exist—otherwise they would not exist—God has forbidden them, so that they are not morally right. Clearly, while in most cases an ethical sense is not coextensive with what God commands, in this specific case of sin and unbelief ethical significance is coextensive with what God wills.

The debate about moral capacities had implications in the area of the basic procedures of juridical methodology to deduce prudent decisions for human choices in matters that presented ethical dilemmas in areas that were not adequately covered in the revelation. Can God compel humanity to conform to the moral and legal requirements of the religious system without allowing freedom of choice in matters of religion? Although the question remained true to core traditionalist understandings concerning divine omnipotence, it had trajectories in directing the middle path that, on the one hand, sought to maintain God's absolute sovereignty over creation and legislation and, on the other, left enough autonomy for humanity to exert its free will to be obligated to obey divine commands and earn deserts.

The debate engaged the intellectual energies of Muslim thinkers to resolve the disputes encompassing the ontology and the epistemology of moral acts. What is the nature of good and evil? How do humans learn about them? Muslim theologians were divided into two major camps, depending upon their appraisal of good and evil. The rationalist Mu'tazilite theologians maintained that good and evil are rational (*'aqlī*) and objective categories that can be known through reason, independent of revelation. In other words, the knowledge of good and evil is naturally available to *all humans* capable of morally good acts, and God is justified in holding people responsible for their choices. Innately, ethics is independent of religion. To be more precise, through the innate ability created in human nature (*fiṭra*) God has empowered humans to know self-subsistent good and bad. Moreover, being rational categories, they are autonomously and fundamentally independent of scriptural authority and are directly related to human experience and reasoning ability.

In contrast, the traditionalist Ash'arites maintained that the two ethical categories of good and evil are ontologically related to God's commandments (legislative = *shar'ī*) and epistemologically known through scriptural sources (transmitted = *naqlī*) revealed through the Prophet. Good and evil depend upon God's will and attain authority only through God's revealed commandments about instituting the good and preventing the evil (*al-'amr bi al-ma'rūf* and *al-nahy 'an al-munkar*). All acts attain value through God's commanding will that specifies their desirability or reprehensibility or prohibition. Accordingly, it is only the divinely revealed scriptures that determine the nature of good and evil.

Inevitably, the Ash'arites had to take up the critical assessment of the two central theological precepts to fortify the monotheistic absolutism in the area of ethics: (1) the principle of causation and (2) the doctrine of God's justice. They did not deny these doctrines as such; rather, they ruled them to be meaningless outside God's provenance and command. The command to do good and abstain from evil cannot inherently determine the reason why a certain act was ruled permissible or forbidden, nor can such a command on its own establish the goodness or the evilness of a particular act since both justice and injustice are determined by God's command. Justice for God is to be God. It is outside human prerogative to rule about the morality of divine acts. Whatever God does or commands is just, without any question, since God is bound by no rule or obligation. It is entirely within God's omnipotence to decide to punish a believer or reward a disbeliever. All God's actions are right and just, and therefore there is no need to search for reasons such as to rationalize or explain the ultimate decisions of God.

To summarize, Mu'tazilite and the Shī'ite ethics fall under rationalist-objectivist ethics, and Ash'arite ethics fall under traditionalist-subjectivist ethics. The admission of reason in their methodology was dependent upon discovering the extrarevelatory proofs that formed part of the evolving toolkit that comprised information, resources, and advice derived from revelatory sources that functioned as principles and rules needed to determine the permission/prohibition of a specific activity with legal-moral consequences. This toolkit constituted both textual as well as rational resources for resolving the nature of commandment, whether it was an imperative duty (*farḍ*) or simply a recommended (*mustaḥabb*) act. Both the rationalists and the traditionalists were engaged in determining the principles and rules that could provide reliable criteria to deduce predictable judgments in all areas of interpersonal relationship. Central to this discussion was the analytical treatment of the twin ethical concepts of justice (*ʿadāla*, usually defined as "putting something in its appropriate place") and obligation (*wujūb*, meaning "morally obligatory" or "logically necessary"), sometimes defined as "promulgation of divine command and prohibition." The concept of justice provided a theoretical perspective on the question of human responsibility in obeying divine commands and the extent of human capacity in carrying out moral-religious obligations (*al-takālif al-sharʿīya*). The concept of obligation defined the nature of divine command and provided deontological grounds for complying with it.

The Ashʿarite doctrine about God's commandments being for the good of humanity became gradually less different and eventually the same as the Muʿtazilite doctrine about God's essential moral attribute necessitating that God do what was most salutary for humanity. Both traditionalism and rationalism appeared to iron out the rough edges of exclusively moral or scriptural procedures that continued to profoundly challenge both the Ashʿarite traditionalist divine command ethics and the Muʿtazilite rationalist objectivist ethics when it came to the analysis of the ontology and epistemology of human understanding of the moral accountability in the context of a number of fields in applied ethics in Muslim societies in modern times. The basic Muʿtazilite thesis that human beings, having been endowed with an innate capacity to know right and wrong and having been equipped with free will, are responsible for their actions before a just God could not be sustained when the reality on the ground showed tensions in evaluating the consequential dimensions of historical events.[4] Furthermore, as per their epistemology, good and evil are rational categories that can be known by intuitive reason, independent of revelation. According to the Qur'an, God created all humans in such a way that they are capable of acting justly and perceiving good and evil objectively (Q. 91:6–7). In the absence of any notion about congenital tendencies to do evil, the rationalist conclusion about human nature being innately moral emboldened the Muʿtazilite argument in support of human moral agency. Freedom of will then functioned as a corollary to the main Muʿtazilite thesis, namely, that God's justice depends on creating and conferring on human ability to act morally. Divine justice also presupposes the human aptitude to extract moral principles based on expressions of attitude and feelings about ethical decisions and volition to determine the right course of action related to one's social relationships. Without such an endowment of natural ethical knowledge, and in the absence of any contact with a prophet or sacred scriptures, no human being can be held accountable for his deeds. To state it differently, the Mu'tazilites asserted the efficacy of natural reason as a source of spiritual and ethical knowledge, maintaining a form of rationalist objectivism. In this way they emphasized complete human initiative and responsibility in responding to the call of universal ethical guidance through natural reason, which was further elaborated by guidance through revelation.

The Ash'arites challenged the Mu'tazilite rationalist theory. In fact, they rejected the idea of natural reason as an autonomous source of religious-moral guidance. They maintained that good and evil are as God commanded them in the scripture, and it is presumptuous to judge God's action restricted by God's justice, on the basis of categories that God has actually provided in the scripture for directing human life. For the Mu'tazilites, the Ash'arites argued, there is no way, within the bounds of ordinary logic, to explain the relationship of God's power to human actions. It is more realistic to maintain that everything that happens is the result of God's will, without explanation or justification.

However, argued the Ash'arites, it is important to distinguish between the actions of responsible human being and actions attributed to natural laws. Human responsibility is not the result of free choice, a function that, according to the Mu'tazilites, determines the way an action is produced; rather, God alone creates all actions directly. Then how do human beings become accountable for their actions? This was the source of their moral quandary. If human acts are predetermined by God's will, then what is the purpose of the Day of Judgment and the final reward or punishment? This doctrinal predicament had to be resolved in the light of the Qur'an's constant reference to the day of reckoning and human destiny in the hereafter being dependent upon human performance on earth. Human beings are agents of their voluntary actions in a secondary sense, because if God does not create the act and the ability in the agent to act, there is no human action. On the basis of the traditionalist usage, one needs to make a distinction between "creation" and "acquisition": God's action is a creation (*khalq*); a human being's voluntary act is an "acquisition" (*kasb*). In some actions a special quality of "voluntary acquisition," which allowed humans to engage in performance of an act, was superadded by God's will, thereby making the individual a voluntary agent and responsible for his actions. Consequently, human-acquired responsibility is the result of God's will that is known through scriptural guidance, i.e., the Qur'an and the Tradition. Otherwise, moral values have no foundation but the will of God that imposes them. This attitude of the Ash'arites to ethical knowledge is identified as theistic subjectivism. This means that all ethical values are dependent upon determinations of God's will expressed in the form of revelation, which is both eternal and immutable.

Both these theological standpoints were based on the interpretation of Qur'anic passages, which undoubtedly contain a complex view of human responsibility in procuring divine justice on earth. On the one hand, the Qur'an contains passages that would support the Mu'tazilite position about human free will, which emphasized the complete human responsibility in responding to the call of both natural guidance and guidance through revelation. On the other hand, it has passages that could support the Ash'arite viewpoint, which upheld the omnipotence of God, and hence denied humans any role in responding to divine guidance. Nevertheless, it allows for both human volition and divine will in the matter of accepting or rejecting faith that entailed the responsibility for procuring justice on earth.

However, the role of ethical norms in deriving moral judgments was articulated in greater detail by the theologians who were divided along the same lines as the jurists: those who supported the substantive role of reason (*al-ijtihād al-ʿaqlī*) in knowing what is right and obligatory and those who argued in favor of the scriptural sources (*al-ijtihād al- sharʿī*) as the primary foundation of ethical knowledge. To be precise, moral reasoning is directly related to religious epistemology based on textual evidence in Islamic thought. Ethical objectivism or deontological theory, with its thesis that human beings can know much of what is right and wrong because of the intrinsic goodness or badness of actions, is connected with the rationalist ethicist, Mu'tazilite theologians; ethical voluntarism, the traditionalist ethics, which denied anything objective in human acts themselves that would make them right or wrong, is connected with traditionalist Ash'arite theologians.

The traditionalist reactions to rationalist ethics resonated with the jurists' apprehension of independent reason (*ijtihād*) in deriving deontological judicial decisions (*aḥkām*) that had to be obeyed unquestioningly. The arbitrariness of human reason, as the traditionalists pointed out, could not guarantee a right solution to the complex moral dilemmas faced by human beings in everyday situations. Moreover, if reason was capable of reaching the right ethical judgment unaided by the revelation, then what is the need for God's guidance through the revelation? Hence, according to the upholders of traditionalist divine command ethics, it was more accurate to maintain that God's command in the form of revelation is not only the primary source of the moral-religious law; it is also the sole guarantee for avoiding contradictions that stem from reason's arrogation of the function of revelation.

This cautious and even negative evaluation of rational methodology in traditionalist ethics had a parallel in the systematization of juridical theory among Muslim jurists. The ethical-juridical problem-solving method was in search of a fundamental rational-scriptural principle that could function as a template for the formulation of up-and-coming ethical-legal decisions. There was a tacit recognition that evaluative judgments related to moral issues uncovered expressions of juridical preference, subjective expressions of jurist's attitudes, or personal feelings, not only rendering them relative but also, in some cases, contradicting scriptural guidance. For instance, the pre-Islamic institute of temporary marriage, although endorsed by the Qur'an (Q. 4:24) and tolerated by the Prophet during the conquest of Mecca in 630, was repudiated by a number of early jurists who regarded it as immoral.[5] The expansion of Muslim political rule beyond Arabia raised questions about the application of the rulings provided by the revelation that had come in the specific Arabian tribal context. The jurists were quick to realize that such absolute application without considering specific social and cultural contexts of these rulings was not without a problem. After all, the rulings provided by the revelation emphasized specific human conditions related to custom, everyday human behavior, and ordinary language used to convey moral precepts and attitudes to life in Arabian tribal society. In other words, even when a moral precept is wholly promulgated through divine legislation (e.g., gratitude to one's benefactor = *shukr mun'im*) in the Qur'an and the Tradition, such a precept inferred on the basis of factual elements is also objective because of its universal application in diverse cultures.

In delineating the scope of juridical tradition that integrated ethical tradition in its interpretive enterprise, Muslim jurists distinguished between two areas of Sharī'a precepts: duties to God (*'ibādāt* = ritual duties) and duties to fellow human beings (*mu'āmalāt* = social transactions). Performance of ritual duties was required when the necessary conditions were met. In addition, they were to be performed as part of one's religious duty, regardless of differences in culture and time and place. In contrast, social transactions were necessarily conditioned and evaluated by reference to everyday human life experience under specific cultural, social, and political conditions, and, hence, their implementation was adjustable to the needs of time and place. It was in the latter sphere of interpersonal relations that the jurists needed to provide fresh rulings generated by the changing human circumstances. As a consequence, the range of deontological ethics in Islam is extensive and covers all people, regardless of their faith identification. Accordingly, the interpersonal sections of jurisprudence are firmly founded upon principles and rules that can be generalized and applied to all matters dealing with relational ethics. However, authoritative decisions in matters of social justice could not be derived without first determining the nature of human acts under religious-moral obligation (*taklīf*). The divine command, understood in terms of religious-moral obligation, provided the deontological ethical code of conduct and a teleological view of humans and the world. The idea of obedience to the divine commands was equated to one's spiritual and moral progression toward final salvation. Intractably, violation of divine commands, as Muslim jurists taught, is not only immoral on the grounds that it interferes with the pursuit of the human goal of achieving happiness (*sa'āda*); it is also sinful because it results in loss of prosperity in this and the next life. Ultimately, human salvation in revelation is directly connected with human conduct—the subject matter of Islamic ethics and jurisprudence.

Islamic Ethics in Juridical Methodology (*uṣūl al-fiqh*)

Every category of religious-moral act, whether classified as obligatory (*wājib, farḍ*), recommended (*mandūb, mustaḥabb*), permitted (*mubāḥ*), disapproved (*makrūh*), or forbidden (*ḥarām*) in the Sharīʿa, is founded upon explicit or implicit moral principles and rules extracted from the apparent or metaphorical sense of the Qur'anic passages or the *ḥadīth*-reports. The basic principles of a voluntarist theory of ethics, as maintained by Sunni theologian-jurists, is based upon the doctrine that the source of value is God and that that value is known to humans through the divine commands in the scriptures. Thus, Sharīʿa, as a deontological and teleological ethical system, is theoretically able to discover the religiously ordained judgment on every category of human act in the area of human-God relations (ritual duties, *ʿibādāt*) and human-human relations (social transactions, *muʿāmalāt*) and learn about the awaiting accountability. However, jurisprudence also scrutinizes the religious sources (the Qur'an, the Tradition, and the consensus of the learned [*ijmāʿ*]) for their admission as validation in concluding fresh cases occurring in a different contexts. This part of the juridical inquiry is related to the science of "juridical principles" (*uṣūl al-fiqh*), or interpretive jurisprudence. The juridical principles serve both moral and religious analysis in identifying the applicable principle of normative ethical judgment on external human acts. The emphasis at this level is to bring to light moral details as part of corroborating analysis and conclusion. The moral assessment of human behavior is applied to derive judicial decisions that are directly concerned with fundamental questions about the role and cognitive validity of rational inquiry on its own to pronounce (*ḥākim*) moral-religious obligation as necessary (*wājib*) or simply good (*ḥasan*) or to be discarded as evil (*qabīḥ*).

Take, for instance, the case of autopsy in interpretive jurisprudence. It is one of the most sensitive issues in the Sharīʿa dealing with two conflicting obligations: respect for the dignity of the dead and the need to determine medical causes of death. The case presents fundamental divergence between two sets of evidence that claim equal importance and application to resolve a highly delicate matter in Muslim cultures. It goes beyond the interpretive jurisprudential inquiry to assume culturally explosive moral-ethical problems concerning respect for the dead. The source of the disagreement reverts to juridical methodology that has an explicit clause that in such cases, in order to resolve the divergence between two authoritative proofs, only *one* set of evidence can be admitted as the basis (*milāk*) of authorizing a judicial decision (*ḥukm*). Moreover, the choice to perform the duty is upon the agent under obligation (*mukallaf*) to decide on the preference of one over the other proof in fulfillment of the responsibility regarding the dead.[6]

Islamic tradition regards bodies and spirits as God's gift. Human beings do not possess absolute ownership of their body or spirit. They are like stewards charged with preserving and dignifying their life by following the guidance provided in the revealed texts. Stewardship in the Qur'an suggests freedom of action, while recognizing that this freedom is not unlimited. To be a steward is to acknowledge responsibility and accountability to the ultimate source of life and sustenance, God, the Almighty. Accordingly, suicide is a criminal act and strictly forbidden in the Sharīʿa. A person who commits suicide is not accorded full burial rites. Moreover, suicide constitutes denial of God's creation and desecration of human personhood made up of integrated body and spirit.

A major source of controversy in Islamic jurisprudence is the modern medical practice of making an incision in the body of the deceased.[7] A living individual who donates a kidney must undergo surgery that requires a twelve-inch incision. Performing the same procedure on a cadaver, however, poses a host of theological and ethical problems for Muslim jurists. In the Sharīʿa there was never any objection to performing an autopsy for the purpose of understanding the cause of death in specific cases or to advance medical knowledge in general. Autopsy is a well-established procedure of modern medicine. It is performed to correlate clinical aspects of disease for diagnostic and therapeutic evaluations to determine the cause of death as well as to serve an educational function. With the spread of modern medicine all over the world, Muslim countries have more or less allowed postmortem biopsies under certain conditions. In comparison to the traditional complete or limited chest- or abdomen-only autopsy, contemporary postmortem tissue sampling through a nonmutilating procedure performed immediately after death seems to have overcome religious and cultural opposition to postmortem in many Muslim societies.

Nonetheless, modern advancement in tissue sampling through needles and other nonmutilating procedures notwithstanding, public perceptions about postmortem dissection and postmortem examinations continue to carry the stigma of mutilation, which affects public opinion in many societies. Current medical diagnostic techniques that tamper with the corpse or delay its burial are often viewed by the public as mutilation of the dead. The Prophet emphatically advised his followers to bury their dead promptly, "not waiting for morning to bury if the person died at night; and not waiting for nightfall if the person died in the morning. Make haste in taking them to their resting place."[8] Muslim regard for the dignity of the dead entails both prompt burial and respect for the dignity of the corpse. Still, the rule of arranging objectives in an ethical hierarchy—*qāʿida bāb al-tazāḥum*[9]—provides the needed justification to make an incision in the corpse when such a procedure may help resolve any dispute about the cause of death or the settlement of a bequest or when it might help to save a life by providing a vital organ, like a heart, lung, or cornea, for transplantation.[10]

It is worth remembering that the search for paradigm cases in this connection was prompted in modern times by the use of cadavers in the training of medical students. The increasing use of this practice early in the twentieth century prompted a number of articles written in response to questions posed to the religious authorities in Cairo, Egypt, or in Najaf, Iraq, about the possibility of desecration of the dead. The search for paradigm cases supporting such use of cadavers led to the identification of two sections of jurisprudence where such cases involving limited desecration of the dead had been resolved. The two sections that provided the rulings dealt with the burial of the dead (*al-janā'iz*) and the distribution of the inheritance (*al-irth*) left by the dead.

Since there are no specific text-proofs that address the modern issues connected with dignity of the dead or making incisions in cadaver to determine the cause of death, most of these decisions are based on juridical principles and rules (*qawā'id fiqhīya*) that are essentially derived from moral analysis of the case. Hence, interpretive process depends on a number of possible solutions based on rational analysis of one's claim to ownership (*milkīya*) of one's body. The overriding concern in these rulings is to avoid granting easy permission to slit open the dead body because the inviolability (*ḥurma*) of the human body proportionally weighs heavier than medical forensics. Consequently, it is only to determine the cause of death to protect or redress the legitimate claim of the heirs that the incision in the dead body is tolerated. No incision should be made based on the rule about the inviolability of the human body at all times. Hence, if the cause of death is under investigation, the heirs have no right to speed up desecration of the body to claim their inheritance. In any event, desecration of the body should be avoided except as a last resort to satisfy a legitimate resolution connected with the heirs' claim over the estate of the deceased.

Today anatomical dissection and postmortem examinations are a routine part of medical education and diagnostic techniques that stress the need for such procedures in understanding illnesses and evaluating incompletely known disorders or discovering new diseases. Accordingly, the scope of clinical diagnosis requiring autopsy has expanded beyond the three traditional justifications mentioned in the classical juridical formulations in Islam.[11] An additional aspect of increased instances of desecration facing a dying person and his family is the possibility of donating organs for transplant. This means allowing surgical procedures that constitute a desecration of the dead in the Sharī'a in order to retrieve an organ. A visible incision into the body and the removal of externally visible or internal organs represent true desecrations. Muslim jurists have had to search for a moral principle or a rule that could permit an incision or mutilating procedure for the immediate saving of the life of a patient who is dying of organ failure. Such permission depends upon establishing that the donor is dead at the time the organ is removed for transplantation.

In the context of organ retrieval from brain-dead patients, it is important for jurists to determine the end-of-life criteria. The brain-death criteria are still being contested by some prominent Sunni and Shīʿite jurists. The critical issues in such cases are quality of life and the withholding of care from those for whom treatment is assumed futile or whose right to consent is overlooked because of the patient's inability to participate in the decision about her treatment. These issues speak to some of the urgent legal and societal matters in Islamic medical ethics. Since medical practice in the Muslim world continues to be paternalistic, there is hardly any reference to the enforcement of the ethical principle of autonomy. As a matter of fact, ordinary Muslims have only a vague understanding of informed consent in a clinical setting. What does this consent involve? Is it just signing a legal document to the affirmative? Under such circumstances, informed consent pays no heed to the most fundamental principle of Islamic medical ethics, namely, "No harm, no harassment" (*lā ḍarar wa lā ḍirār*), which promotes beneficence and distributive justice. And although the Islamic Juridical Council, representing Muslim communities worldwide, in Mecca has permitted the turning off of extraordinary life-support equipment in the case of brain-dead patients, there is no agreement among scholars that organs can be removed while the patient is on artificial life support.

The possibility of organ transplantation for saving a critically ill patient did not exist until recently, when surgical techniques and immunosuppressive drugs made this an option and thus a serious moral-religious issue for Muslim jurists. The relatively high rate of success in organ transplantation has encouraged Muslim jurists to search for legal-ethical justifications to formulate their rulings to keep pace with the demand for such medical procedures, which are already a de facto practice in many hospitals in Muslim countries. In their rulings in this area, some jurists have relied on the principle of public good (*maṣlaḥa*), which allows postmortem dissection following a stillbirth and for the purpose of retrieving a swallowed valuable object belonging to someone other than the deceased. Yet the Prophet's well-known tradition states, "Breaking a bone of a dead [person] is like breaking a bone of a living person,"[12] and this tradition has served to remind Muslims to show deference to honor the dead and forbid the desecration of the body unless required to promote the larger good. All jurists agree that saving a life, as the Qur'an requires, makes it possible to approve the lesser evil of desecration for the larger good that such an act promises. More pertinent, desecration carried out in aggression is certainly different from a clinical incision to retrieve an organ made with the deceased's permission in advance directives. This latter procedure is still within the accepted treatment of the dead.

A Muslim Scheme of Categorizing "Obligatory," "Good," or "Evil" Acts

Islamic ethics and the Sharīʿa rulings share value terms like "obligatory," "good," and "forbidden."[13] However, their definition depends on the way human agency is perceived doctrinally in juridical theology. Among traditionalist jurists, all the Sharīʿa categories (obligatory, recommended, permitted, disapproved, and forbidden) are defined in relation to actual divine command and prohibition and religiously promised rewards and punishments by God in the next life. In contrast, among rationalist jurists these categories are defined in terms of their relation to human ability and freedom to perform them as a part of humans' infused moral nature. Since humans are endowed with intuitive reasoning and the power of deliberate action, they are under the divinely ordained obligation of the Sharīʿa. After all, as justificatory reasons go, the revelation assures people that God does not impose any duty beyond human ability to perform it (Q. 2:233).

The rationalist theologians maintained that the expression of a command or prohibition by the revelation to do or to avoid doing something, as maintained by the traditionalists, is in itself inadequate to render the act obligatory or forbidden. The ontological reference to human acts is either to an act's essential nature or category or to the circumstantial course that leads to its occurrence. In the latter sense, the agent is regarded as simply morally responsible for the act as she caused it to come into being or has knowingly and intentionally caused it to occur in a particular way. Hence, these characteristics have to be indicated by other words additional to the command (*ʿamr*) or prohibition (*nahy*). Accordingly, the divine command or prohibition should read, "Do it, because it is your duty to do it" and "Don't do it, because you will be worthy of blame if you do it." Supposedly, the commands and prohibitions that originate as part of the rulings of the revelation are actually in possession of intrinsic ethical properties of their own, over and above being commanded and forbidden by God.

In the context of orthopraxy, Muslim jurists define the category "obligatory" or "prudentially necessary" in terms of the juridical category of the "obligatory" (*wājib*, *farḍ*) act from the standpoint of self-interest of the agent (*mukallaf*) who, by means of her intellect, determines the performance of action to its omission on account of the harm connected with omission. Thus, an act is obligatory when it is necessary for the agent to do it if she is to avoid harm. It is also prudential because the act serves the practical interest of the agent. In fact, expected harm in this life may be recognized by intellect, whereas expected harm in the next life is known only by revelation.

The ethical nature of this concept becomes evident when one considers the objective-subjective aspects of an obligatory act, as maintained by the Muʿtazilites and Ashʿarites, respectively. An act's objective aspect is rationally determined by the facts of the world rather than the opinion of some judge or observer about it. In this sense, this type of ethical knowledge is autonomous and self-validating, having been established by reason as obligatory. On the other hand, an act's subjective aspect is determined by the opinion of some judge or observer. To be precise, reason does not determine anything to be morally or religiously obligatory, nor are goodness and badness generic or essential qualities of action that can be known through reason. Rather, it is God who, through divine command and prohibition, determines an act to be good or bad, respectively.

Furthermore, the Muʿtazilite definition of "obligatory" looks at the relations of praise and blame to the agent for the act. Accordingly, "obligatory" as applied to an act is that for whose omission the agent deserves blame. For instance, when a man fails to fulfill his spousal responsibility of providing enough means to manage a home, the failure to do so is not simply deplorable; it is a failure of performing the essential duty that affects adversely the entire family—the fact that legitimately declares that person as deserving of blame. The failure to attend to the familial duty is based on empirical facts about his being the breadwinner. Hence, the relation of blame that he deserves is obvious. "Deserving blame" suggests the result of the events that made such a negative evaluation of his sense of duty necessary. This failure is objective because "deserves" introduces a fact, which is truly predicated regardless of anyone's opinion. This was the doctrine firmly held also by the Shīʿite rationalist jurisprudents.[14] The Ashʿarites, on the other hand, denied the objective nature of obligation based on some objective attributes of acts in themselves, which were then commanded by God for human beings to perform. On the contrary, they maintained that God's commanding certain types of acts provided the essential characteristic that made them obligatory. As noted earlier, the human agent's performance belongs to her and is ascribed to her as her act by virtue of its correlation to an ability to act which God creates at the time of the performance of the act.

The Ashʿarites denied the Muʿtazilite thesis that an obligatory act had an ontological reference in human reason and ability. The agent's ability is verified and is true only with respect to performance that actually occurs when God creates it at the time of performance. The Ashʿarites are accused of holding that God imposes upon humans the obligation to do what in fact they are, in some instances, incapable of doing. On the basis of the observed facts, there was disagreement among prudent and intelligent persons regarding the obligatoriness of particular acts under varying circumstances. This observation-based rejection served as the fundamental characteristic of theistic subjectivism or voluntarism among the Sunni jurist-theologians, particularly, by the Sunni law schools of Shāfiʿī and Ibn Ḥanbal. For them an obligatory act is that for which there is a threat of punishment, and a forbidden act is one whose omission is necessary, as prescribed by the revealed law.

It is important to state that the Qur'an distinguishes objective ethical concepts from God's acts of commanding and forbidding. Thus, when it says "[B]e forward in good works," the category of "good works" is clearly founded on a universally recognizable moral good (*al-khayr*). It was only through the development of Islamic jurisprudence, and more specifically its adoption of the limited senses of ethical concepts of the Qur'an and their transformation into expanded meaning of legal categories of the Sharīʿa, that defined good in terms of commanded and evil in terms of prohibited. Gradually, the Sharīʿa categories, such as "act of disobedience" (*maʿṣiya*), were widened in application, and they came to replace the original ethical terms like "abominable" and "detested" (*munkar*) themselves, giving rise to ethical voluntarism (theistic subjectivism). This theory, as discussed earlier, maintains that it is the revelation that provides the ontological grounds for categorization of a particular instance of good and evil, thereby equating the objective ethical categories of good and evil with God's commanding and forbidding, respectively.

The thrust of the Ashʿarites' argument is based on their expositions of the conditions that control what is "obligatory" in the actual world. These conditions are created by the will of God. In addition, the human's natural ends are enforced by inescapability (*jabrī*) of divine forces in creation. In this way, God not only determines but also commands the obligatory acts for the natural ends of humanity. This is the traditionalist theistic ethics, which relates moral acts to the divine prescriptions and proscriptions provided in scriptures.

God promises rewards and imposes sanctions for obeying the divine commandments, which renders performance of these acts compulsory if one wants to avoid God's punishment. In general, there is no attribute in addition to God's commandment that renders acts obligatory for humans to perform in their own interest.

The second important category in the Muslim scheme is the "good" (*ḥasan*), in general meaning "agreeable" or "fitting to an end" or even supernatural good. In relation to acts, "good" is that for which the agent does not deserve blame. In relation to a purpose, the purpose of undertaking a "good" act may be that of the agent, as in the commonest usage, or that of other persons, or of the agent in one respect or one time but not others. Thus, good is relative to the specified purpose, and what is good for one person may not be so for another person, or even for one of them in different respects or times. Thus, an unbelieving person may call adultery "good" because he approves of it.

The technical meaning of "good," as adopted by the Muʿtazilites, is whatever is fitting for any end in this life. However, the Ashʿarites have adopted the second technical meaning, namely, what is fitting only for the ends of the next life that deals with ultimate salvation. In this latter sense, "good" signifies the ends and the means that are determined and that are assigned to everyone by the revelation. However, jurists inclining toward Ash'arism have extended "good" to cover anything that agents are permitted to do. The Mu'tazilites and the Shī'ites, on the other hand, define "good" with reference to acts for the performance of which the agent does not deserve blame.

"Evil," "ugly," or "bad" (*qabīḥ*) is in many ways identical with, though completely opposed to, "good" in its various meanings. Thus, in the general sense, the Ash'arites view "evil" as whatever is repugnant or inappropriate to an end, with attention to its relative rather than absolute character. But the evilness of an act is determined by divine command and not by its inherent nature that merits blame when committed. In structure these definitions of "good" and "evil" resemble that of "obligatory." Instead of referring to what is necessary to do for this life or the hereafter, as in "obligatory" acts, "good" refers simply to what is serviceable to an end, "evil" to what hinders attainment of an end.

Mu'tazilite belief in the autonomy of the human intellect to discern good and evil, unaided by the directives of revealed law, led them to object that the meaning of "good" in common usage is not restricted to what promotes an end, nor the meaning of "evil" to what hinders attainment of an end. People perform some acts as good on their intrinsic merits, when they cannot possibly foresee any advantage to them, and likewise they avoid other acts as evil even when they can see no disadvantage to themselves. As an instance of intrinsic good sought, someone gives help and comfort to a dying person with no expectation of reward; she does it simply because it is good in itself to help others in distress. As an instance of intrinsic evil avoided, a physician without belief in religion, and thus in no fear of punishment in the hereafter, refuses to help a terminally ill patient to commit suicide, even under threat of execution for his refusal; such a physician regards suicide as evil not merely in relation to ends but in itself.

The Ash'arites, believing that good and evil have no objective value, offered their rebuttal of these instances. They explained that the first instance could have been motivated by natural sympathy between human beings or by love of praise or by the association of ideas which leads one to do in an abnormal situation what would serve an end in a normal one. In the case of a woman helping others in distress, one can detect a motivation based on the expectation that the patient would live and show gratitude. Hence, the Ash'arites rejected the explanation of a rational desire for good. The second instance was explained by the agent's love of praise for not succumbing to the pressure or by an association of ideas: taking a life, however indirectly through physician-assisted suicide, is normally followed by harmful consequences. Hence, they ruled out a rational avoidance of evil. In other words, Ash'arites looked for self-interested or emotional causes for the acts mentioned in order to avoid admitting attributes of good and evil intrinsic to the acts themselves and acceptable or unacceptable to the rational mind regardless of personal ends. Their view of ethics is based on extrinsic relations of acts to good and evil. Their overall understanding of the process to evaluate a possible relationship between factual elements and moral decisions avoids the law of causation; instead they emphasize moral evaluation in connection with an agent's righteousness. That is to say, an act is good when it promotes human ends; moreover, it does so not by direct instrumental causation but because God has decided upon rewards for certain acts and punishment for others.

The primary means to attain human ends are of two kinds: performance of external acts of obedience in accord with the rules of conduct, revealed in scripture, and internal cultivation of the virtues of the soul. External acts are helpful both because obedience is rewarded directly for its sake and because these acts contribute to the acquisition of virtues. But the inner state of the heart is more important than any external acts in the eyes of God and more conducive to reward. None of the relations just described is causal. Acts do not cause virtues; they do not cause rewards in the next life. Even virtues do not cause rewards. In all cases, God, through divine benevolence (grace = *luṭf*), bestows rewards or moral progression. Here, once again, God is the only cause and God is under no obligation to do the most advantageous for humanity. Religious enlightenment consists largely in understanding these revealed truths. The secondary means are principally knowledge and motivation; these are necessary for the effectiveness of the primary means to happiness. The mission of the prophets is designed to provide these aids, for scripture gives guidance and inspiration, both to acts of obedience and to the virtues. Finally, the Muslim community, when it is working properly, sustains the individual in various ways through its organization and leaders.

Ethics and Law in Sharīʿa-Oriented Orthopraxy

Corresponding to the primary and secondary means to happiness are two practical sciences: *fiqh* (interpretive jurisprudence), which sets forth the principles and rules to derive laws from the scriptural sources, and *akhlāq* (ethics), which guides the formation of agents' moral and spiritual character. Traditional Sunni jurisprudence was based on the application of ethical predicates, such as doing "right" and doing "wrong," to concrete actions, and the way the predicates derived from these sketches are applicable to the agent responsible for the act under its ethical explanations. The core of that theory was to indicate that even when every agent acts by virtue of an ability to act, it is God who wills and creates whatever occurs. Whatever comes into being exists as the realized God's eternal ability to act and God's eternal volition. God is in an absolute sense the agent of all that occurs in the world. In view of that, the value terms applied to action, such as "right," "wrong," "obligatory," "good," and "evil," have no meaning in themselves; hence their application to action cannot be intuitively known by reason. However, since these categories acquire ethical meaning only when related to the commands (*awāmir*, plural of *ʿamr*) and prohibitions (*nawāhī*, plural of *nahy*) in revelation, knowledge about their applicability can be acquired exclusively by investigating the revelatory sources.

Their opponents in this regard were the Sunni rationalist Muʿtazilites and the Shīʿites with their thesis about the objective nature of moral values intuitively accessible to human minds with the power of autonomous action. The objectivist position was the rational understanding of ethical attributes that empowered human beings to deliberate action and made them subject to moral obligations. According to these theologian-jurists, people in any society, in general, engage in moral evaluation and develop specific terminology to express their deep-seated attitudes and feelings about human behavior and character. Furthermore, they maintained that most people believe that when they describe someone else as "just," "wicked," and so on, they are describing a real quality of that person (however hard to analyze), not merely some relation of obedience or disobedience to God's commands. The presumption is that a common ethical language is being used, understood clearly and in the same way by the speaker and the addressed parties. Such a language could not depend on their prior acceptance of the particular scripture being delivered by the speaker. Many of the terms used have definite objective meanings as far back as can be traced. Yet, there remained a critical question about the role of revelation in their rational-objectivist theory of ethics.

From the beginning of Islamic theology, the revelation emphasized the overwhelming power of God. The traditionalist thesis did not admit that human beings could ever determine on their own, without aid from the revelation, what was right and what was wrong in the world, still less what was obligatory for God to do or not to do with God's creation. The traditionalists obviously felt this way since the rationalist claim undermined the utility of their scriptural sources that were used as the principal source of paradigm cases for moral-legal deliberations to derive authoritative judicial decisions. The Sunni schools of interpretive jurisprudence increasingly inclined in this direction, until ethical voluntarism became part of the basic procedures of jurisprudence under the most thoroughgoing logic by Shāfiʿī (d. 820). In his work on methodology, Shāfiʿī demonstrated that the entire juridical procedure could be derived from the revelatory sources, that is, the Qur'an and the Tradition, without resorting to intuitive reason in the form of the "sound opinion" (*raʾy*) of a jurist. On the side of juridical theology, voluntarism, with its theistic subjectivism, found a champion in Ashʿarī (873–935) and his successors.[15]

In the sphere of ethics, the conservative spokesmen of Islam, who referred to themselves as "the people of tradition and the community" (*ahl al-sunna wa al-jamāʿa*), continued to react against Muʿtazilite rationalism. The main reason is probably that the Muʿtazilite theory was the only articulate theory that could be set in contrast to the prevailing traditionalist trend of Islamic thought that dominated interpretive jurisprudence in juristic circles. In addition, Muʿtazilite rationalist-objectivist ethics was firmly based on the major question in juridical methodology, which was determined to establish the permissibility of any act that did not contradict the ethical presuppositions of the revelation. This latter conclusion would advance interpretive jurisprudence to formulate religious-ethical action-guides for future contingencies.

The Muʿtazilites defined an act deontologically in terms of its character without reference to consequences. The main terms of their ethics affirmed the human ability to rationally know which acts are good and which evil. Hence, "obligatory" as an attribute of acts is defined as that for the omission of which the agent deserves blame, and "evil" as that for the doing of which the agent deserves blame, and so on. The blame can be known by any person of sound reason, as in cases of suicide and infanticide, without reference to consequences. God has endowed the normal maturity of intelligence that is common to all intelligent persons (*ʿuqala*ʾ), who know the absolute and universal principles of moral judgment. This capability of discovering and recognizing those aspects that make an act obligatory or evil or good, and realizing that they have the ability to act freely and deliberately, makes them morally responsible for it. God thus imposes duties on the people whose fulfillment on the basis of the universal moral principles earns them high praise and fitting compensation. This sharp turn from teleology to deontology in Muʿtazilite ethical theory was marked by the new prominence of obligation in Islamic legal-ethical thinking that sought application in interpretive jurisprudence.[16]

The prominence of obligation in revelation is underscored by the requirements of religious law. These duties, as the Sharīʿa explains, ought to be performed by virtue of a contractual agreement between God and humanity. As God's creatures, human beings ought to serve the divine purpose by obeying God's commands. In return for this obedience God promises rewards. Hence, judged on the basis of the Sharīʿa, every human being will receive what they deserve. In such a contractual relation between God, as the Benefactor, and humans, as the servants, obligation in the proper sense of duty occupies a pivotal role. The Muʿtazilites, thus, did not explain obligation wholly in terms of the interest (*maṣlaḥa*) of the subject and its good consequences. Rather, they were concerned to show the essence of deontological perspective in ethics of action that actions become obligatory because of the inherent characteristic of "obligatoriness" in them (i.e., commitment to promises, truthfulness, and justice).

Duty to Uphold Justice in Human Relationships

A major academic component of interpretive jurisprudence is to determine principles and rules that can be applied to cases requiring cognitively valid judicial decisions. At the center of this scholarly activity is categorization of revelation-based principles and rules in the moral assessment of an action from many different perspectives, including those of the agent, the act itself, the objective, and the consequences. There are different viewpoints about the meaning and nature of moral principles and rules as they are applied to different types of moral dilemmas. In fact, many disputes in ethics stem from disputes about the generalizability and applicability of more than one of these normative principles that function as moral and religious action-guides, categorizing actions as morally required, prohibited, or permitted. For example, in the case of a sick infant's irreversible medical condition, the principle of "preponderance" (*tarjīḥ*) has a limited application to choose termination of the treatment that does not alleviate the ailment but only prolongs suffering. The rule about preponderance can be weighed against the principle of "No harm, no harassment" (*lā ḍarar wa lā ḍirār*) that can be generalized under all perceivable harmful or repulsive conditions of the patient to determine the cessation of extraordinary treatment. Moreover, there exists a variety of principles-oriented approaches that take into consideration general moral principles as sources of rules, and rules that specify types of prohibited, required, or permitted actions, before any particular judgment can be derived in controversial moral cases like the right of the terminally ill patient or her family to end her life.[17]

Moral Concepts Assimilated in Juridical Methodology

The beginning point of the juridical methodology (*uṣūl*) was to identify moral concepts that were embodied in the rulings provided by the scriptural sources. The Ash'arite thesis about the divine command ethics was essentially founded upon the moral language of the revelation that reflected the fundamental concern of the early leadership to provide norms for a new social-political life under Islamic governance. Ethical evaluation of human conduct and accruing moral responsibility in the context of major political and social changes under Muslim rule proved to be the basis of a legal theory for the elaboration of the morally responsive methodology extracted from the moral usage of the revelation and subsequent commentaries that advanced interpretive jurisprudence. The importance of promoting ethical good and preventing evil as known to the sound mind made the legal doctrines adaptable to contemporary legal problems and issues. The ultimate objective of the juridical deliberations entailed doing justice and preserving people's best interests in this and the next world. How was that purpose to be fulfilled when all possible human contingencies in the future were not covered in the revelation, whether the Qur'an or the Tradition? The simple and yet significant reason-based philosophy of deriving the future action-guides that rationalist ethics affirmed was based on a well-known dictum among jurists. That dictum established the permissibility of any act on principle, unless it was specifically forbidden, or as forbidden on principle unless it was specifically permitted. More pertinent, this dictum launched an investigation into the sphere of moral values embedded in scriptural norms. Hence, in treating the question of inheritance, the Qur'an laid down general rules founded upon just distribution that were acceptable in the tribal context of Arabian society in the 7th century. However, complying with Qur'anic guidance in the matter of justice was a universal norm that could be generalized and applied under different circumstances to any case that involved equity and fair distribution in all areas of interpersonal relations.

The predictability of the judicial decision was dependent upon the generalizability of the norms presented in paradigm cases (extracted from the direct commands of the Qur'an and preserved in detailed form in a *ḥadīth*-report). These generalizable cases played critical role as discoverers of the lawgiver's objective in these acts that benefited humanity and human institutions. Contrary to commonsense expectations that the application of judicial decisions must be posterior to the prior elaboration of legal-ethical theory, Islamic jurisprudence actually antedated the genre of paradigm cases by undertaking the analysis of moral aspects of a case that required immediate response. By applying the ad hoc rules inferred from the moral cases in scriptural sources, Muslim scholars were able to resolve more immediate cases intuitively by paying attention to the prevalent practice of the early community as preserved in the Tradition. The norms preserved in these precedents mark a transition point for the subsequent moral cases wherein the cumulative tradition, the Sunna, was utilized to document substantive law. As precedents for subsequent ethical-legal decisions, these cases also indicated the underlying moral principles upon which the final judgment in those cases depended. In addition, these precedents turned out to be the critical grounds for further development of juridical principles and rules. The novel issues were then settled through the evocation of these principles and rules. Essentially the methodology developed rules and principles by discovering the moral aspects of a case that could be evoked in the future resolution of a growing number of problems in the area of interpersonal dealings.

The Qur'anic norms dealing with distributive justice or equity, like other values, such as avoiding causing harm or reciprocating harm with harm in interpersonal relations, were stated in the most general terms to allow jurists to develop their applicable boundaries as demanded by different cases in changed circumstances. Accordingly, the scholarly charge of a Muslim religious expert included providing the definition of religiously prescribed norms by elaborating the criteria that could determine their applicability in the given context of a similar, but new, case. Moreover, in specifically familial or societal disputes, he had to determine factors that could reveal the scale of violation necessitating financial or other forms of compensation recognized in the penal system. Technically, a major part of a Muslim jurist's training dealt with learning these principles and rules in the context of the Qur'an and the Tradition to offer an analogical method to problem-solving in society.

The scope of the present work does not permit me to enter into detailed examination of the entire juridical practice that impacted orthopraxy. I have determined the most important juridical doctrines and principles that have been evoked historically and in the contemporary situation to provide the necessary acumen to adapt the classical formulations to novel issues in the realm of religious-moral action guides.

Ethical Principles and Rules in Interpretive Jurisprudence (*al-fiqh*)

It is important to keep in mind that the status of human reason in deriving the principles and rules in juridical methodology was always contested. The form of permissible and legitimate rational investigation (*ijtihād*) was always text-based, that is, traditional. It was generally admitted that reason recognized the contingency of the world, the existence of the Creator, and the necessity of the institution of prophecy. The traditionalist-subjectivist ethicists belonging to the majority of the Sunni Ash'arite theology assigned a formal role for reason to discover the correlation between divine command and human good. Ethical reflection occurred within the boundaries of the Tradition as a process of discernment of principles that were embedded in propositional statements in the form of rulings as well as approved practice of the earlier jurists. The relationship between religious-ethical judgments and the principles in such cases is overshadowed by reference to the religious text, however far-fetched it might appear. To be precise, for Sunni Muslims knowledge of rules of law and ethics is anchored in divine revelation and not in human intuitive reason. The process of deriving rules from the revelation is founded upon interpretation of the relevant texts. In this sense, Islamic religious law is a body of positive rules by virtue of the formulations of jurists extrapolated by referencing the religious texts rather than the dictates of their own intuition. The exposition of orthopraxy depended on this text-oriented approach, although a great deal of positive law in the area of interpersonal relations was derived from the individual discretion of a jurist in employing intuitive reasoning.

The substantive role for reason was proffered by the Sunni Muʿtazilite and Shīʿite schools of thought, which saw human reason capable of not only discovering the divine purposes for human society but also establishing the correlation between human moral judgment and the divine commandment. They identified the major principles and rules ensuing from both the revelation and rational sources that could be utilized to make fresh decisions in all areas of interpersonal relationship. In theory, these principles and rules became general religious-moral action-guides to determine the ethical valuation of an act and declare it as incumbent or necessary, prohibited, permitted, recommended, or reprehensible in the context of specific circumstances. But the process of ethical deliberation did not necessarily involve ahistorical norms from which other norms or judgments were deduced. Rather, it involved a dialectical progression between the insights and beliefs of the contemporary jurists and the paradigmatic cases preserved in the juridical corpus of the early jurists who had relied heavily on the revelation that embedded principles and rules for solving specific cases. At any rate, the revelation provided certain principles that could be universalized and applied for solving contemporary moral dilemma.

Two such analytical and practical procedures in jurisprudence were *istiḥsān* and *istiṣlāḥ*. Both these procedures were indicative of the independent juristic judgment of expedience or public utility. Nonetheless, the legitimacy of employing these reason-based procedures depended upon their assimilation into the textual sources. The jurists were aware that the inherent nature of religious law was to insist on text-based indicators to determine a particular course of action. It was important to develop hermeneutical strategies whose language was closer to the moral impulse of Islamic revelation. Hence, for instance, the duty to avoid literal enforcement of the existing law, which may prove detrimental in certain situations, gave rise to the principle of *istiḥsān* (juristic preference). This juridical method of prioritization of ethical rulings considering the concrete circumstances of a case at hand has played a significant role in providing the necessary adaptability to religious law to meet the changing needs of society. However, the methodical strategy is founded upon an important principle derived from the moral directive of "circumventing of hardship" stated in the Qur'an in no uncertain terms: "God intends facility for you, and He does not want to put you in hardship" (Q. 2:185). This directive is further reinforced by the prophetic tradition that states, "The best of your religion [*dīn*, meaning 'praxis'] is that which brings ease to the people."[18]

Strictly speaking, the principle of "juristic preference" allows formulation of a decision that sidesteps an established precedent in order to uphold a higher obligation of implementing the ideals of fairness and justice without causing unnecessary hardship to the people involved. The obvious conclusion to be drawn from God's intention to provide facility and remove hardship is that the essence of these moral principles is their adaptability to meet the exigencies of every time and place on the basis of private and public interest. To put it differently, juristic discretion—i.e., the use of a jurist's own judgment to determine the best solution to a religious problem—provides relief to the agent that cannot be solved by simply citing sacred texts.

There are numerous examples that one can cite to demonstrate how *istiḥsān* has facilitated solutions to the moral dilemmas encountered by the faith community living in changed circumstances in different parts of the world. There are numerous religious rulings in the classical formulations which can be construed as being unfair to a woman's right to initiate and seek divorce in Muslim family law. Today the most pressing issue in family law has been to curb this one-sided right and provide equability by recognizing the right of a woman to initiate and demand divorce in a repulsive marriage. Whereas Muslim marriage/divorce is customarily formalized by Muslim religious authority, in a number of unpleasant decisions involving divorce, specifically in settling the financial obligations for both parties, certain cases have been referred to and validated by a secular court. In such cases, the question of the validity of secular court's decision to formalize divorce arises. On the strength of juristic preference and, more pertinent, to avoid further unethical bitterness arising from the contested circumstances of legal separation, Muslim jurists have ruled the secular divorce sufficient and legitimate.[19]

Istiṣlāḥ (Promotion of Public Good) and *Maṣlaḥa* (Public Good)

"Promotion of public good" (*istiṣlāḥ*) is traditionally aligned with "Prevention of corruption" (*mafsada*). "Promotion" (beneficence) inevitably leads to "prevention" (maleficence). There are a number of subsidiary rules derived from these two essential principles advocated by the revelation. Thus, for example, "aversion of harm has preponderance over promotion of probable good" is one of the critical rules in social and medical ethics. Both promotion of good and prevention of corruption and wickedness provide sound procedures to evaluate all moral judgments that deal with the factual elements in a given situation within a specific culture that require simultaneously and consistently an exercise of intuitive reason to formulate a cognitively valid judgment. Muslims speak about a collective obligation (*farḍ kifāya*) that must be fulfilled by those responsible for maintaining public order to formulate practical rulings to discourage people from individually as well as collectively spreading corruption. A number of structural ethical principles in Islamic ethics are in some direct and indirect ways discerned through the general juridical principle of *maṣlaḥa*, that is, "public good" or "interest." This principle is invoked in providing solutions to the majority of novel issues in social ethics.

The scope of juridical methodology includes interpreting the rationale (*'ilal*, plural of *'illa*) that underlies some legal-ethical decisions that deal with self-evident moral obligations like interpersonal justice. Islamic moral principles overlap in important respects but differ in others. For instance, the two distinct obligations of beneficence and nonmaleficence are, sometimes, viewed as a single principle of nonmaleficence (*mafsada*), on the basis of the overlapping between the two obligations in the famous *ḥadīth*-report: "In Islam there shall be no harm inflicted or reciprocated" (*lā ḍarar wa lā ḍirār fī al-islām*).[20] In other words, causing harm or countering harm with harm is ruled out in this famous tradition. The principle of "protection against distress and constriction" (*'usr wa al-ḥaraj*) applies universally to social relations and transactions, regardless of one's affiliation with a particular faith community. The point that emerges from this moral principle is that human beings must learn to deal with one another in good faith and forgiveness. There are also a number of rules inferred from the principle of public good which are an important part of the Islamic ethical system.

Consideration of the public interest or common good of the people has been an important principle utilized by Muslim jurists for accommodating and incorporating new issues confronting the community. *Maṣlaḥa* has been admitted as a rationally derived principle, firmly founded upon religious text, to infer new rulings or to suspend earlier rulings out of consideration for the collective interest and welfare of the community. Nonetheless, its ostensible resemblance to the secular principle of utilitarianism that leads the principle to obtain relativism in rulings has been treated with caution among Muslim jurists. The utilitarian doctrine, as understood in secular ethics, maintains that actions are right if they are useful or are for the benefit of a majority. This is a source of controversy among Muslim religious scholars. More pertinent, the doctrine that an action is right insofar as it promotes the greatest happiness of the greatest number raises the question about the authority that can interpret its scope to include its admission as a source for moral-religious action-guides. Some Sunni and Shī'ite jurists have contested the doctrine's competence to provide cognitively valid judicial decisions.

Looking at the majority of Muslims, who belong to the Ash'arī school of thought in their understanding of God's plan for humanity, one needs to understand the Ash'arite view of what is the best for people. The Ash'arites, who maintained the divine command ethics (the theistic subjectivism), confined the derivation of *maṣlaḥa* strictly from the revelatory sources, that is, the Qur'an and the Tradition. Ghazzālī, as an Ash'arī theologian-jurist, elucidates this position in his major work on legal theory:

> *Maṣlaḥa* is actually an expression for bringing about benefit (*manfa'a*) or forestalling harm (*maḍarra*). We do not consider [*maṣlaḥa*] in the meaning of bringing about benefit or forestalling harm as part of [God's] purposes for the people or [God's] concern for the people, in order for them to achieve those purposes. Rather, we take *maṣlaḥa* in the meaning of protecting the ends of the Revelation (*al-shar'*). The ends of the Revelation for the people are five: To protect for them (1) their religion, (2) their lives (*nufūs*), (3) their reason (*'uqūl*), (4) their lineage (*nasl*), and (5) their property (*māl*). All that guarantees the protection of these five purposes is *maṣlaḥa*; and all that undermines these purposes is *mafasada* (detriment).[21]

According to the Ash'arites, justice is what God wills and commands; for humans it is to do what God commands. Humans do not have to know the constitutive reasons for obedience and disobedience to enable them to rationalize or explain the divine purpose in creating a human person under obligation (*mukallif*). As a matter of fact, as the traditionalists assert, God is not bound by any rule or obligation; humans ought to simply obey God's commands. Hence, human obligation lies in the commission and application of what God had declared to be good and the avoidance of that which God had forbidden in these sacred sources. Moreover, ruling an action good or bad depends on the consideration of the general ethical principles laid down in the revelation. Consequently, human responsibility is confined to the course ordained by God by seeking to institute what God declares good and shunning what God declares evil.

In principle, the appraisal of the Mu'tazilite Sunni thinkers, who maintained objectivist rationalist ethics, was at variance with the Ash'arites. They regarded human reason as capable of knowing *maṣlaḥa*, the consideration of public interest that promoted benefit and prevented harm. For these scholars, *maṣlaḥa* was an inductive principle for the derivation of fresh decisions in the area where the scriptural sources provided little or no guidance at all.

The moral reasoning that undergirds interpretive jurisprudence maintains that regardless of whether the principle of public good originates in the scriptural sources or human reason, no Muslim scholar questions the conclusion that religious-ethical judgments are founded upon concern for human welfare (*maṣāliḥ*) and human protection from corruptive aspects (*mafāsid*). In theory, the divine lawgiver legislates with a purpose of doing that which is most advantageous (*aṣlaḥ*) for people, even when the exact method of deducing this general doctrine is in dispute among the rationalists and the traditionalists. The Ashʿarī-Sunni scholars maintain that they have inferred the doctrine through the examination of the judicial decisions themselves, and that in legislating them the lawgiver has certainly the welfare of humanity in mind.[22] In contrast, the Muʿtazilite-Sunni and the Shīʿite scholars maintain that the welfare of humanity in legislation and its protection from corruption is established through the very obligation upon God to do that which is most advantageous for people. These rationalist theologians claim that there is a consensus among scholars of religious law that legislation by the lawgiver is actually to advance that objective.[23] Some theologian-jurists have, for all intents and purposes, related all the ordinances back to the doctrine of "public good." Hence, for example, the Mālikī jurist Shāṭibī (d. 1388) maintains that all judicial decisions were founded upon "public good" and asserts that the Qur'an provides humanity with the knowledge of good of this and the next world in such a way that, through God-given ability, it can acquire the good. In addition, the scriptural sources have made the corruptive aspects of this and the next world known to humanity so that it can protect itself from them. If one looks at the Tradition, reminds Shāṭibī, one will find nothing but the fact that all religious and moral duties (*al-takālīf al-sharʿīya*) point to God's concern for the welfare of humanity.[24]

The scholars of juridical methodology identify this doctrine of public interest as *al-maṣāliḥ al-mursala*, that is, the common good whose rules are derived on the basis of a rationally suitable benefit not protracted by the Qur'an or the Tradition. This perspective is close to the Shīʿite doctrine of rational good and evil that leads to similar conclusions regarding the divine purposes for humanity. In particular, it is close to the Shīʿite doctrine about "rejection of harm (*ḍirār*)." It is certain that application of this latter doctrine requires a rational or, at least, reason-based approach, even when this application is not exclusively derived by rational procedures. The textual proofs support the doctrine of rejection of harm to oneself and to others. The doctrine provides wide-ranging interpretation of the textual proofs in order to provide solutions to a variety of problems faced by the people in their everyday life.

What Kind of Issues Does "Public Good" Cover?

The principle of public good has been meticulously expounded in terms of its scope. Hence, public good covers (1) all matters connected with human life on earth and (2) all matters connected with life in the hereafter. Although God's commands and decree cover benefits of both worlds, there is a difference in the "good" of the two realms:

1. Ordinarily, the good connected with the life in this world is not morally so, because there is a possibility that every good is accompanied by the cause of its corruption and every cause of corruption has some good in it. Hence, in any matter connected with the good or evil of this life, if the cause for good has preponderance over the cause for evil, then the good becomes the effective cause (*'illa*) for concluding a matter, whereas if the cause for corruption has preponderance, then the matter is construed as evil.
2. Customarily, when people regard a thing to be good they have this preponderance in mind.[25] On the other hand, the good of the next life is regarded as authentic, except in one instance: when a person believing in one God is placed in Hell. Reason cannot fathom that inconsistency.
3. Ordinarily, the good of this life is known through reason and experience of the factual elements, expressions of attitude and feeling, whereas the good of the next life and its description are known through revelation. Reason has no access to that information, which is strictly derived through faith in the revelation.[26]

Evidently, even though public good covers matters related to this and the next life, the good in the next world is associated with all practices of worship related to the human-God relationship (*'ibādāt*). In contrast, seeking the public good—*istiṣlāḥ*—as a method of legislation is connected with social transactions related to interhuman relationships (*mu'āmalāt*) in a general sense. Technically, all purposes stated for the validation of the principle of public good cover social transactions and penal codes.

The principle has been examined in the light of those who benefit from it in terms of collective or individual good. In the juristic principle of *istiḥsān* (juristic practice), the criterion is essentially based on public good that is unrestricted and that reaches the largest number of people. However, it is sometimes likely that an individual benefit could become the source for a ruling that could give rise to incongruity with another ruling that has better consequences. In principle, the sole criterion for the divine lawgiver in legislation is the potential for general good that is, in most cases, contained under a specific good. The foundation of primary judgment is this kind of good. But personal welfare is essentially the context of change of a ruling from primary to secondary so that it can benefit that particular individual in a specific situation. Self-evidently, elimination of the primary injunction and its change to a secondary ruling takes place in a specific situation. In this sense, specific considerations function as criteria for legislation, whereas individual benefits function as the context for secondary rulings. The latter situation that looks at individual benefit as a source of conclusive ruling causes disagreement among the jurists in determining the good and evil of the circumstances under consideration.

For instance, Shāṭibī, after explaining what covers the good of this and the next world, opens up a new section in his estimation of public good and elaborates on its aspects that lead to corruption. He goes on to clarify that if the public good and corruption happen to be outside customary law, then the juridical process requires further investigation before any conclusive ruling can be given. He goes on to provide examples of the prohibition connected with eating a dead body or other contaminated foods that become licit under dire circumstances. In addition, out of necessity, cutting a limb that has been infected by an incurable disease becomes obligatory. Nevertheless, jurists have disagreed on adopting one or the other course of action on the basis of divergence between the good or interest and potential corruption that might occur while analyzing aspects of the problem under investigation.[27]

As a rule, discussion about *maṣlaḥa* takes place under one of the following rubrics.

Public Good in Matters of Orthopraxy, Promulgated by God as the Divine Lawgiver

This occurs when the lawgiver has in fact determined the public good in the laws enacted in the interest of the people, regardless of whether these laws are related to human-God or human-human relationships or are simply connected with customary matters and regardless of whether or not this good is determined by human reason. Hence, public good, in this sense, is accepted in all matters connected to religious or social dimensions, without requiring that reason to discover the criteria and the merit(s) of public good in all the obligatory and recommended duties in orthopraxy, and without necessitating that reason uncover the corruptive dimension of all the forbidden and reprehensible actions. This is where the public good takes on a theological dimension by actually sitting in evaluation of God's actions and laws whether they are necessarily or through a special favor in the interest of humankind. This dimension brings to mind the rule about the correlation (*talāzum*) between that which is ruled by the revelation and that which is judged by reason. Accordingly, the matter of public good and public corruption are subjects for philosophy of law in Islam today, just as the subject of instituting the good and preventing the evil was central to the classical juridical tradition. In the classical as well as contemporary rulings, instituting the good was connected to the moral duty of promoting the public good and preventing the evil that was related to public corruption of society.

Public Good in Encountering Fresh Rulings by Jurists

Discovering new rulings occurs when jurists confronted with a new situation give their rulings in reference to the public good or that which ought to be done in the interest of people. This type of public good is, in major part, pivotal to the principle of "seeking and promoting the welfare" (*istiṣlāḥ*), in its specific meaning of instituting the good through enactment of the laws that are in the interests of the people. It is also under this kind of public good that jurists have raised the question about the dependability (*ḥujjīya*) of the principle of public good. As discussed earlier in the typology of public good, sometimes the good is collective and general, and at other times it is individual and specific. When public good is admitted as a valid source for the derivation of a new decision, the ruling is not given because of sheer necessity (*ḍarūra*). Rather, as a secondary and derivatively necessary ruling, it is open to further discussion when full investigation of the factual elements, including expressions of attitude and feeling secured by rational procedure, are carried out to evaluate its applicability to the public interest. If it is determined that individual interest is at stake, then secondary consideration assumes the primary role in formulating a final judgment. The jurist at this stage is engaged in deriving the secondary ruling connected to the specific circumstance of the case. Hence, he could rule, for instance, in a case of emergency connected with a woman's health condition, that she can be examined by a male gynecologist on duty in the clinic. The woman who obtains this ruling allows a male physician to investigate her condition, making it possible for her to abstain from that which is actually required by the orthopraxy, that is, to be examined only by a female physician. It is important to keep in mind that although the ruling denotes the welfare of the female patient involved, the ruling is made independent of this specifically gender-related consideration in Islamic ethics. What actually reverts to the principle of public good is the secondary ruling by the lawgiver and the application of the ruling by the person who knows that doing otherwise was not in her best interest. The consideration regarding her gender is a critical part of the orthopraxy, and yet, in this case it assumes both a primary as well as a secondary concern extracted by reference to the principle that "seeks and promotes the good" (*istiṣlāḥ*). However, the jurist has recourse to the principle of necessity (*ḍarūra*) to bolster the applicability of the public good to give the ruling that surpasses specific individual good to collective good of others like her. By doing so the ruling attains permanence and is afforded the status of universal custom. It is valid to assume that the principle of public good applies in all those cases in which the question of an individual's welfare can be generalized for all the people under consideration. However, this criterion applies only to the social issues connected with interpersonal relations; it cannot be admitted in matters that are done essentially as part of one's obligations connected with the human-God relationship.

Public Good When the Principle Encounters Corruption

This occurs when the good and corrupt aspects come together in a single case affecting public life. Sometimes this happens when religious leaders are opposed to a state policy they deem harmful to the public. For example, from time to time the World Health Organization has supported and funded preventative public health measures in the interest of the public in Third World countries. Unfortunately, the flow of foreign funds from WHO has led to corruption among public officials. The public good and ensuing corruption, in such cases, appear factually in the same instance. In order to stop the illicit practices of the political leaders, Muslim jurists have often ruled against the preventative health measures to combat corruption at the leadership level. In such cases, it is critical for jurists to revisit their earlier negative rulings and reassess the important criteria to the greater benefit of the preventative public health measures. The approach to solve this moral dilemma is for the leading Muslim juridical authority to rationally prioritize the applicable criteria in order to determine, through risk-benefit analysis, the necessity of issuing a new ruling in the interest of the public.

Diverse Views about Public Good

Since its introduction in interpretive juridical procedures, *maṣlaḥa* has been defined variously. Some have regarded the principle of public good as being outside the scope of juridical documentation—largely textual—that is admitted in derivations of fresh rulings. Others have argued for its admission among valid proofs for the derivation of religious-ethical rulings. Moreover, the classification of public good into general and particular has also given rise to its incompatibility under different circumstances, especially when these circumstances are open to pluralistic interpretations. Following are some significant views about this principle:

(a) The view that unconditionally rejects *maṣlaḥa* as having evidentiary value in religious-ethical decision-making. Most the Sunni jurists hold this opinion about *maṣlaḥa*.[28]
(b) The view that categorically accepts *maṣlaḥa* as having evidentiary value in religious-ethical decision-making. A number of leading Sunni jurists

and theologians have ascribed to this opinion. Among them one can count Mālik,[29] Juwaynī, Shafiʿī,[30] and Aḥmad b. Ḥanbal, the founder of the Hanbali school of orthopraxy. Some Ḥanafī scholars, known for their reason-based jurisprudence, have also inclined toward the principle of public good.[31]

(c) Those who do not admit public good as a source for the derivation of orthopraxy point to the lack of any textual endorsement of the principle in the Qur'an or the Tradition as the main reason for its abandonment. Moreover, they maintain that decisions made by reference to public good are necessarily based on conjectural (*ẓann*) procedures, which tarnishes the cognitive validity of the ordinances thus extrapolated.[32]

(d) Some jurists object to this principle simply because they reject the doctrine that God's injunctions are teleologically based on their good and bad consequences. It is only human actions that are the result of such considerations. In fact, they contend, human beings always weigh benefit and risk in doing or avoiding an action. God's actions are not limited by such considerations. They furthermore argue that the analogical deduction founded upon humans' and God's actions leads to the false doctrine that God's actions are informed by their ends. God does not act in accord with good or bad consequences. God, being omnipotent and omniscient, does not need to evaluate all the divine acts in terms of their good or bad consequences for humankind.

Theoretically, there is nothing in the world of contingencies that invalidates the conclusion that what is good for one could be harmful for another. Hence, God is not under obligation to do what is most beneficial for humankind or to do what is worst for them. God being God is bound by no rule or obligation. The obedience and disobedience of human beings is not based on rational procedures. God wills what God commands, absolutely and immutably. More pertinent, if one were to believe that God works in the interest of humanity based on public good to protect people from possible harm, the possibility of such speculation and its application in the matter of divine ordinances would and could lead any ruler or scholar to change or introduce a fallacy in these ordinances.[33]

On the other side of the spectrum are those jurists who have supported the doctrine of *maṣlaḥa* and defined its juridical and ethical scope and parameters. They have appealed to reason in order to argue for its cognitive validity. The divine lawgiver has willed the interests of humanity in all the ordinances of the Sharīʿa. Even when it is understood conjecturally that in doing something such a benefit will accrue, it is valid to admit *maṣlaḥa* as an important source of investigating the level of benefit. Such a conjecture is necessary, and it is only through this process that one can evaluate and calculate what should be done considering the needs of everyone affected by such a ruling. This is the denotation of "promotion of good" (*istiṣlāḥ*) to seek and to promote public good in order to maximize benefit and minimize harm. This has been regarded as one of the two arguments in support of the public good that Mālik has offered.[34]

The other rational argument is the one in which supporters of *maṣlaḥa* have engaged in assessing the greatest good in most certain terms so that this consideration can intrinsically defeat the negative value. They regard this process as approved by the revelation. This certainty can overcome the conjectural aspect of the ruling and render it firmly based on maximal good and minimum harm, as endorsed by the revelation. To act on such a conjecture is obligatory because any sound mind weighs the preponderance of good over harm and sanctions the maximal good. This has support in the Tradition, where it quotes the Prophet saying, "I judge on what is apparent."[35]

In searching for textual proof in support of the principle of public good, jurists have found abundant historical precedents to show that at different times the Prophet and early leaders made necessary adjustments to the rulings by taking into consideration changed circumstances. In one such instance the Prophet sent ʿAli on a mission and asked him to assess the situation first and then implement his instructions. If need be, ʿAli should make necessary adjustments to accommodate the situation as he assessed it. In other words, the instructions given to ʿAli worked as precedent, making it permissible for him to go beyond the specific instructions of the revelation and rationally extrapolate the ruling in the best interests of the people.[36] On another occasion the Prophet instructed his army not to institute the legal penalty on a thief by cutting off his hand during the war in enemy territory for fear that a Muslim soldier might seek refuge with the enemy and endanger the Muslim army.[37] Even more to the point is ʿAli's statement about the Prophet's instruction about dyeing one's beard with henna and to avoid appearing like Jews, who, apparently, did not dye their beards. When ʿAli was asked about this he replied, "The Prophet of God (may God's mercy and salutations be upon him) gave this instruction when there were few Muslims. Now that Islam has become widespread, and has attained firmer ground on its own, people can do [with their beard] what they want."[38]

The Change of *Maṣlaḥa* and the Change of Rulings

One of the consequences of employing the public good in juridical procedures is the inevitable change of judicial decisions in accord with the change of circumstances requiring reassessment of what serves the people's interests and what causes corruption among them. Many precedents in the early history of the community, which serve as documentation in support of public good and which have been used as paradigm cases by jurists to extrapolate fresh decisions, are rooted in this principle. If it is accepted that religious ordinances are based on considerations that look into increasing positive value and minimizing evil, especially in matters that deal with social ethics, then we must also regard these ordinances relative to the situations, mutable and, hence, in accord with the logic of time and space. A number of prominent jurists have accepted this relative dimension of the ordinances dealing with all matters connected with interhuman relationships. They have also asserted that alteration and adaptation are permissible, even if they go against the religious texts or if there is an agreement among jurists contrary to the terms of the text. However, a large number of jurists permit modification and adaptation in the ordinances dealing with specific topics about which there does not appear to be a textual proof or an agreement among the scholars.[39]

In general, Sunni jurists were connected with the day-to-day workings of the government. Accordingly, they were required to provide solutions to every new problem that emerged in the society. In order to do this they devised methodological stratagems based on analogical reasoning (*al-qiyās*), well-considered opinion (*al-ra'y*), seeking and promoting the good of the people (*istiṣlāḥ*), and choosing the most beneficial of several rulings (*istiḥsān*). Through these methodological procedures they were, to a large extent, able to respond to the morally and legally complex situations that arose in the social and political contexts. In many aspects, the Shīʿite juridical system paid attention to individuals rather than corporate groups. It is not until the Iranian Revolution in 1978–1979 that we find Shīʿite jurists taking up the question of admitting the public good as an important source for legal-ethical decision-making. The direction followed by these jurists in Iran, Iraq, or Lebanon is not very different from the one followed by their Sunni counterparts throughout the political history of Sunni Islam.[40]

4

Scriptural Sources of Ethical Methodology

In the previous chapter I endeavored to propound the thesis that although the traditionalist Ashʿarite ethics ruled out a meaningful role for human reason to determine ethical good and evil, in jurisprudence, following the rationalist Muʿtazilite ethics, Sunni jurists endorsed a critical role for human reasoning as the discoverer of the divine purposes embedded in the scriptures. The method developed a linguistic-rationalist theory of knowledge of the rules of action (*uṣūl al-fiqh*) that was founded upon the interpretation of scriptural sources. The rules governing orthopraxy are dependent upon three kinds of authoritative revelatory sources, collectively known as "proofs" (*adilla* pl. of *dalīl*): the Qur'an, the Tradition, and consensus (*ijmāʿ*). The consensus is to be that of the learned scholars (*mujtahid*s). A jurist had no choice in employing independent reason to determine the rules of action that were already mentioned in revelatory sources. Accordingly, the fourth method, namely, analogical reasoning (*qiyās*) based on independent reason (*ijtihād*), was not regarded as a primary source in the sense in which the first three are. Technically, analogical reasoning was employed to infer the probable connotation of the text (*al-naṣṣ*) related to investigation in the language of revelation to derive orthopraxy (*al-ijtihād al-sharʿī*). The language of the scriptural sources had to be rationally understood through the analysis of their changing context (*taghyīr al-aḥwāl*) and, where feasible, discovering the scholarly consensus (*ijmāʿ*) regarding the probable linguistic and lexical inference.[1] As a rule, there was no short-cut available to adaptation (*iqtibās*) of scriptural rules without indispensable rigor and clarity by expounding essential ethical objectives (*maqāṣid*) of the Sharīʿa (identified by Ghazālī in his definition of the "public good," discussed in Chapter 3) that stood independent of any specific textual evidence. Consideration of public interest or common good of the people, as discussed in Chapter 3, has been an important principle utilized by Muslim jurists for accommodating and incorporating new issues that the community encountered. Public interest (*maṣlaḥa*) has been admitted as a principle of reasoning to derive new rulings or as a method of suspending earlier rulings out of consideration for the interest and welfare of the community. However, its admission as an independent source for legislation, as discussed in Chapter 3, has been contested by some Sunni and Shīʿite jurisprudents. Undoubtedly, the common good is based on the notion that the ultimate goal of the Sharīʿa necessitates doing justice and preserving people's best interests in this

Islamic Ethics. Abdulaziz Sachedina, Oxford University Press. © Oxford University Press 2022.
DOI: 10.1093/oso/9780197581810.003.0004

and the next world. But who defines justice, and what is the most beneficial for the people? Here ethics based on scriptural materials was utilized to define the parameters of the common good.

The majority of Muslims belong to the Ashʿarite school of thought in its understanding of God's plan for humanity; therefore, one needs to understand the Ashʿarite view of what is the most advantageous for people. The Ashʿarites, who maintained the divine command ethics (theistic subjectivism), confined the derivation of *maṣlaḥa* strictly from the revelatory sources, that is, the Qur'an and the Tradition. Ghazālī, as an Ashʿarī theologian-jurist, elucidates this position in his juridical theory regarding *maṣlaḥa*. He takes *maṣlaḥa* in the meaning of protecting the ends of the revelation for the people, which are, according to him, five: to protect for them (1) their religion, (2) their lives (*nufūs*), (3) their reason (*ʿuqūl*), (4) their lineage (*nasl*), and (5) their property (*māl*). All that guarantees the protection of these five purposes constitutes the public good, and all that undermines these purposes is *mafasada* (a source of detriment). Nevertheless, God is bound by no rule or obligation. No creature can have any claim of right with respect to God, for this would imply that there is something that God ought to do. It is not incumbent on God to do what is most advantageous for the people.[2]

Hence, according to the Ashʿarites, justice for God is to will what God commands for humanity, and for humanity to do what God commands. Moreover, ruling an action good or evil depends on the consideration of the general principles God has laid down in the revelation. Consequently, human responsibility is confined to the course ordained by God by seeking to institute what God declares good and shunning what God declares evil. As far as the derivation of fresh rulings is concerned, the Ashʿarites maintain that the principle of public interest is internally operational in the rulings that reveal with certainty that in legislating them God has the welfare of humankind in mind. The obedience and disobedience of the agents do not constitute reasons; they cannot be rationalized or explained. The agents ought to obey without seeking elaboration of God's commands.[3]

The Muʿtazilite Sunni thinkers, who maintained objectivist rationalist ethics that essentially recognized human intuitive reason as capable of deliberate action, were understandably at variance with the Ashʿarites. The consideration of public interest that promoted benefit and prevented harm was essentially common to all intelligent people. Intelligent people know the absolute and universal principles of moral judgment. They are capable of discovering the intrinsic characteristics which render an act obligatory or good or bad. By creating human beings God effectively places them under moral obligation. Accordingly, these rationalist thinkers regard recognition of public good as an inductive process for the derivation of fresh decisions in the area where the scriptural sources provided little or no guidance at all, and where moral judgments had to depend upon factual elements that take into consideration previous moral preferences, tensions, and reflections derived from particular cases and circumstances.

In the context of matters connected with social ethics, which deal with everyday contingencies of human life, it is important to keep in mind that, regardless of whether the principle of public good originates internally in the scriptural sources or externally through intuitive reason, no jurist questions the conclusion that religious-ethical judgments are founded upon concern for human welfare (*maṣāliḥ*) and in order to protect people from corruption (*mafāsid*) and harm (*ḍarar*). In other words, they maintain that God provides guidance with the purpose of doing what is most beneficial (*al-aṣlaḥ*) for people, even when the exact method of deducing this general principle is in dispute.[4]

Some jurists have, for all intents and purposes, related all the ordinances back to the principle of public good by employing case-based reasoning that compared cases and analogically inferred moral-legal conclusions. Hence, for example, Shāṭibī (d. 1388) maintains that promulgation of the ordinances took place by referring to the paradigm cases in the scriptural sources like the Qur'an and the Tradition that took into consideration the welfare of the people (*li-maṣāliḥ al-ʿibād*) in this world and the next. This assertion that God has the interest of people in mind is dependent upon an authoritative proof that could determine the validity of the claim that the paradigm case reflects an underlying doctrine that God is bound to do what is most beneficial for God's creatures. However, as Shāṭibī correctly points out, regardless of the doctrinal aspects of the principle of public good, which are treated in theology proper (*ʿilm al-kalām*), it is important to emphasize that the application of this principle in juridical theory (*uṣūl al-fiqh*) permits and even fosters new moral insights and judgments in the Sharīʿa. Most contemporary jurists endorse the latter view and have produced evidence in their work on juridical theory in support of the specific legal-ethical decisions analogically inferred on the basis of the common good.[5]

Shāṭibī provides several examples of ordinances from the Qur'an and the Tradition that were instituted by God in keeping with people's interests in this and the next world. Thus, in justifying the rules of purity and ablutions, God says in the Qur'an, "God does not intend to make any impediment (*ḥaraj*) for you; but God desires to purify you, and that God may complete God's blessings upon you" (Q. 5:6). In addition, the scriptural sources have made the corruptive aspects of this and the next world known to humanity so that it can protect itself from them. If one investigates the Tradition, asserts Shāṭibi, one will find nothing but the fact that all religious-moral duties (*al-takālīf al-sharʿīya*) point to God's concern for the welfare of humanity.[6]

To recapitulate, in Sharīʿa the objectives (*maqāṣid*) are understood as human interests and the ends of human purposes which, as Ghazālī expounded, are fivefold: the preservation of their religion (*dīn*), lives (*nufūs*), intellect (*ʿaql*), lineage (*nasl*), and property (*māl*). These five purposes are known by induction, through numerous proofs that cannot be limited to the revelatory sources and their contexts. As the Ashʿarites understood and argued, God had provided all that humans need to obey the prophetic guidance in the form of revelation. All that humans need is expected involvement to advance their interests (*manfaʿa*) and avert their harms (*maḍarra*). According to jurists like Ghazālī and Shāṭibī consideration to promote public interests were construed intuitively on the basis of divinely endowed nature that directly depended upon legitimate human intellectual elaborations to underscore their relevance and significance by engaging in analyzing the rule that is known exclusively from revelation. In theory, reason in juridical-ethical methodology was circumspectly restricted to the adaptation of scriptural sources without any reference to natural experience and intuition. It is only by using the revelatory information as the major premise that analogical deduction becomes a legitimate method of inferring the divine reason to safeguard human interests. More important, as divine command ethics taught, God is bound by no moral obligation or rule and can in effect command rules with or without reasons.[7] In cases where God provides reasons, it is legitimate for human beịngs to discover and apply that knowledge to other, similar cases.

Scholarly analysis of the textual materials from its inception was founded upon the logical necessity of discovering the underlying moral connotation of divine commandments to determine whether these prescriptions could be used as precedents to extrapolate other, related ordinances. To verify the reliability of the judicial decisions thus arrived at, justificatory reasoning had to make plain the correlation (*talāzum*) between scripturally and rationally derived moral values that formed an integral part of orthopraxy in the two major fields of Islamic jurisprudence: human-God (duties of worship) and human-human relationships (duties accruing from natural and contractual familial or societal connection) as manifestations of divinely approved religious-moral action-guides (*taklīf*). Rigorous investigation in religious-ethical justificatory reasoning has regarded the performance of religiously and morally required action as a fundamental aspect of God's purposes for humanity. The Sharīʿa repeatedly emphasizes performance of righteous action (*ʿamal ṣāliḥ*) as the sole guarantor of human prosperity in this life and an efficacious criterion for salvation in the hereafter. It is plausible to assert with confidence that as long as human life is distinctively geared toward a life in the hereafter with compliance and extensive power over adaptation in this life, then conceivably the first obligation that humans have to themselves is to get accustomed to living a morally upright life so that they can personify virtues. The Qur'an captures this personification profoundly when it affirms the essential responsibility of human personhood to work toward a divinely endowed constitution (*fiṭra*) by remaining committed to moral self-advancement in order to deserve God's extolling in the following passage:

> God changes not [the ability to become virtuous], which is [infused in] a people [by God's will], until they change what is in them [naturally]. Whenever God desires evil for a people [for abandoning their infused nature], there is no turning it back; apart from God they have no protector. (Q. 13:12)

Evidently, the Qur'an desires to guide humanity to become responsive to its infused moral nature without making unconvincing excuses for its poor performance on earth. In another place the Qur'an asserts the immutability of divine endowment in the form of infused divine nature (*fiṭrat allāh*) with which God has created human beings:

> So orient yourselves to the divinely ordained regulation (*dīn*) [and do not deviate in the slightest], a human of pure faith. [Act in accordance with the dictates of] your God-given nature and follow the pattern of creation established by God. Indeed, this pattern does not change nor do God's laws (*sunna*) ever become obsolete. That is the desirable directive (*dīn*), but most humans know it not. (Q. 30:29)

As pointed out earlier, analogical deduction was a syllogistic method of inferring the meaning of the text related in revelatory sources that needed to be understood through their context (*taghyīr al-aḥwāl*) and agreed upon by scholars (*al-ijmāʿ*). In other words, Sunni-Ashʿarite jurists like Ghazālī introduced *istiṣlāḥ*—the ethical principle of promoting beneficence through consideration of social interests of the people and their ends beyond the piecemeal evidence of the revelatory texts. In principle, Ghazālī treated promotion of the common good as a presumed derivative that lacked concrete textual proof expected for the derivation of Sharīʿa rulings.[8] This consideration brings into focus extended independent rational inquiry (*ijtihād*) based on reasoning that correlates human interests with the divinely ordained Sharīʿa. I introduced "public interest" as an extrarevelatory ethical principle in Chapter 3, when I discussed the interdependence of the two principles in secular bioethics: beneficence and maleficence.[9] Actually, the Sharīʿa indicates that consideration of public good has validity in the revelation when it introduces the prohibition about intoxicants because of its adverse impact upon human sanity (*ḥurrimat li-ḥifẓ al-ʿaql*).[10] By extension, this analogically deduced prohibition can be applied to all other intoxicating drinks. Conversely, in other instances the revelation in reality snubs public interest to preserve the collective interests of the individual. Nonetheless, in both these situations, the jurists were engaged in ruling on the basis of their personal understanding of the collective or individual interests based on their appraisal of equity and public good.

Evidently such an application of human intuition was problematic in interpretive jurisprudence which questioned the validity of freely derived judgments. Such matters, as discussed in detail in Chapter 3, were identified as *al-maṣāliḥ al-mursala*, that is, the benefits that were independent of the required link to the revelatory sources. The practical aspects of such decisions affecting public interests could not be ignored by those working in the public sectors of Muslim societies. Scholars like Ghazālī, while explaining the original sense of *maṣlaḥa,* which signified "deriving benefit (*manfaʿa*) and repelling harm (*maḍarra*),"[11] adhered to the technical sense of "safeguarding the purpose of the revelation (*al-sharʿ*)." In other words, the revelation approves promotion of human interests and elimination of causes of harm.

The Relativity of the Interpretive Enterprise and the Universalism of Ethical Values

In my search for universal moral dimensions of Islamic tradition that could engage in a meaningful conversation with other religious and nonreligious traditions, I begin with a critical assessment of the historical Islamic juridical tradition in the context of juridical-theological ethics.[12] My aim is to explore the ethical doctrines that undergird the juridical methodology in deducing fresh rulings in the area of interpersonal relations as defined in the context of changed circumstances of modern national and international relations. As I will argue in this chapter, it is the ethical dimension of the Islamic juridical methodology that holds the potential for an inclusive universal language that can engage the common morality of modern secularity. The public good cannot be assessed simply based on an interpretation of benefits and harms covered in Ghazālī's and Shāṭibī's expositions of the principle. What's more, the language of *maqāṣid*-oriented jurisprudence cannot be circumscribed to its traditionally endorsed areas of application. Like the evolving social relations and social-political concerns of modernity, Islamic ethics needs to extrapolate new values and resolutions to the extensive relationships and interactions of modern society. Accordingly, what is critically needed in Islamic ethics is to make evident that carefully formulated judicial decisions of the Sharīʿa are organically integrated within the moral consideration of the juridical methodology that aims to provide solutions to the moral dilemma encountered in everyday living. To disregard the moral sources on which judicial decisions are based would be to foreclose any opportunity to fathom the ethical worldview of the revelation that aims to protect human dignity and advance peace with justice in the world. Hence, taking an instance in ethics of the end-of-life decisions in bioethics, which are based on rational and utilitarian aspects of medical care, and comparing these with religion-based bioethics that closely adheres to the revelatory guidance in evaluating the sanctity-of-life principle, disagreement occurs regarding the right of surrogate decision makers to decide whether to continue or discontinue the futile treatment. The analysis is centered on the pros and cons of "prolongation" of futile treatment versus "allowing" nature to take its course toward relieving the patient's suffering. The revelatory guidance in cases of futility is explicitly against prolongation of treatment when there is no hope for cure, whereas secular bioethics emphasizes the moral obligation of saving life. The moral dilemma in such cases cannot be resolved by the prevalent juridical methodology in interpretive jurisprudence alone; the case demands full appraisal of the factual and cultural elements in the context of the terminally ill patient. The scriptural and rational framework of Islamic ethics provides the guidelines to derive a morally viable solution in cases of futility of further medical intervention.

As a rule, ethical inquiry connected with moral epistemology or moral ontology is underdeveloped in the seminarian curriculum, which is in large measure religious- and legal-oriented. This lack of interest in the theological-ethical underpinnings of juridical methodology that deduces rulings in all areas of human activity is a major drawback of seminary education in the major centers of Islamic learning. As a matter of fact, this lack of interest in moral principles that undergird interpretive jurisprudence to deduce fresh decisions is grounded in conceptual misinterpretation of theological-juridical ethics. In a recently published work on practical ethics (*akhlāq-i ʿamalī*), Ayatollah Muḥammad Riḍā Kanī has denied any relationship between interpretive jurisprudence and ethics, neither in the methodology nor in the application to derive judicial decisions in all areas of social ethics that includes sexual relations, hoarding of wealth, and so on. He essentially and restrictively deals with virtue ethics which impact one's decision about a moral course of action, as if Islamic jurisprudence does not deal with the rightness or wrongness of action.[13]

A number of Western scholars of Islamic legal tradition, following the antirationalist attitude of mainly Sunni jurists, have erroneously ignored any organic relationship between theological and legal doctrines in shaping juridical methodology and application. In contrast, Shīʿite legal studies have not severed their epistemic correlation with, for instance, the theological question of whether or not good and evil are objective categories that can be known intuitively by an agent's divinely endowed reason. The moral consequences of raising such questions about ethical epistemology are enormous since they lead to larger issues about the human ability to comprehend justice and to assume moral agency to take responsibility to effect changes in social and political realms. Moreover, theological-ethical deliberations have led to moral categorization of human acts based on rational understanding of one's duties and reciprocal responsibilities. It is important to keep in mind that juridical categorization in jurisprudence has simply followed what was rationally estimated as necessary (*wājib*), recommended (*mandūb*), or forbidden (*ḥarām*) in ethics.

My other aim in pursuing the ethical foundation of Islamic juridical tradition is to emphasize the human dimension of the juridical enterprise in Islam so that the normative essentialism attached to interhuman relationships in the juridical corpus of the classical age is understood in its historical and relative cultural and social circumstances. Having spent more than four decades of my academic life in becoming proficient in Islamic legal tradition, I have concluded that the reason legal reforms in the Muslim world during and after the colonial period lacked cultural legitimacy was because the challenge to rethink legal methodology in order to appreciate universal content of its ethical underpinnings was ignored in favor of textual proof for fresh rulings in the area of interhuman relationships. Modernization through Westernization forced Muslim countries to adopt Western civil codes to respond to the changing social and political conditions of modern men and women living as citizens of a modern nation-state rather than as believers. There was no dearth of conceptual resources in Islamic ethics for deriving universal moral principles to guide the life of a citizen who needed to be treated equally, first as a human being endowed with rationality and dignity, and only then differentiated as a member of a specific faith community.

The prevalent text-based hermeneutical methodology (*al-ijtihād al-shar'ī*), by not seriously paying attention to the moral values that rationalize the classical juridical rulings and extrapolations, has rendered the traditionalist approach to problem-solving inconsequential, and even incongruent. Textual proof has always depended on the legitimate hermeneutics that related the text to the changing circumstances of modern living that have absolutely no comparable rubrics in the classical juridical corpus. The adopted text-based approach, without ethical analysis that demands intellectual rigor in defining the moral philosophical underpinnings of past rulings, leads to logical inconsistencies in determining the relative framework of historical judicial formulations. Chronologically moral reasoning precedes and substantially supplements the scriptural sources by correlating the conclusions of two foundational sources—revelation and reason—for guiding human action. Hence, for example, on a number of occasions, using the classical rulings on permissible divorce between married couples, jurists have ruled that a man has unilateral rights to divorce his wife, even without reasonable justification. To be sure, such a ruling seems to have ignored meticulous moral analysis, which would have required taking into consideration the ethics of the marital relationship and the impact of its dissolution on a divorced woman's future in Muslim culture.

The most striking example of the failure to undertake rigorous ethical analysis to produce an inclusive human rights document that would promote the fundamental rights of all citizens in a modern nation-state occurred in the drafting of the Cairo Declaration of Human Rights in Islam in August 1990. The almost irrelevant citations from the Qur'an and the Sunna to argue about the equal rights of all humans as humans failed to convince secular analysts of the document's universal appeal that needed to go beyond the boundaries of the faith community to include all human beings regardless of their race, creed, or color, based on their inherent dignity. In fact, without including the critical revelation-based articulation of universal morality, as I have argued in my previous research on the challenge that Islam faces in promoting human rights, it is impossible to convince the international community of the inclusive moral intent of the Islamic tradition, much less that its exclusionary theology is capable of treating all humans as humans first. The history of modern juridical reforms in the Muslim world since the 19th century is replete with examples that indicate lack of interest in ethical analysis among Muslim jurists engaged in formulating fresh rulings within the larger context of a modern, secular social-political reality of a nation-state. Without recognizing the moral agency of all humans and their freedom of religion and conscience, as extracted from the Qur'an, it is ludicrous to speak about inherent human dignity and inalienable human rights that apply to all citizens equally in the Muslim world.[14]

Let me be clear that Islamic ethics awaits the search for antecedents in the juridical tradition of Islam. Without succumbing to the temptation of regarding the human analytical mind as the only arbiter of just public order, and without denying revelation the power of correlating the human understanding of justice with revelatory guidance in the matter of just social order, it is not far-fetched to argue that there is consonance between the truths of the revelation and the demands of human intelligence in discovering a standard of just interaction that would be reasonably accepted by all in some suitably defined public order. Moreover, although interpretive jurisprudence accommodated the separate jurisdictions for spiritual and secular through its notions of human-God (*'ibādāt*) and human-human (*mu'āmalāt*) relationships, it carved out a particular role for ethics to guide the universal moral and particular spiritual lives of the people living under its public system.[15]

Religious Reason in Muslim Ethics

The world-embracing posture of Islam necessitates that Islamic ethics develop both scripture-based and public reasoning to analyze and offer solutions to the sociopolitical realities that make the religious and the secular inseparable in

Muslim societies. Of all the world religions, Islamic tradition, with its notion of a universal religious-political community—the *umma*—directed its adherents to institute good (*al-ma'rūf*) and prevent evil (*al-munkar*) by creating a political society committed to govern comprehensive human life in all its manifestations and prepare its followers for the hereafter. This ethical-political obligation connected with public order in Islam has been identified by some Western social scientists as "political Islam." So interpreted, "political Islam" is an active response to implement that worldly vision that seeks to counter internal decadence and political corruption in Muslim states. Further, and incongruously, "political Islam" is intrinsically open to manipulation as a militant ideology to press for political and social reforms in order to make them compatible with Islamic teachings about the ideal public order, which also includes the implementation of the divinely ordained Sharī'a.[16]

However, from its inception Islamic tradition was concerned about the tension between universal and communitarian ethics, and therefore it undertook to address the issue on several occasions. The strategy employed by the Qur'an to connect humanity as a single community under its universal moral order, even when it recognizes the plurality of scriptural guidance given through various prophets in history, is to relate them through the "innate nature" that is capable of recognizing a moral good (*al-khayr, al-ma'rūf*). This innate or infused nature is the source of the very first qualities in virtue of which someone becomes human:

> So orient yourselves to the divinely ordained regulation (*dīn*) [and do not deviate in the slightest], a human by nature upright. [Act in accordance with the dictates of] your God-given nature and follow the pattern of creation established by God. Indeed this pattern does not change nor do God's laws (*sunna*) ever become obsolete. That is the desirable directive (*dīn*), but most humans know it not. (Q. 30:29)

God's laws (*sunna*) never change or become obsolete. This reference is to the order of nature. In addition, God honors humanity with a "noble nature" (*karam*). As part of their noble nature, all humans are endowed with an innate scale with which they can weigh the rightness and wrongness of their conduct. This innate scale is connected with universal ethical cognition, as stated in another reference to human creation: "By the soul and that which shaped it and inspired it [with conscience of] what is wrong for it and [what is] right for it. Prosperous is he who purifies it, and failed has he who seduces it" (Q. 91:7–10).

Hence, "human by nature upright" or created in "God-given nature" (*fiṭrat allāh* = "God's nature") is endowed with a morality that cannot be arbitrary. Ethical knowledge that is "inspired by God" does not require any justification independent of the naturally endowed innate scale. The Qur'an leads humankind with "upright nature" to achieve a balance between the "known" (the convictions determined through the process of reflection) and the "unknown" moral judgments by placing the known in history and culture at the same time. Consequently, the Qur'an anchors moral norms in the reflective process and invites human beings to ponder the consequences of their actions and learn to avoid any behavior that leads to perilous ends. Moreover, it appeals to the human capability for learning from past destructiveness preserved in historical accounts in order to avoid it in future. The assumption in the Qur'an is that there is something concrete about human conditions that cannot be denied by any reasonable persons endowed with "hearts to understand," that is, a conscience to judge its consequences (Q. 22:46).

The concept of a known pre-revelatory moral language in the Qur'an does not fall short of acknowledging the concrete historical and social conditioning of moral concepts. But it stipulates that people living in different cultures must seek to elicit the universal ideal out of the diversity of concrete human conditions—a common foundation upon which to construct an ethical language that can be shared cross-culturally in the project of creating a just public order. Both the clearly stated and the implicit moral values in the Qur'an point to concrete ways of life in different cultural idioms that must be understood in order to extricate the universal values and to apply them in other contexts. The moral and spiritual awareness that ennobles human existence and leads it to carry out duties to God and other humans functions as a torch of the divinely created innate human nature, enabling it to discover the universals that can build bridges of understanding across cultures.

With the weakening of the critical emphasis on ethical reasoning in Muslim cultures, although Muslim societies are traditionally religious-minded, the importance attached to past juridical formulations without understanding their generalizable moral justifications has led to the neglect of undergirding moral norms as the most fundamental aspect of the overall scriptural guidance. This means that a religious worldview comprised of exclusionary Islamic beliefs about the supernatural and orthopraxy has continued to shape social and political attitudes and interpersonal relationships and to provide existential meaning as well as security in the ever-changing human relations in modern life. Nonetheless, the major source for the secular skepticism of the religious worldview and scriptural reason in general, and Islamic tradition in particular, is the historically disruptive character of religious politics, and the endless religiously inspired violence in many parts of the world that disrupts normalcy beyond repair.

Historically, religion in the public domain has been disruptive of necessary social cooperation and cohesion based on some consensus about the equality of all citizens in a modern nation-state. The classical interpretive jurisprudence has not been able to respond to the need for a modern political order promoting citizenry. As I write this chapter, I am aware that the Islamic juridical tradition has not provided an alternative to the classical division of the world into domains of faith and disbelief. Obviously, without extracting the universal ethical norms that regard human beings essentially and primarily as human, based on inherent moral agency and dignity taught by the Muslim scriptural sources, it is hard to fathom critically needed reform of the juridical methodology that is firmly based on moral presuppositions of the Qur'an. Thus far, rethinking the methodology has recovered what is popularly known among Sunni scholars as *maqāṣid*-based interpretive jurisprudence. However, these objectives, five or more, as introduced by Ghazālī and others, stem from the rationally, morally, and naturally recognized interests and ends of all people. In other words, attention needs to be drawn to the ethics of interpretive jurisprudence that is firmly founded upon the four sources (*adilla*) of judicial decision-making (*fatwā*), namely, the Qur'an, the Sunna, consensus of the scholars, and analogical reasoning. It is worth remembering that Ghazālī in his major work on methodology introduces these naturally (read "rationally") derived principles (like "common good" = *maṣlaḥa*) as *al-uṣūl al-mawhūma* ("presumed" = a method believed to be correct even when there is no proof of it, but on the grounds that it is extremely likely).[17] Undoubtedly, Sunni jurists introduce "public good" as a justificatory moral reasoning that functions as an antecedent for other, similarly deduced norms to enable the jurist to look beyond the immediate changing circumstances to formulate future rulings with wider application. Furthermore, modern life has reached a point when existentially it has not been able to provide necessary meaning to life to motivate an active response to demanding reciprocity and responsibility in human relationships.

At the core of a religious message is a concern with developing just and fair relationships among peoples. Coexistence and cooperation among human groups with variant belief systems is so central to the advancement of religious faith and its spread among all peoples that scriptural sources of the major faith traditions are embedded with rules that govern just and fair dealings among the followers of particular community and with those outside it. Yet these very sources have been misappropriated to impose discrimination against and unfair treatment of the religious and cultural "other." Islamic juridical tradition is just one example of the way a universal tradition that can treat all humans as humans can, for whatever reason, end up becoming a starting place of institutionalized discrimination against all those who are religiously reduced to some sort of "second-class" citizenship.

Hence, the purpose of this chapter is to argue for rethinking the role of ethics in jurisprudence to advance the moral philosophy that undergirds juridical theory. In the Islamic context, I need to critically assess the theoretical problems before

I can advance solutions to the lack of academic or religious interest in moral philosophy among Muslims in general, and their traditionalist leaders in particular. The problem, as a number of non-Muslim and Muslim authors on the subject have pointed out, is with the Islamic juridical corpus that is in stark contradiction with the ethically informed methodology. While it is true that Islamic juridical sources need to be meticulously reinvestigated for their discriminatory laws based on religious and gender differences, in my opinion it is the investigation of the ethical underpinnings of the revealed texts that can usher in the necessary reform of these laws to meet the universal standards recognized in, for instance, protection of religious and cultural minorities living under the domination of majority Muslim states. The major objective of this chapter, then, is to explore the Islamic ethics that serves as the foundation of Islamic legal thought. Muslim theological ethics, in its deontological-teleological forms, promises to bring to light a universal language of ethical necessity (*ḍarūriyāt*) in Islamic revelation—a language that has the potential to become inclusive through its universal moral requirement of moral necessity (*al-ilzām al-khulqī*) founded upon natural morality (*al-akhlāq al-fiṭrī*) infused in all human beings because all human beings are provided with the ability to know right from wrong.[18]

Islamic religious thought is based on the human ability to know right from wrong. Through God's special endowment for all of humanity, each and every person on earth is endowed with the nature (*fiṭra*), the receptacle for intuitive reason, that guides humanity to its spiritual and moral well-being. Moral cognition, in this notion of divine endowment, is innate to human nature, and because of this cognition human beings are capable of discerning moral law. There is no discussion about natural law or natural rights in Muslim theology. But the Qur'anic notion of universal morality with which all human beings are blessed and held accountable to God, regardless of their particular faith commitment or even lack of it, as I will elaborate in Chapter 5, makes it legitimate to speak about an Islamic idea of natural law. The moral law that is discernible through naturally endowed minimal knowledge of good and evil, then, is universal and can be discovered by all due to the simple fact of sharing a common humanity through creation. Further, the moral law guides humans in all matters, spiritual and temporal, private and public.

Islamic and secular presuppositions about the universal ethical norms are in agreement about infused human dignity and inherent human moral agency, and the role intuitive reason plays in ethical cognition receives its main thrust from my argument founded upon comprehensive doctrine about God's purposive creation with political implications. In this sense, religious premises in Islam carry political implications. However, there is no standardized Muslim theology representing the "official church" of Islam because there is no "church" in Islam to represent God's interests on earth. In fact, God's interests are commensurable with human interests in the Qur'an. Although claims of "official creed" are not lacking among some Muslim traditionalists, who have downplayed any plurality of religious thought based on different interpretations of the Islamic revealed texts, it is futile to search for a "generic" and "official" Islam that can be regarded as the standard version of moral philosophy, applicable to all places and circumstances.

The Roots of Universal Morality in Revelation

The negative impact of relativity of religious meaning and the growing dissension because of divisive interpretations create a formidable hurdle in contending for the universal application of the genuine sense of moral requirement that touches all human conditions, including, at times, incapability and impossibility generated by certain contexts. The traditionalist scholarship has, on the one hand, asserted the conclusiveness of the traditionalist interpretation as the *only* valid interpretation of Islamic thought; on the other, it has regarded ethical pluralism as a major source of political and ethical instability in society. This traditionalist strategy has led these scholars to negatively evaluate the role of human reason in deriving a universal ethical necessity based on authentic interpretation of authoritative religious texts. In addition, they have dismissed the rational approach. Whether in support of the congruency between some common concerns for justice and fairness shared by changed contexts and Islam, or in support of building a social-political system based on constitutional governance in Muslim countries, traditionalist scholars have construed modernist arguments in support of pluralistic moral and religious interpretations and the tolerant democratic system as a threat to the religious integrity of an exclusivist Islamic public order.

Consequently, taking the example of Islamic discourse regarding the legitimacy of and compliance with the UN's Universal Declaration of Human Rights (which has from its inception avoided entanglement with religion and God's rights regarding humanity) and the secular norms that undergird this document, the traditionalists are faced with the critical question of how exactly to generate necessary confidence that compliance with the secular international declaration will not lead to compromising one's faith in the divine command ethics as the only source for promoting global justice. This lack of confidence in secular ethics founded upon rationalist objectivism gives rise to the tension and disagreement between religious wielders of power and the advocates of constitutional democracy, with its doctrine of inclusive citizenry. Advocates of ideological Islamic government discern a hidden threat to its faith-based character if it were to work toward the implementation of equal rights by making religious governance comply with democratic politics. In fact, those who derive their political might religiously maintain that such a political process will end up denying the religious basis of Islamic governance, which will, in turn, lead to a rejection of a public role for religion. It is for this reason that they have preferred nondemocratic religious governance, which also ends up denying rationalist objectivist ethics cultural legitimacy among traditionalists.[19]

Theoretically, Islamic philosophical theology, based on its readings of the scriptural texts on matters that have solely to do with human activity and well-being in this life (*al-dunya*) and matters pertinent to human attainment in the life to come (*al-dīn*), allows or denies the concept of the autonomous individual, who acts by virtue of her ability to act freely, exercising her rights and determining the object of her ability to act. The disagreement between the rationalist objectivists, who regarded human being as a free moral agent of God, and those traditionalist subjectivists who denied her autonomy to deliberate her moral course of action except through obedience to divine commands, has had a bearing upon the religious-ethical formulations that are critical in understanding the Islamic sources for consequential reforms in the realm of the changed social and political environment. Accordingly, in maintaining rule of law, for instance, the upshot of the reform is logically connected with democratization of governance, which, on the basis of rationalist objectivist ethics, holds itself accountable for upholding the rights of its citizens.

The fundamental question that needs to be raised in the context of Islamic ethics is not very different from the one that has been raised in the context of secular ethics dealing with the secularization of public space by excluding religion from political debates. The main question is whether religious convictions should be allowed to engage public reason in a political debate about a certain policy that morally affects all citizens, regardless of their religious or cultural affiliations. The moral inclinations need to be closely examined so that people with religious convictions do not become estranged through unfair denial of their right to express freely what deeply touches them as members of the human race. Nevertheless, religious conviction that neglects to update its sociological context by engaging in a meaningful interpretation of the religious heritage by going beyond the normative texts might become irrelevant to the emerging consensus about citizenship as the sole criterion for empowering citizens in a nation-state today. By itself, this fresh interpretation is not possible without considering all other forms of human knowledge which actually clarify and enhance the understanding of the normative texts and their application in a totally different sociological framework. In working out the details of Islamic law, Muslim jurists in their own time and place went beyond the authoritative texts to find solutions to pressing issues in the community as it expanded beyond the Arabian Peninsula. Today, more than ever, Muslims are in search of appropriate interpretation of Islamic revelation to make Islamic interhuman ordinances more humane and inclusive in those sections of juridical tradition where there have been problems of discriminatory justifications to make Muslims a privileged class. The ethical norms that undergird the juridical methodology evidently disclose the deontological and teleological ethics rooted in some key religious concepts like public good (*maṣlaḥa*), averting harm and harassment, and doing what is most advantageous (*aṣlaḥ*) to human interests and ends. These concepts are unanimously upheld, and they can stimulate and engage secular ethics in a profound conversation to appreciate an inherent secularity that exists in the Qur'anic norms regarding the equality of all human beings on the basis of their inherent dignity and moral worth.

Ethical Necessity in the Context of Universal Human Dignity

Where and when does an unconditional and genuine sense of moral requirement in Islamic ethics express itself as practical necessity that takes into consideration what Ghazālī identifies as presumed capacity or incapacity to uphold revealed obligations? Is God required to heed the moral needs of the people? If an "obligatory" (*wājib*) act is one whose omission brings harm to the agent or whose contradiction is impossible, then the doctrine that upholds allowing for "dignity" (*karam*) to benefit all humans is obligatory on God and is nonadmissible. God is under no obligation to do what is most advantageous for people. Depending upon their theological stance, Islamic scriptural sources take either a universalistic or particularistic view of human dignity. The rationalist-objectivist Mu'tazilites, in this sense, were inclusive of all human beings in their conception of inherent human dignity. In contrast, the Ash'arites, who maintained divine command ethics, afforded dignity only to believers in Islam. To be sure, as discussed earlier in this book, rationalist theology upheld the inherent universality of the infused moral nature of all humans in all situations or purposes; in comparison, traditionalist theology restricted ethical knowledge relating to and affecting or including everyone in a group or situation. It is plausible to argue that rationalist ethics, with its emphasis on human dignity and moral agency, was universal, present and prevalent everywhere, whereas traditionalist ethics was particularistic, relating to those in a particular group, for instance, Muslims. According to the rationalist advocates of moral universality, human beings are endowed with intuitive reason, which, according to the doctrine of the public good, as maintained by Ghazālī, is one of the five purposes of the Sharī'a that the state ought to protect. Human reason, liberated from its religious or metaphysical antecedents, is free to negotiate its potential and creativity without any restrictions. Human beings, with their ability to reason, are the ultimate locus of knowledge, including knowledge about the moral truth, which enables human beings with moral reasoning to determine the parameters of the moral life that incorporates responsibilities along with rights to advance political justice.

In secular rationalist ethics, in order to derive a universal principle that could serve as the criterion for the equal moral worth of all human beings, human reason was made the sole criterion for moral cognition. As such, reason had to be separated from its divine origin, as maintained by religion. Furthermore, to avoid any confusion with religious reason, public secular reason was severed from its bedrock in natural law, which provided all the necessary guidance to achieve the divinely ordained purposes for human life on earth. Secularization of reason coupled with economic and social development led to depreciation of the role of natural law and its religious and metaphysical foundations. This undermining of the metaphysical aspects of secular ethics has been intentional and was covered up until recently, when questions about universal acceptance of international biotechnological and medical codes and cultural relativity have flared up between Western healthcare providers and local Muslim healthcare institutions.

As I will elaborate in Chapter 5, in Islam reason is firmly acknowledged in its metaphysical source established through the divine act of creation and endowment in human nature (*fiṭra*), the receptacle for intuitive reason. Moral cognition is innate to this nature, and because of this human beings are capable of discerning moral law. This law is universal and can be discovered by all due to the simple fact of sharing a common humanity through creation. However, such an inclusive and universal view about moral law outside the revelation was not endorsed by all Muslim schools of thought, especially when such a view was perceived to separate morality from its religious bedrock and render religious reasons for just public order superfluous. In general, Muslim theologians, even the rationalist-naturalist among them, could not endorse a separation of religion and morality in the public domain when the Prophet's political career had set the precedent for the integration of the religious and political to establish a just public order. Hence, Muslim jurists, whether proponents or opponents of the substantial role attributed to reason in moral epistemology, were thoroughly grounded in revealed texts that were appropriated through a rational or traditional hermeneutical approach to support their theses. The core issue that engaged Muslim thinkers was God's justice that comprises God's purposes for humanity in attaining prosperity in this and the next world. If as a human being I ought to espouse a religious life based on scriptural guidance in my personal life as well as in the public domain, how ought I to act if I have never encountered a revealed religion or an inspired prophet who can guide me? This particular question arose in the pluralistic sociological environment of Islamic civilization, where different Abrahamic and non-Abrahamic religious traditions had established their communal presence much earlier. Surely Islam was not the only religion in Baghdad or Damascus of the 8th and 9th centuries. How was Islam then to maintain a relationship with other religions in the public domain?

The dominant view among traditionalist scholars was to make Islam the sole repository of religious truth and the ensuing political guidance that regulated the relationship of Muslim dominance over non-Muslims in the public domain. As a matter of policy, the only way of maintaining good relationships among all races and creeds in the empire was to seek a comprehensive doctrine that could override the particularistic bent of the dominant theology to make room for other faiths and peoples as equally blessed and in possession of a guidance that did not solely depend upon scriptural sources to derive moral norms. These moral norms guided intercommunal and even intracommunal relations in Muslim societies.

At the risk of oversimplification of the complicated theological debates among different scholars living under different political circumstances, I have identified two major ethical trends among Muslim theologians. The first trend was set by the majority Sunni-Ash'arī thinkers, who did not allow human reason an ability to understand the rightness or wrongness of an act independent of God's revelation. Consequently, the concept of the autonomous individual, freely exercising her rights and determining the course of her life, was rejected by these theologian-jurists. The human being was born to obey God, who alone determined what was good or bad for her. In fact, without God's intervention there was no way for a person to know the moral worth of her actions. God's commands and prohibitions establish the good and the evil, respectively. The logical conclusion of such a doctrine about human moral cognition and volition was the legitimation of authoritarian politics of the Muslim empire and its autocratic dominance over subject peoples. This traditional, majoritarian Sunni position is void of an inclusive doctrine of human moral worth and denies inherent human dignity outside the communal faith boundaries. It is not far-fetched to suggest that religious extremism in the Muslim world today can be traced back to this hegemonic theology which does not hesitate to treat dissenting groups within the larger community (like the Shī'ites, for example) as less than human and, hence, worth killing. Whether in Afghanistan, Pakistan, Saudi Arabia, or Iraq, untold atrocities and violence against minority Muslim and non-Muslim groups in the past four decades has gone unnoticed by such human rights organizations as Amnesty International.[20]

The second trend was set by the Sunni-Muʿtazilite and Shīʿite theologian-jurists, who form a minority school of thought in Islam. These thinkers recognized reason as God's gift to humanity to develop moral consciousness and acknowledged human moral agency. The main doctrine propounded by these scholars was about God's justice. God is just and God is bound by God's rule and obligation to do what is beneficial for humanity. Part of God's justice requires God to guide humanity to attain the goal for which it is created, namely, establish justice by combating injustices on earth. In theory, the rationalist doctrine of justice is a comprehensive conception that specifies an entire program for the spiritual and moral development of an individual in society that reflects God's will and purposes for humanity.

Accordingly, God's purposes for humanity include providing necessary guidance to all human beings, without exception, to achieve the stated goal of establishing a just society. Endowment of innate moral cognition and volition to carry out its intimations is part of God's justice so that no one can escape the responsibility for working toward just public order, regardless of religious affiliation. This doctrine is foundational for a comprehensive political system based on the equality of all human beings endowed with minimal, and yet comprehensive, moral apprehension as part of their nature that actually precedes revelatory guidance that comes through God's envoys, the prophets. Muʿtazilite and Shīʿite natural-rationalist theology, although attuned to innate human capacity to know right from wrong, did not develop a theory of natural law as such, but their doctrine of human moral agency explicitly made humans the locus of reason and moral law by the very act of God's creation. Moreover, human nature was acknowledged as essentially social, requiring the fulfillment of moral duty to institute the good and prevent the evil in both personal life and the public domain. In fact, this latter doctrine was one of the major principles of the Mu'tazilite-Shīʿite political ethics.

Although the Muʿtazilite rationalist thesis was defeated by the Ashʿarite divine command traditionalism, their attribution of legitimacy to human reason as a critical source of moral epistemology has resurfaced among Sunni Muslim modernists and continues to influence their advocates of democratic governance and equality of all citizens based on a rationally extracted notion of inherent human dignity.[21] The traditionalist and rationalist positions, as they stand, are based on selective retrieval of Islamic revealed texts, which deprives a modern reader of gauging an inclusive worldview of the Qur'an and its impact upon two contradictory interpretations. It is important to point out that even when the Muʿtazilite rationalist-naturalist interpretation of the inclusive moral language of the Qur'an resonates well with the universal morality that undergirds secular ethics, it is on its own insufficient to convince those traditionalist theologians whose divine command ethics is thoroughly anchored in the revealed texts. What is evident, however, is that without reconciling the two positions on human moral agency to a common denominator needed to garner the support of all Muslim scholars to accept the challenge of upholding the equality of all human beings, it would be difficult, if not impossible, to engage the traditionalists in conversation with the secularists to protect basic freedoms with the religiously negotiated moral worth of humans as humans.

Internal theological contradictions regarding the status of reason notwithstanding, it is not possible to dismiss the theological enterprise as insignificant in formulating a foundational theory of ethics in Islam simply because traditionalist or rationalist ethics cannot resolve its internal contradiction. As a matter of fact, both theological positions were compatible with the complex portrait of humanity presented by the Qur'an, in which, on the one hand, God's overpowering will was in control of everything God has created and, on the other, human beings, endowed with cognition and volition, interacted with God's will to assert their ability to choose among the possibilities offered by the earthly contingencies. The revealed texts demonstrated the multivalent connotations, open to variant interpretations, as part of the divine purpose in endowing humanity with intuitive reason as a critical instrument for comprehending the purposes of creation. Rational inquiry into the meanings and connotations of Islamic revelation was an individual endeavor and naturally prone to divisive subjective interpretations. Controversies and disputes among various scholars served as a critical intellectual exercise to uncover God's purposes for humanity. Further, these disputes led to the formulation of a theoretical apparatus for extrapolating principles and rules for the derivation of laws that regulated all interhuman relations, both interfaith and intrafaith. Hence, in the context of the specific political climate of the Muslim society in which the hold of religious law, the Sharī'a, was necessary to provide order and stability, theological disputes underscored the pluralistic nature of Islamic religious inquiry. In this pluralistic interpretation of the revelation, the belief in the omnipotent God, who required people to obey the divine commands as part of their fulfillment of the obligation imposed in the revelation (*al-taklīf al-sam'ī*), could not rule out the human moral agency as an integral part of the Qur'anic doctrine about human accountability. If the Qur'an included a doctrine about human belief as part of divine guidance, it also recognized the human's freedom to negotiate her spiritual destiny without any compulsion.

The rationalist-traditionalist divide among theologians did not lead to a drastic distortion or conclusion about a divinely ordained plan for humanity. According to them, religion established the connection between private and public, individual and society, spiritual and mundane. Humans' progress was guaranteed if they could manage to balance contradicting demands of various spheres of human existence. Two positions on morality did not in any significant way undermine the ability of ordinary people to understand this balance between the demands of reason and revelation. Revelation depended on reason for its validity, and reason sought to validate its conclusions by showing their correlation to the revelation.

Theological Underpinnings of Juridical Discourse

In Islamic philosophical theology, the opposing conceptualization of human moral agency and ethical responsibility has paradoxically served as a conversation stimulator among Muslim modernist-secularist and traditionalist religious thinkers.[22] These thinkers have confirmed or negated Islam's ability to withstand modernist demands for the reformation of discriminatory rulings of classical juridical formulations about interhuman relationships to accommodate, for instance, constitutional democracy and universal human rights. The ongoing debates among traditionalist and modernist scholars about the relevance of certain questionable juridical decisions in the area of intercommunal relations and their disagreement about extending the notion of human dignity and the ensuing equality of all humans reveal a complex and contemporary development of Islamic religious thought's preoccupation with individual autonomy in the context of the dominant traditionalist divine command ethics.

Islam, as Muslims understand it, is a comprehensive system of beliefs and practices that relates private and public, individual and society, spiritual and mundane. The best interests of humanity can be preserved when the two realms of spiritual and temporal work together in providing the values that regulate interhuman relationships in the public sphere. As a matter of fact, the prevalent doctrine about moral obligation in the scriptural sources speaks about the sense of responsibility generated by God's creation of humanity on earth. Human creation in the Qur'an reminds humanity about the two elements that make up the responsive human person, namely, the divine spirit (*rūḥ*) and the earth. These two elements serve as naturally endowed potentials to inspire a person to work diligently toward disciplining the self internally and providing imperatives of interaction externally by discharging responsibilities in society. Additionally, this reference has epitomized the union of body and spirit that generates the sense of accountability for maintaining equilibrium between the demands of the spirit and the body.[23] In view of that, human relationships are at the heart of religiously inspired morality in which people learn to balance the challenging demands of mutual rights and obligations toward one another. As such, contradictory theological doctrines about moral epistemology do not undermine the naturally instilled need for fairness and justice in building social and political institutions that reflect that balance.

The groundwork for an inclusive foundational conception of equality of all human beings in the Sharīʿa, then, can begin with a search for pluralistic formulations of the moral principle of public interest (*istiṣlāḥ*, *maṣlaḥa*) in juridical tradition and inherent human dignity and moral agency in theological interpretations. That there is room for such a foundational source for universal morality and human moral worth based on some of the pluralistic features of

Islamic revelation and Muslim culture is dependent on the authenticity of my presentation of aspects of the inherited tradition that have been downplayed by contemporary traditionalist Muslim scholarship. Contemporary Muslim scholarship on Islamic creed and practice is oblivious to the Qur'an's universal and, as yet, particularistic, message for humanity. This scholarship has intentionally overlooked or ignored the Qur'anic impulse that inspired juridical-ethical formulations about interpersonal justice in all religiously and morally required conduct. More important, political theology that was once geared toward internal criticism of Muslim social and political performance has been turned into justificatory discrimination against perceived enemies of the community.

The political-ethical movement that was spurred by the Qur'an in its early years was founded upon preservation of the message's phenomenological integrity about the interdependence of this and the next world in its soteriology, while acknowledging a critical need to provide principles that would regulate fair and just relationships between Muslims and non-Muslims. Since there was no justification to impose uniformity in spiritual response to God because of the individuality of such responsiveness, a functional recognition of separate jurisdiction for religious and secular to regulate interhuman relations was the only way to guarantee peaceful and harmonious coexistence between peoples of various religious traditions. The Qur'anic emphasis that not even the Prophet could compel people in choosing their spiritual destiny was the cornerstone of the Islamic notion of tolerance and cooperation in the public domain. The Qur'anic declaration "No compulsion is there in religion" (Q. 2:256) served as the foundation for Islamic functional secularity—a notion that marked the immeasurable potentiality of Islamic political theology to provide doctrinal validation for the institutionalization of ethical consensus on public values that met the demands of multifaith and multicultural realities of the Muslim world.

World religions have a lot to say about human dignity and inalienable human rights. In the ongoing debate on whether human rights from religious perspectives can be posited without the enunciation of a divisive ontology underlying them, the point that needs to be emphasized is that religions create and sustain communities with a vision and a sense of unity within the faith community and with other faith communities. The secularist emphasis on the fiction of social contract theory as a universal, rational foundation of human equality in creation misses the point that there were already communities founded by religions before society was formed, as it were, through a social contract. Religions brought together the bearers of different cultures to form a universal community bound together in faith and practice. There was already an overlapping consensus in place that regulated relations between different communities believing in different comprehensive doctrines long before the call to abandon the particularities of these traditions in order to endorse moral universality was raised in modern times.

Functional secularity that was instituted within these communities made it possible for them not to press for unanimity in matters of faith beyond one's own community. Instead, human relationships were allowed to determine cooperation within and between faith communities based on the common moral ground that existed to guide and affirm innate human decency. This was the practical solution to avoid entanglement with ontological foundations of one's tradition which would have made moral cooperation impossible without imposing doctrinal uniformity on others. The secularist emphasis on moral universality outside religious doctrines for the advancement of equality in civic order needs to sit in dialogue with the religious ideas and comprehension of inherent human dignity as the sole criterion for claims of inalienable entitlements. Islam, along with other Abrahamic traditions, has something to say about a just society, good government, and the rule of law. No religion will accept a secular solution to privatize its voice and eventually lose its influence in nurturing compassion and forgiveness as keys to sustainable human relations. For its part, religion needs to voice its concerns for justice without becoming self-righteous and self-congratulating for its glory in the divine. Reciprocally, the public domain provides an opportunity for religion to become a source of moral guidance that is conducive to just human relationships.

Let me now turn to the Islamic juridical-ethical tradition, where I hope to find evidence for my thesis regarding the moral nature of interpretive enterprise dealing with social transactions regulating interpersonal justice. It is clear that Islamic juridical theology, with its exclusionary creed that informs its discriminatory legal formulations, cannot guide or govern a secular nation-state made up of different ethnic and religious communities. Muslims in general adhere to a historically inherited dogma that Islam must not only guide but also govern a political order by providing a comprehensive guide to human life. This is not conceivable in view of the challenges that must be overcome in order to institute democratic governance and implement the notion of equality of all citizens regardless of their race, creed, or gender. Are there within historical Islam paradigm cases that can be tapped for the creation of a nation-state that is also a member of the international public order and a signatory to the international conventions? In other words, in light of the changed contexts (*taghyīr al-aḥwāl*), documented and endorsed by jurists like Ghazālī and Shāṭibī, is it possible to argue for the existence and extension of relative moral and religious action-guides from which to derive universal guidelines in juridical methodology?

Let us trace our steps back to Ghazālī's criticism of the rationalist-objectivist theory of ethics promoted by the Muʿtazilites in his work on theology, *al-Iqtiṣād fī al-I'tiqād*. In the third section of this work, he raises his objections to the rationalist thesis about God being under rational obligation to guide humanity to what is most advantageous for it. Quite to the contrary, according to Ghazālī, God is under no obligation to reward obedience or punish disobedience, as maintained by the Mu'tazilites. In order to absolve God from any rationally imposed obligation for the betterment of human society Ghazālī undertakes a detailed explanation of the meanings of ethical terms like "necessity," "good," and "evil."[24] What follows in his exposition is the Ash'arī stance on moral relativity based on variant interpretations and the application of moral values to deduce religious action-guides.

Ghazālī adamantly maintains that moral values are derived from revelation (*shar'*), and not from reason (*'aql*), as maintained by the rationalists. In other words, the only source of moral law is the revelation, and that revelation has been given to a specific community, whose salvation depends upon carrying out the dictates of the Sharī'a. More relevant, Ghazālī rejects even minimal rational explications of value terms and criticizes the Mu'tazilites and other rationalists who have sought to interpret these terms erroneously as morally self-evident. As for the Prophet's claim to prophethood, Ghazālī maintains that it is exclusively corroborated by performance of the miracles. Hence, the entire section is devoted to establish that God is omnipotent and free from any obligation. Such a doctrine raises a serious question about the universality of Islamic guidance: Is it founded upon revelatory proof only? Or does human reason have any role in its authentication?

Let me make clear from the outset that, being fully aware of the problems of cross-cultural translation and terminology, I am not extraneously imposing functional secularity on Islamic tradition; rather, separate jurisdictions (*niṭāq sulṭa*) constituting human-God (spiritual) and human-human (secular) have informed religious-ethical deliberations when structuring purely religious and largely social-political institutions. The language of separation of "church" and "state" did not exist in the sacred law of Islam, the Sharī'a. If there was any power struggle to represent God's interests in the Muslim empire, it was between the two public institutions: the rulers and the religious leaders in seminary (*madrasa*). As far as the public was concerned, it was the seminarian leadership that represented the authentic transmission and preservation of the Islamic tradition. The state throughout the classical period (9th–12th centuries) suffered from lack of sufficient legitimacy to exercise its will with public consent. Hence, it resorted to political authoritarianism.

Although I will be discussing the Islamic notion of natural law in Chapter 5, let me briefly underscore the significance of the Qur'anic universal discourse calling upon humanity to respond to its original nature capable of moral discernment. No human endowed with reason can fail to understand this moral language.

More important, as a source of unity that transcends religious differences, this language establishes the necessary connection and compatibility between private and particular spiritual, and public and universal moral guidance. Hence, the Qur'an binds all of humanity to its natural predisposition not only to be aware of the meaning of justice but also to will its realization. In this universal idiom, no human being, then, can claim ignorance of the ingrained moral sense of wrong and right; it follows that none can escape divine judgment of a failure to uphold justice on earth.

However, in a multicultural and multifaith society, insistence on agreement on matters of belief as a precondition for social organization is highly problematic. The solution offered by secular advocates of democratic politics is that effective governance arises not from shared belief but from a system of government incorporating pluralistic politics based on relative moral order. International relations today are conducted without any reference to the substantive beliefs of the member states because religious premises are considered "nonpublic." Whatever their irreconcilable differences in matters of faith, all communities are legally bound to do their part in maintaining peaceful social relations. The resolution of conflicts does not require people to uphold certain religious beliefs, nor does it mean that they do not or cannot share a vision of a future community that is inspired by belief in transcendence. According to this line of secular thinking, judgments based on religious reasons are "inaccessible" to people outside the faith community because "some of the crucial premises that underlie such judgments are not subject[s] of general acceptance or of persuasive demonstration by publicly accessible reasons."[25] Islamic political theology has much to contribute to our understanding about the desirability of inclusive universal argument founded upon a spiritual-moral challenge calling for human cooperation in establishing a just public order.

Let me reiterate that the purpose of divine revelation is to provide norms and values that will guide humankind toward constructing a viable system of governance. When the Qur'an honors human beings with divine deputyship, it is speaking about potentialities and challenges that await humanity as it struggles to establish a just order. Political theology which endorses human moral agency that is purposive as well as responsive to duty underscores the fact that it is going to be a struggle rather than a predetermined success. In order to reach its final end humanity will have to utilize the divinely conferred abilities and potentialities to assume the critical responsibility of exercising authority in order to establish an ethical political order. Religious guidance provides activity and creativity in moral agents to advance them in virtuous life as routine orientation. The moral life in the Qur'an requires continual responsiveness and vigilance to God's guidance in order to fulfill morally commendable goals and to overcome the tendencies that hamper the realization of an ideal society founded upon fair treatment of people and respect and protecting the rights of those who stand outside one's kindred and faith community.

More than any other world religion, at one time or other Islam has succumbed to the political ambitions of Muslim rulers and has in the process sacrificed its core values of interfaith tolerance and coexistence. Such an alliance between an exclusive and hegemonic theology perpetrated by court theologians and political power has actually led to the disregard for the universal, inclusive ethical foundations of Islamic tradition. Surely, Islam includes among its theological doctrines of divine justice and human moral agency concepts of individual and collective responsibility to further a divinely ordained ethical public order. Moral agency in Muslim religious ethics is both teleological and deontological. In its teleological emphasis, human beings are called to realize their full potential as spiritually moral persons by undertaking acts of worship as part of God's right (*ḥaqq allāh*) to them, and acts of interpersonal justice as part of the reciprocal rights of human beings (*ḥaqq al-nās*) to one another.

The Qur'an does not teach that humanity has fallen through the commission of "original sin." But it constantly warns human beings about the egocentric corruption that can weaken the determination to carry out divine purposes for humankind. Human pride can infect and corrupt undertakings in politics, scholarship, everyday conduct, and theology. The last is the most sinful aspect of egocentric corruption because it is done in the name of God.

The Ethics of Human Dignity in the Qur'an

Earlier I identified the two basic elements in human personhood: the divine spirit and the earth. The Qur'an sets its believers as undertaking a new prophecy of life stemming from the dual constitution of humanity. This duality, composed of spiritual and material, became the cornerstone of *taqwā*-oriented guidance of the Qur'an. *Taqwā*, in the Qur'an, signifies moral-spiritual consciousness in human beings that actually precedes a declaration of faith (*īmān*).[26] *Taqwā* being connected to human nature (*fiṭra*) is infused with the capacity to experience the spiritual and ethical in developing an ideal human society. The Meccan, that is, the earliest sections of the Qur'an contain numerous moral injunctions, urging purity, chastity, and generosity. The specific moral ideals in the revelation reinforce the moral norms that were upheld in Arabian society in the form of the "known" (*al-ma'rūf*) moral practice. What was new was the way these norms generated the need to develop a strong sense of moral responsibility in the context of a new, divinely ordained religious system that regarded humankind as collectively representing (*khalīfa*) God on earth.

Moral responsibility, according to the Qur'an, originates in the innate sense of obligation (*ilzām*) related to attainment of an objective connected with divine deputyship (*khilāfa*). Accordingly, the fulfillment of delegated authority creates moral-religious obligation (*taklīf*) that must be carried out as ethical necessity (*al-taklīf al-'aqlī*), the obligation imposed in intelligence. As the deputy of God on earth, besides stressing the "noble nature" (*fiṭra*) that guides and promotes human being to perform all those acts that are morally obligatory while avoiding those that are blameworthy, based on the common ethical responsibility that humans have toward one another, the Qur'an emphasizes mutual expectations and relations fostered by universal parentage. This additional ontological reference to common parentage urges people to do what is obligatory and good and to avoid what is bad. There is no mention of the creation of human being in the image of God in the Qur'an, although there are traditions that speak about that.[27] A focal point of Muslim theology is the divine endowment of special benevolence (*luṭf*) in those who are under moral obligation to achieve the reward God offers them in the revelation. Human beings are endowed with distinctive qualities by God through this benevolence to enable them to exercise the capacity to perform obligations as God's creatures and relate to one another as members of the human community. In this sense those who will do all that is obligatory and avoid whatever is bad with or without the aid of revelation will merit the ultimate reward for which they were created. Divine benevolence functions as the sole repository of moral worth. Each individual has value and dignity by nature, and as a member of a faith community every person is the bearer of inalienable rights.

In the context of the social and political life of believers with the "other," the question that needs to be raised is the role of ethics. Does the religiously generated quest for moral purity determine the manner of treating other human beings? Is the morality in the scriptures integral to revelation that seeks expression through just and fair human interaction? To put it differently, can moral order be realized without considering religious imperatives about the highest end of human existence on earth? According to the Qur'an, human beings, although not born with original sin, face a choice that requires God-given natural principles to stabilize the infused moral capacity to know the right from the wrong in order to advance humanity on its path to bidimensional perfection of spirit and earth. Natural principles (*qanūn ṭabi'ī*) generate moral and intellectual virtues that are needed to attain the secure wholeness promised by faith in God. At this stage in moral development the infused moral law and the public good determined by reason correlate to produce the intended human salvation by keeping faith in God alongside moral action. Without moral action founded upon faith-generated natural principles, the ideal spiritual-moral society cannot be realized. Human cooperation for the public good is a collective effort that brings about a common end when widely different religious beliefs and even irreconcilable individual interests are traced back to the universal and supernatural source of moral interaction that stems from the infused constitution of humanity. In other words, according to the Qur'an, the revelation and reason—the supernatural and natural—are at work to provide a balance of divinely ordained comprehensive relations between this and the next world.

The rational moral paradigm based on intuitive reason seems to sustain an irreconcilable conflict between revelation and reason in generating the necessary disposition to acquire wholesome ethical life that promotes the spiritual and earthly good in accordance with scriptural sources. Evidently, the revelation-based ethical theory, with its unmistakable emphasis on this-worldly connection, is proposing a practicable solution between rationally acquired principles of character formation, founded upon different ends of life, and the universally endowed moral principles that conflate this and the next world in its ideal moral order: "O humankind! We have created male and female, and appointed you races and tribes, that you may know one another. Surely, the most honored among you in the sight of God is the most god-fearing [spiritually and morally aware] of you. God is All-knowing, All-aware" (Q. 49: 13). Undoubtedly, the Qur'an indicates that human beings cannot achieve moral purity without the power of God. People, having been endowed with moral-spiritual consciousness (*taqwā*), need to affirm their choice by turning to God and attaining the moral life that has been imprinted in human nature by obeying God's guidance through the prophets, who come to remind human beings about their divinely ordained nature and its potentials. In contrast, secular ethics requires people in public to appeal to the independent rational basis when dealing with matters of justice. Whereas one has the freedom to choose between competing doctrines and pursue one's belief in private religious institutions, in the public domain, where one is linked to others in common citizenry, one is bound to select fair principles that would support a system of social cooperation.

Abrahamic traditions are characteristically founded upon the scriptures that locate justice in history through community. This ideal of justice in a divinely ordained community is a natural outcome of the belief in an ethical God who insists on justice and equality in interpersonal relations as part of the believer's responsiveness in accepting the fundamental moral challenge of turning to God in faith. The indispensable connection between the religious and ethical dimensions of personal life predictably introduces religious precepts into the public arena. In other words, moral responsibility generated by agreeing to obey divine command ethics requires the involvement of the individual and the community in taking the responsibility for law and order.

In spite of this emphasis on obedience to God's will manifested in the creation of ideal order and rule of law, the Muslim political order historically remained susceptible to dissent and disagreement in matters of faith and practice. In the absence of any religious institution resembling a church in Islam, religious dissent went unnoticed unless it manifested in violence and damage to public good. Consequently, violent dissent within the Muslim community was treated with intolerance. As a rule, the judiciary was thoroughly institutionalized and empowered to deal with religious heresy and apostasy as political and civil insurgence. Islamic interpretive jurisprudence has preserved numerous cases in which the moral dimensions of "no coercion in matters of religion" were ignored to impose severe penalties, including capital punishment, for violating the "pale of Islam" (*bayḍat al-islām*). In modern times, with the creation of nation-states with equal rights for all citizens, there is ample evidence that contemporary Muslim jurists have not engaged in a conceptual investigation of the moral presuppositions of certain commandments in the Qur'an. In particular, the absence of a thorough analysis of the Qur'anic ethical-legal categories on the one hand, and the ethical-religious on the other, has generated rulings that fail to recognize separate jurisdictions for human-God and interhuman relationships. For instance, the Qur'an assigns Muslim public order the obligation of controlling "discord on earth." This phrase is part of a long verse that prescribes the most severe penalties for rebellion:

> The punishment of those who fight against God and His Messenger [Muslim state], and hasten to do corruption, creating discord on earth: they shall be slaughtered, or crucified, or their hands and feet shall alternately be struck off, or they shall be banished from the land. This is degradation for them in this world; and in the world to come awaits them a mighty chastisement, except for those who repent before you lay your hands on them. (Q. 5:33–34)

That the Qur'an presents comprehensive commandments in which the moral, religious, and civil are not always easy to distinguish is demonstrated by the equal gravity under civil law accorded to moral and religious transgressions by Muslim jurists.[28] Moreover, interpretive jurisprudence treats these transgressions as affecting not only humans but also God. There is a perception in which both humans and God may have claims in the same infringement, even if the episode seems to harm only one of them. Although punishment of crimes against religion are beyond human jurisdiction, the juridical body in Islam is empowered to impose sanctions only when it can be demonstrated beyond doubt that the grievous crime included an infringement of a private claim (*ḥaqq ādamī*). The sovereign duty of the political authority is to protect the public interest, a function for which the religious law afforded the authority an overriding personal discretion (*ta'zīr*) to determine how the purposes of God might best be served in the community.

Corelating Objectives of the Sharīʿa with Ethics

The Qur'an introduces the word *sharīʿa* as a system of values which God provides for the Prophet to implement in directing the totality of human acts imposed as normative categories (*al-aḥkām al-sharʿīya*) that must be obeyed to deserve ultimate salvation. The five categories that classify human acts into obligatory, recommended, neutral, reprehensible, and forbidden apply to religious as well as moral categorization. The criteria to distinguish the religious and moral are the same since the Qur'an uses a universal moral idiom to convey obligatory and forbidden in all areas of human interaction. In theory, juridical categories appeal to the infused morality with which humanity is created in such a way that God's commandments announced through revelation appeal to reason for the comprehension of the rationale behind the normative guidance. Hence, the scope of juridical procedures (*uṣūl al-fiqh*) that investigate scriptural sources includes rational exertion to discover and correlate the rules of morality to the deduced rules of orthopraxy, like "averting a probable harm" (*daf ʿḍarar muḥtamal*) or "promoting public interest" (*maṣlaḥa*).

The Qur'an emphasizes dual responsibility for establishing justice on earth. One aspect of that responsibility is related to administering the justice in society for which the rudimentary categories of the penal code are mentioned in the Qur'an and the Tradition; the other aspect, and perhaps the crucial one in a religious system, is to prepare humanity to face the comprehensive divine justice which will consider the total performance of human activity while on earth. Even as law guides specific human activity in the day-to-day encounter with real-life conditions, morality lays down the rules of understanding good deeds and weighs them against evil ones. The engagement of morality is with epistemology and ontology of human action, whereas the juridical procedures discover the judicial ruling based on the deontological and teleological aspects of humans' decisions to act and bear the consequences of their course of action.

The foundational question about universal morality in Muslim political theology provided the opportunity to delineate the relative adequacy of teleological and deontological models of human moral agency that undergird the juridical tradition in Islam. As I have argued in this chapter, it is the ethical component of the Islamic juridical methodology that holds the potential for the materialization of inclusive moral language in interpretive jurisprudence—the language that can contest the secularly derived universal morality of the secular international order. Islamic ethics shares common moral terrain with modern secularity on several levels. To disregard the merit of the Muʿtazilite-Sunnite and Shīʿite deontological-teleological model that has an effect on responsive duty or purposive human action would be tantamount to foreclosing any opportunity to dialogue with Muslim traditionalist scholars on the need to develop the rules of morality alongside the rules of law to protect human dignity and to advance peace with justice in the world.

The classical administrative document that was written by the caliph ʿAlī (d. 660) at the time he appointed his governor for Egypt and its provinces necessarily reveals the universal moral language that can be adopted in Islamic ethics. It is important to bear in mind that the document was issued when Muslim conquerors were a minority in Egypt. Egypt had a large Christian population, to whom a proper status had to be granted for administrative purposes. To reduce the majority to a "non-Muslim" tolerated people was detrimental to the development of a sense of civic responsibilities to the conquering Muslim army. In this context, the idea of civic equality was introduced in the following document written by the caliph himself to underscore the fact that communitarian membership was not incompatible with civic equality based on human dignity. As long as the role of faith was to instill moral and spiritual awareness leading to responsible behavior in society, the government could be founded upon a more universal principle of recognizing other humans as one's equal in creation.[29]

The status of non-Muslims as "equals in creation" can certainly be accorded to citizens regardless of their religious affiliation. The role of religion, then, is to foster norms, attitudes, and values that can enhance peaceful relations among different ethnic and religious communities. Norms such as "your brothers in religion or your equals in creation" can and should serve as the founding principle of governance through the creation of a civil society.

Can secular theories of human entitlement serve as a self-sufficient canon for the universality of contemporary international human rights without full assessment of the psychological and religious appeal of the religion-based moral universality of the common humanity, who are "equals in creation"? As a matter of fact, the concept of "equality in creation" simply reiterates the Qur'anic foundation of the plurality of religious paths of salvation while endorsing the common moral grounds that could function as the fundamental source of human interaction and cooperation:

> For every one of you [Jews, Christians, Muslims], We have appointed a path and a way. If God had willed He would have made you but one community; but that [He has not done in order that] He may try you in what has come to you. *So compete with one another in good works.* (Q. 5:48, emphasis added)

The Qur'an allows religious pluralism to exist in human societies as a divinely ordained system that builds its global community firmly based on humans' need to coexist despite their differences and to find a common moral cause for mutual respect and cooperation. According to this fundamental decree, what unites peoples of different faiths is the call to advance the common good of all.

5
Natural Law and Ethical Necessity

Now that I have established an inherent connection between juridical methodology and Islamic ethics in interpretive jurisprudence, I need to elaborate in the broadest creedal contexts juridical theology based on humanity's egalitarianism in decoding the basic moral law infused in human nature through reason. The Qur'an regards the human capacity to know the right from the wrong as essentially part of human nature that can be known through the divinely enacted moral law. This inherent ability resides in a moral agent. Human actions, whether involuntary or intentional, mental or physical, are the result of the human ability to act and produce acts. Ontologically predicates of actions refer to an action's class (e.g., speech or movement) or to the mode of its occurrence (false or harmless). An agent's moral culpability is measured in relation to causing that action to come to existence simply involuntarily or knowingly and intentionally. The aim of this theology of human actions is to teach humanity how to behave as humans living in private and in public. The fundamental aspect of the universal principle known to all human beings is to emphasize to all intelligent agents that one ought to avoid what is harmful to one's own being (*daf' al-ḍarar 'an al-nafs*) and to seek what is beneficial (*al-ṣalāḥ*). This rational inducement is the consequence of the natural cognition to realize one's accountability to an authority who has made humans subject to ethical duty to know their Creator by recognizing life beyond this world. The infused morality functions as the main entry point for searching and inquiring about the all-powerful and all-knowing authority that exercises a discretionary mandate over the welfare of humanity. The basic conditions for the fulfillment of the rationally imposed obligation are given intuitively so that its consequences are understood innately.

Islamic political theology, with its goal of establishing an ideal public order, had laid the doctrinal groundwork for the Muslim community to work toward reaching a consensus about the need for a peaceful and just relationship with other faith communities on the basis of common human nature under obligation to obey the universal divine law of justice. For the Qur'an it was a given that different communities and groups ought to come to terms with the fact of cultural and religious diversity and regulate interhuman relationships on the dictum that functioned as a toleration-generating principle among various claims of exclusionary religious truth. The Qur'anic guidance in this matter was clear: "To you your religion and to me my religion" (Q. 109:6). In God's wisdom, humans

Islamic Ethics. Abdulaziz Sachedina, Oxford University Press. © Oxford University Press 2022.
DOI: 10.1093/oso/9780197581810.003.0005

were to be left alone to exercise their volition in the matter of religion (Q. 2:256). Nonetheless, even though coercion in the matter of one's choice of spiritual path was ruled out, the Qur'an did not overlook the necessity of providing some workable principle like universal human nature (*fiṭra*) to serve as a foundation for what *is* good and what we *ought* to do to manage just interhuman relations. To avoid any dispute about whose religion is superior, the principle to bring peoples of diverse religious and cultural backgrounds to respect and treat one another as equals had to be based on some rationally understood sense of religious-moral duty (*al-taklīf al-ʿaqlī*). Providing such an extrarevelatory principle that could be acceptable to all faith communities and groups was a challenge for the Qur'an that included both universal and particular aspects in its message. The manner in which the Qur'an addressed the generality of humanity was clearly marked off by the universal address "O humankind!" When the substance of the message dealt with the ultimate objective of everyone's well-being, then the Qur'an proceeded with its universal insinuation, as the following passage explicitly underscores: "O humankind, We have created you male and female, and appointed you races and tribes, that you may know one another. Surely the noblest among you in the sight of God is the most morally and spiritually (*atqā*) aware of you. God is All-knowing, All-aware" (Q. 49:13).

In contrast, when the well-being of those who had formed a community of faithful was the objective, the Qur'anic message specifically addressed the Muslim community as "O believers!" The following passage underscores this particularity: "O believers, be aware of your spiritual and moral duty (*ittaqu-llāh*) and fear God as He should be feared, and see that you do not die save in submission [to God]" (Q. 3:102). Hence, the Qur'an is engaged in guiding all humanity as well as its particular faith community, making sure that the latter group becomes exemplary by avoiding extremism of all sorts and following the path of moderation to earn the title of a "median community" (*umma wasaṭa*) so that it can serve as God's witness to other peoples (Q. 2:143).

The two forms of Qur'anic address evidently point to the comprehensive ambition of the Qur'an to serve as the "Reminder" (*dhikr*) to all human beings, regardless of their race, gender, or creed. Although submission to the divine will together could serve as a uniting principle, God's decision was not to coerce people into accepting religion under duress. Consequently, the Qur'an sought to provide a source of guidance which any person with common sense could adopt as a strategy to benefit from individually as well as collectively to advance toward justice. Such a universal dimension of Qur'anic guidance always appears with God's creation of the world and humanity as a pure act of gratuity. As the Ashʿarites remind Muslims, God could have chosen to create a different world or nothing at all. Creation of everything, including humanity, was not without purpose. God created a humanity endowed with a nature (*fiṭra*) that is morally hardwired to sense right and wrong, a humanity that is endowed with intuitive reason as autonomous moral agents, a humanity that shares a common parentage to claim equality, a humanity upon which is bestowed nobility and dignity to assume God's work on earth. Even more in the ambience of universal concern is the moral admonition that calls upon all human beings to follow the innate predispositions of our being and work for the common good (*al-khayrāt*) of all beings in the environment despite their religious differences (Q. 5:48), to deserve reward for their good work in future in the world to come. To be precise, the Qur'anic universalism is thoroughly spiritual in the sense that it essentially responds to the claim of God as the Creator, who sends prophets to inform humanity of the life to come and to impose upon them duties based on ethical principles that can be extracted from autonomous reason.

However, this claim of God requires humanity to respond to the revelation that transmits further incentives to do what is essentially right and imposes specific duties that foster the habit of performing right action. The divinely endowed nature and the revelation together provide our senses with the ability to appreciate what is right and what is wrong in relation to others in the temporal order to actualize God's purposes. The divine purposes in religion are closely linked to the perfection of the temporal order in which human beings, assuming autonomous moral agency, striving (the true sense of the term *jihād*) to become fully and authentically human by undertaking the duty to be virtuous: "God commands you to deliver trusts back to their owners; and when you judge between the people, that you judge with justice. Good is the admonition God gives you; God is All-hearing, All-seeing" (Q. 4:58–59). The substance of the divine command in this passage reflects social convention based on an intuitively derived sense of duty to deliver trusts back to their owners and of justice in dealing with others. At the same time, it appeals to the community of faithful, who have agreed to live under the religious system that also regulates the community's relations with other communities living under its governance.

This characteristic of Islamic public order seeking to build common ground that is similar to the modern search for overlapping consensus between religious and secular premises for a political order was underscored by Ghazālī (d. 1111) in his chapter on political leadership (*al-imāma*). Speaking about the rationally as well as religiously inferred absolute necessity of political power to manage human affairs, he writes:

> Existence of absolute authority (*sulṭān*) [who is obeyed] is necessary in managing the religious public order (*niẓām al-dīn*); and secular public order (*niẓām al-dunyā*) is necessary in managing the religious public order (*niẓām al-dīn*). The religious public order is indispensable (*ḍarūrī*) in realizing the happiness in the hereafter, which has been the absolute goal of the prophets.[1]

Ghazālī is at pains to demonstrate that religious and secular public orders are interdependent in achieving the objectives of both reason and revelation. Moreover, secular public order cannot be achieved without the imam (leader) who is obeyed (*al-imām al-muṭā'*). Ghazālī suggests that while religious faith is essential for managing the success of religious public order structured on the principles of secular order, it is insufficient to manage an inclusive religious public order built on political consensus on religious premises only; rather, it must look for public reason to hold onto the legitimate power structure. Remarkably, the source of public reason in the Islamic temporal order is correspondingly derived from the scripturally prescribed moral duty to exercise authority with justice and dependent upon the specific capacities of knowing and choosing freely one's spiritual destiny. It is in this particular spiritual and temporal sense that all human beings are universally enjoined to treat one another as being fully capable of knowing the basic moral law and recognizing the divinely ordained principle that strongly advocates freedom from coercion in the matter of faith (Q. 2:256).

It is important to emphasize that the reservoir of overlapping consensus in traditional communities was drawn from divine revelation, which, on the one hand, excluded other communities from its particular brand of salvation and, on the other, insinuated its own community to benefit from an innate sense of human moral worth to forge a practical consensus to treat other faith communities with respect and fairness. The oft-repeated Qur'anic commandment to Muslims to pray regularly and to engage in charity was ordained to inculcate self-discipline in the community. This discipline was geared toward attaining the ultimate freedom from seeking to harm others and to deprive them of their inherent dignity. The main objective of the infused moral law was to advance inherent ends of human nature by developing spontaneous concern for social justice, including care of the downtrodden and disabled in society under the obligation imposed by intuitive reason.

In earlier sections I demonstrated with much evidence that the purpose of the revelation is to provide belief in objectivity of moral norms and values that will guide humankind toward constructing an advantageous system of governance. When the Qur'an bestows God's deputyship (*khilāfa*) on human beings, it is speaking about the human ability to understand the potentialities and the challenges that await humanity as it struggles to establish an ideal public order. The purpose of revelation is to provide spiritual and moral incentives to enact social and legal sanctions in the light of general ethical principles that become available by exploring the workings of nature (*fiṭra*), more particularly under the impact of its stated objectives, on the one hand, and against the relative background of their social milieu, on the other. In other words, although the relativity of its application could undo the universal aspect of natural law, it is still in a position to reveal the abnormalities of the rational procedures that have been employed to promulgate certain disabilities in terms of naturally regulated inequalities.

This is an ontological inquiry about intuitive reason as an independent source of human morality grounded in the revelation. Are human beings ontologically inclined to apprehend moral truths or develop moral virtue, regardless of attending to the scripturally ordained duties (*aḥkām*)? More precisely, is intuitively guided nature sufficient and adequate to provide moral indicators and procedures to reason independent of the revelation? Technically, these questions lead to a teleological interpretation of nature that endeavors to corroborate inferred norms that are universal in appeal to all peoples across cultures and traditions. Further, the revelation is also conducive to a teleological approach that appeals to all the faith communities to obey God's commands in support of the divine project of pursuing justice in human relationships. However, this rationalistic thesis about an innate sense of right and wrong, which is binding on all agents, insinuates a doctrine that appears to be incongruent with a rational principle. The divine command ethics extends the absolutely binding characteristic of divinely imposed obligation (*al-taklīf al-samʿī*) upon all human beings to God's acts. In view of this scripturally imposed obligation the question arises: Are God's acts subject to the same ethical standards that apply to humanity? Surely human beings act for what they perceive to be in their own best interest. Does God act with any special interest in mind? Can one hold God bound to absolute moral obligations that are suitable for humans qua humans?

My thesis thus far has been to contend that morality is intrinsically related to revelation, and interpretive jurisprudence is a human endeavor to extricate ethical norms that are anchored in rationally inferred moral assumptions of divine revelation. In reality, reason and revelation have functioned as two interlocking sources of values and systems of categorizing the level of absoluteness related to acts (their being good and bad, obligatory and forbidden) that have existed side by side in all human communities, regardless of time, place, and culture. Every religious tradition is provided with both universal and particular ethical standards which have, on occasion, both converged with and contradicted each other. In the history of interaction with the intricate realities of human existence, each religiously informed moral dilemma has caused fresh thinking in the area of application in the changed social and political contexts, requiring the developing religious-ethical ruling (*ḥukm*) to stand in dialectical harmony with moral-religious action-guides (*taklīf*). Revelation, for its part, through its hermeneutical potential, has endeavored to guide the juridical tradition by striking a balance between the ideal and the real and linking the communal beliefs and ideals to the formal legal-moral structures and processes for the implementation of concrete solutions to the problems, largely in the ethics of human relations (*muʿāmalāt*).

The juridical methodology developed a refined procedural structure that decoded the enduring principles of Islamic faith into evolving precepts of human action. It sought to infuse Islamic ethical standards in the form of inductive propositions to emphasize the logical character of juridical categories for indicating the relevance of certain situations and facts from a given normative angle. However, Islamic interpretive jurisprudence has always faced the problem connected with the inherent and consequently immutable religious nature of the procedure and its ability to be consistent with changing social-political conditions. In the modern period, when Islam had to deal with a restatement of the inherited tradition that strikes a balance between religious authenticity and forces of social evolution, Muslim jurisprudence was faced with the task of redefining the relationship between the normative standards ("ought") required by the revealed texts and mundane forces ("is") that activate society. The basic assumption in Islamic ethics is that the rationally knowable value of things is interlocked with the purpose and function determined by the revelatory framework that regards God as the provider of purposive directives. How was this theistic source of natural morality to avoid secularization of its juridical ethics with the unavoidable adoption of secular values, which could not correlate reason with the comprehensive spirit of the religious "ought"?

Contemporary Muslim jurists who wanted to introduce reform the juridical tradition did not engage the theoretical discussion related to the ethical foundations of juridical methodology (*uṣūl al-fiqh*).[2] Bypassing serious theoretical discussions connected with human nature and the divinely ordained moral law was, in all likelihood, the only way to avoid wide-ranging conflict with the traditionalist establishment. Religious scholars at the traditional centers of higher Islamic learning were not open to critically evaluating the classical methodology to provide a firm foundation for the fresh rulings that were demanded from them in all areas of modern human institutions and interactions. Maintaining some kind of historical continuity with the inherited juridical tradition was part of the strategy to maintain a status quo in connection with the irrelevance of past juridical decisions. By sidestepping to undertake critical examination of the highly technical and fundamentally moral principles in Islamic legal theory, Muslim jurists failed to respond to the charges that the entire Muslim juridical establishment was dominated by obscurantism propelled by the dominant conservative spirit in religious studies in traditional institutions in the Middle East. Historically, the early Muslim community was committed to perpetuating a revelation-based legal system by working toward a legal theory that would, at least, render juridical inquiry predictable and contemporaneous in deriving practical rulings in all areas of interhuman relations. Instead, the inherited juridical tradition ceased to be the primary source of precedents that were based on moral-legal analysis, and insofar as its rules survived in modern codes, they ceased to be legitimately founded upon paradigmatic cases or deduced with some sense of conclusiveness.

Apart from this intellectual weakness of modernization of the Muslim religious-ethical heritage, the persistent problem among traditionalists has been to eschew analysis of philosophical issues related to religious thought in terms of prevailing modern philosophical and historical ideas. At the foundational level, it is plausible to maintain that there is no unequivocal language of moral law per se in Islamic sources. Human moral agency, endowed with divinely infused morality, envisions the equality of all human beings in the estimation of the juridical ethics that entitles them to equal concern and respect from the Muslim public order. The modern concept of the citizen is conspicuously absent in the traditional sources of Islam. In addition to this conceptual insufficiency, at the political level the idea of all humans having equal dignity is also lacking.

Technically, the language of Islamic juridical ethics is primarily the language of obligations and accruing responsibilities. Human being is not the ultimate referent of moral agency. It is God who is the end of the moral life: "The ethical valuations (*ahkām*) of actions are grounded neither in the acts themselves nor in their properties; they are grounded simply in what God says."[3] Most of the Sunni ulema, in line with the Ash'arite theological voluntarism that vindicated the primacy of God's will over the intellect, resisted the rationalist impulse of the Qur'an that allowed the Mu'tazilite theologians to speak about the interconnectedness of human beings who were endowed with innate moral worth and autonomous agency. In addition, the Ash'arite voluntarism led to identifying morality with divine positive law and denying that ethical values can have any other foundation but the will of God that imposes them. There was no inherent objective of humanity to develop interpersonal justice. Nature and reason, according to these scholars, were insufficient for ethics. Consequently, a natural system of ethics was construed by Sunni scholars as alien and was discarded as un-Islamic, which ironically denied Islam human dignity and capacity to participate in that moral order. There was no standard of good and evil, however minimal, available to all rational creatures. An action is not good because of its being construed so by the essential nature of human being, but because God so wills it. The notion of God as an unlimited and arbitrary power implied the reduction of all moral laws to inscrutable manifestations of divine omnipotence.

Modern Muslim Social-Political Discourse

The Muslim encounter with modernity has been sluggish. Systematic working-out of Islamic religious thought by taking into consideration the inherited duality between the religiously eternal and the temporally changeable has not been forthcoming. A more persuasive interpretation of normative Islam is indispensable to derive an Islamic worldview that is compatible with the new rational synthesis between relatively static traditionalist, historical interpretive jurisprudence and the constantly changing situation of the world in the modern era. For Muslim thinkers, entry into modern discourse hinges on unmistakably restoring the Qur'an and the Tradition (*sunna*) as the only authentic sources for human guidance, so that the conformities and deformities of historical jurisprudence may be distinctly judged by the original intent of the Islamic revelation, as expounded and preserved by the traditionalists. For instance, identification of the epistemic nature of human conscience in moral valuation and the universal dimension of the common nature of human being in deriving legal-ethical decisions would have provided Muslim jurists with the deontological as well as teleological justifications for some positive legislation required to improve upon classical solutions to interhuman and international relations. More important, recognizing the fundamental equality of all human beings based on having received intuitive reason to guide humanity's initial moral discernment would have served as an important resource for those judicial decisions that require the faith community to work for the common good (*maṣlaḥa*) of all human beings. Rationally inferred just social order, however abstract and inconsistent with human nature seeking to assume the responsibility for creating an ethical political order, is inextricably intertwined with the revelatory demand for just and equitable governance as overall minimal political structure that is necessary for healthy interhuman relationships fostered on the doctrine of equality of all human persons regardless of their gender, creed, or race.

In theory, Muslim thinkers working on political ethics need to engage Islamic juridical theology rather than Islamic legal heritage to challenge the secular advocates of modern political development to take minimalist Islamic moral universalism seriously. Islamic theology in general, and juridical ethics in particular, have the potential of developing the thesis about natural law in Islam and its connection with inherent, inalienable entitlements of human beings based on human equality. Natural law as an indication of intuitively known nature of what is intrinsically good or intrinsically bad is the cornerstone of Islamic ethics. Moreover, the locus of concern in natural law theory with the question of commonsensical good (*al-ma'rūf*), toward which humanity is invited to act in building intercommunal relations beyond those which the Sharī'a norms had projected for the Muslim community, is a logical starting point in searching for a native paradigm of modernity in Islam.

The articulation of humankind as a worldwide community (*umma wāḥida*)—the central doctrine of the Qur'an (Q. 2:213, 5:48, 10:19) based upon the common, immutable and eternal moral nature of human beings—is correlated with the reformulation of the Islamic conception of natural law that has the potential for universal application of values connected with the relationship between God, society, and individual. Reappropriation of the original impulse of human equality in the revelation means finding ways of effecting authoritative transformation in contemporary Muslim thinking about the emerging patterns of human relationship by integrating the inherited communal patterns into new social and political affiliations in the context of modern notions of citizenry.

The most significant revelatory insight about human being is that as an earthly being having needs, perception, and desires, she is capable of pleasure and pain, of joy and grief, and of receiving benefit and suffering harm. Foremost in recognition of gratuitous creation by God is that she has a mind and the ability to deliberate about an action, execute it, and take responsibility for it. The endowment of intuitive reason in human creation establishes the bequest of knowledge and understanding that is common to all intelligent persons. It is this common aptitude that makes all human beings subject to moral obligation. In general, God has created human beings with the capacity of discovering and recognizing those characters that render an act good or bad and assuming moral responsibility for performing it. With the capability of infused morality to know what is right from wrong as part of humans' creation, God imposes duties (*taklīf*) whose fulfillment involves hardship. On the basis of some intrinsic ethical principles connected with the expression of gratitude in performing religiously ordained duties, God rewards agents for performing what is obligatory and good and for abstaining from doing bad. Divine benevolence (*luṭf, tafaḍḍul*) benefits all human beings for having suffered undeserved hardship in performing those duties.

In view of the doctrine of autonomous moral agency in rationalist theology, Islamic natural law evidently touches not only the human's relation to God but also the human's relation to truth, government, family, and neighbor. It affects both private and public domains of human existence. Consequently, in developing and founding universal moral norms that touch all humans, Muslim thinkers must contend not only with the historical juridical system that was promulgated by considering the politically dominant role of Muslim rulers; they must also revisit the theological-ethical foundation of juridical procedures to reform the process to reflect the moral world of the revelation. The revelation-based moral world was part of the community's empirical history that sought its relationship with the challenging aspects of the ethical principles that originated in God's command and decree. The hypothesis that informed this deduction was that human beings know these principles naturally, along with other rational principles, simply because the ethical characteristics of these acts are ontologically authentic attributes. These attributes either originate immediately from the manner of the act's occurrence or human beings unravel true qualities of things grounded in divine commandment by simply obeying them.

The problem of ahistorical treatment of juridical heritage that had separated hands with ethical principles in the revelatory decrees and commands created a moral philosophical vacuum in Muslim encounters with modernization. The intellectual challenge of modernization affecting reformulation of the heritage to derive the universal potential of Islamic ethics in Muslim societies has involved selective retrieval of the traditional past and traditional articulation of the persistent new in relation to the overall objectives (*maqāṣid*-based jurisprudence) of Islamic religious law. While the robust retrieval of the revealed text and its interpretation in conformity with the challenges of the new era has been feared as a threat to an inherited pattern of values and meanings, it has sometimes been acknowledged as an arduous undertaking to create new values and meanings to replace or extend them, especially in the context of democratic governance and protection of the fundamental equality of all citizens. Understanding and communicating about the crisis of modernization for Islamic religious thought and the role religions like Islam can play in negotiating its ethical public order is extremely strategic to an inner Islamic reformulation based on the core doctrines in the social and political settings of a modern nation-state. Consequently, intellectual collaboration between modernizing and traditional elites in the Islamic world is indispensable to counteract any negative effects of traditional religious and cultural values that hold back the emergence of necessary consensus in resolving the crisis of modernization and the emergence of a political environment conducive to the progression of a human rights regime.[4]

My argument is built upon a very straightforward thesis: there is a crisis of epistemology in Islamic juridical sciences. This crisis is the result of a persistent dislocation between theology, ethics, and law in Islamic tradition. Unless the doctrinal and ethical presuppositions of the early juridical tradition are investigated and expounded afresh, the crisis will continue to produce apologetic, intellectually impoverished, and, most important, ethically insensitive Islamic scholarship. Ethical principles rooted in Islamic revelation can be a major source to provide their moral contexts to resolve the epistemological crisis facing the tradition today. Lack of historicism in analyzing the primary materials with incisive ethical tools has led to devaluation of human life caught in the crossfire of political conflicts. When a tradition that once taught respect for the dignity even of an animal becomes the source of legal opinion that justifies the suicide bombing of innocent bystanders, then it is time to reexamine the moral directives of the Qur'an and the teachings of the Prophet, who is reported to have said, "I was commissioned to complete the noble virtues [in humanity]." One of the fundamental noble virtues that the Prophet came to teach was the dignity of the human person as human. According to a well-known narrative, one day the Prophet was sitting in the company of his close associates when a bier carrying a Jew passed. It was his custom to stand up in respect when a bier passed. So he stood up. His companions pointed out that the dead person was not a Muslim; in fact, as some pointed out, he was a Jew. To this the Prophet responded, "Is he not a human being?" Humanitarian aspects of such traditions reveal the conceivability of the moral argument built upon the sufficiency of human dignity as a principle to honor and respect all human beings.

Ethical Necessity in Islamic Theory of Natural Law

A moral action-guide constitutes an obligation that is rationally necessary (*wujūb ʿaqlī*) because ontologically the ethical principles originate not only in divine commands but also through human creation and realization of cognition that knows them naturally along with other rational principles—the major component of natural law. The objective attributes of acts are ontologically factual aspects that depict the way the act is performed. Since they are grounded in naturally endowed reason, God determines the obligatory as obligatory, providing human intellect with the knowledge of ethical values and principles as absolute universals. It is this universally imparted knowledge about the moral quality of acts that requires humanity to find ways to apply them in fostering peace and harmony with one another. This cognition also entails an objective moral mandate grounded in divine will that necessitates establishing a moral society, whose proper appraisal is discernible to human reason. In contrast to the rationally inferred obligation (*al-taklīf al-ʿaqlī*), which is solely related to the everyday aspects of human action, the revelation-commanded duty (*al-taklīf al-samʿī*) that is derived from the doctrine that God's will is the ultimate expression of morality is actually a validation of God's absolute will that determines the deontic nature of morality. Hence, the Muʿtazilite ethics regarded intuitive reason capable of providing moral justification for considering habitually performed duties as constitutive of the fulfillment of God's will; in contrast, the Ashʿarite view regarded only the obligation derived from the authority of revelation (*wujūb sharʿī*) to be capable of attaining comprehensive prosperity (*falāḥīya*) in this and the next life. In theory, both the rationalist and the traditionalist ethical estimation of imposed duty is classified as a religious-moral action-guide (*al-taklīf al-sharʿī*), drawn on the basis of rational and textual procedures to formulate an obligation. According to the Qur'an, God's command and the consequent reward are integral part of the "order of nature" (*sunnat allāh*) (Q. 33:62, 48:23, 17:77). Nonetheless, obligation imposed by command is taught by the Prophet as part of God's total guidance for human prosperity; whereas obligation imposed in intelligence is derived through rational procedures. In principle, a moral action-guide leads one to discover ethical and social norms that are universal and applicable to all humans as human. Moreover, in terms of their goal to advance interpersonal justice, they are derived on the basis of moral norms that follow from essential human nature. Religiously imposed duties lead to the discovery of the deeper signification of duties that are pertinent to human achievement in the matters of religion (*'umūr al-dīn*), whereas rationally imposed duties are pertinent to human well-being in this world (*'umūr al-dunyā*).

This rather simplified description of the two types of necessary action might lead the reader to regard revelation-based necessity in Islam to be comprehensive and with enormous capacity to be inclusive in the public domain. As a matter of fact, taking the case of the 1990 declaration of an alternative Islamic human rights document (written in response to the 1948 secular Universal Declaration of Human Rights) is based on such an assumption that, as a comprehensive system, historical Islam is capable of becoming a source of universal human rights. The critical issue that has been intentionally sidestepped by the Cairo Declaration on Human Rights in Islam is the political dimension of theological evaluation regarding moral human nature and just public order in the historical Islamic tradition. Most of the traditionalist Muslim leaders not only refuse to regard human being as a rational being, capable of guiding herself and deriving from her intuitive reason a standard to judge her environment; they also deny that there is anything intrinsically good or intrinsically bad which can be apprehended by human reason and, as such, does not depend on the revelation. Further, and perhaps negating the Cairo document's claim to be universal, is the denial of a doctrinal basis for the notion that the human is born free and is equal to all other humans in creation.

The traditionalist theory of divine command ethics, which maintains that ethical principles originate simply in God's command and decree, regards the revelation to be the sufficient and sole source of ethical principles. The Sharī'a—an expression of God's will—functions as the comprehensive source of orthopraxy that promises those who follow it salvation in the hereafter. In comparison, rationalist objectivist ethics, which maintains the doctrine of human free will and moral agency, regards human reason, epistemically capable of understanding and undertaking to live a moral life, as a manifestation of the rational will conferred on humanity as part of God's purposive creation. In principle, natural law and ethical necessity are linked to infused morality, which is the source of objective values discernible to human reason. The essential tenet of this infused morality is the equality of all human beings in creation and as recipients of divinely endowed nobility. Humankind is one community (*umma wāḥida*) based upon this commonly endowed constitution as part of their creation. Accordingly, the essence of humanity cannot be at variance with this common constitution, which is also the source of the common good and human responsibility to God for upholding it. It is this moral foundation of human society in terms of the common good in the rationalist doctrine of justice that needs to be emphasized in any universal implication of moral connection among all human beings. To be sure, the doctrine of justice does not prescribe the manner of achieving a just society; it simply underscores the human potential and responsibility to establish a just public order wherein the respect of humans is assured on the rational basis of ethical necessity which rules out discriminatory and unfair treatment of religious or cultural "others."

Muslim traditionalists have not treated Islamic ethics as an independent discipline, separate from juridical studies that deal with God's commands and prohibitions. The main thrust of their creed is that ethical valuations (*aḥkām*) of actions are not grounded in the acts themselves nor in their attributes. They are part of God's plan to provide orthopraxy based on the revelation. Accordingly, developing a systematic theory of natural law, with its rationalist trappings based on naturally endowed morality with its ontologically real characteristics, was not within their scholarly compass. In point of fact, the traditionalist treatment of and emphasis on the revelation as the only valid source of divinely bestowed ethical cognition and volition clashed with their project of working out the entire orthopraxy based on textuality and traditionalist consensus. Unpretentiously, the call for reform (*iṣlāḥ*) of any political institution that perpetrated injustice in the public sphere in Muslim society, as a rule, was the byproduct of this moral challenge of the revelation. Conversely, Muslim rationalists, both the Sunni Mu'tazilites and Shī'ite theologian-jurisprudents, propounded the rudiments of the Islamic theory of natural law when they expounded their moral epistemology in which they contended that ethical knowledge is objective and rationally acquired as part of the infused morality (*fiṭra*). The scriptural declaration about infused morality in human beings was the major evidence in support of their theory about human moral worth as well as human moral agency.

The natural rights language presupposes a person's moral capacity in understanding and exercising her naturally endowed rights. Consequently, a potential moral agency is a prerequisite to exercise one's rights. Without free exercise of will, a possessor of rights cannot be expected to make a moral decision and accept the responsibility for her action. A moral right presumes a capacity for acting in conformity to the natural law. To possess a right is to have a faculty of acting rightfully in some manner; to act in this way is to exercise this right. As an owner of a property I have the ability to rent out part of it whenever I wish; if anyone lacking this ownership rents out the place, her act violates the moral law. But how do I make that other person responsible to recognize my right without any power of causing her to act in that way? It is here that social norms become an important source of conformity to the moral code within the limits of natural law. The informal force of society provides the necessary pressures of morality. The society collectively function as the protector of rights by regulating the rules of law or morality so that no act of injustice occurs without censure.

The *Fiṭra* as the Receptacle of Infused Morality

In tracing the intended significance of the critical source of infused morality I need to demonstrate that even the staunchly traditional and doctrinally Ashʿarite interpreters of the Qur'an could not sever the inherent relationship between universal divine guidance and its implications for the development of natural law thesis in juridical theology. Hence, Sayyid Quṭb (d. 1966), a major figure in the Sunni reform movement in the 20th century, in his commentary on the Qur'an regards human nature (*fiṭra*) as the locus of divine guidance for the purpose of guiding humanity toward the natural order that regulates human action as well as the movement of the entire tangible order, orienting the creation toward the Creator.[5] Accordingly, the purpose of creating human beings is to guide their *fiṭra* in such a way that they attain moral and spiritual perfection through the guidance that God bestows in two forms: practical intelligence (*al-ʿaql al-ʿamalī*) in order to fortify the soul to fathom the purpose of its creation, and guidance to the right path in order to achieve salvation in the hereafter.[6]

The concept of *fiṭra* (nature) in the meaning of "creation" in the Qur'an is customarily connected with the notion of "by nature upright (*ḥanīf*) through creation (*faṭara*)" (Q. 30:30). The act of creation is to cause a thing to come into existence for the first time. It also signifies natural or original constitution with which a child is created in his mother's womb. In this sense *faṭara* is *khilqa*, that is, "originating a thing," as the Qur'an says when it speaks about "originating creation" (Q. 30:27). A similar meaning of "natural or original constitution" is evident in the Prophet's tradition which states, "Every infant is born in a state of conformity to the natural constitution (*fiṭra*) with which he is created in his mother's womb, either prosperous or unprosperous [in relation to the soul]." Evidently, there is agreement among classical Arabic lexicographers that the essential meaning of the word *fiṭra* is something natural, native, innate, original, or another moral quality or property with which humans are created by God.[7] Some lexicographers take the word to imply the ontological reference to the "faculty of knowing God." God has created human beings with a purpose of being known by a morally inspired creature—a human being. In other words, *fiṭra* is the source of a differentiation in the world of creation. It is only the human being who is the recipient of the divine nature (*fiṭrat allāh*). God's universal guidance has come to humanity through morally infused nature. The divinely communicated revelation through the prophets confirms the moral presuppositions of the divinely ordained nature. Religious faith can be sought in two ways: first, by seeking knowledge (*maʿrifa*) through endowed reason and evidentiary signs in nature; second, by learning through revelation inner purification (*tazakkī*) and ascetic practices (*riyāḍa*).[8]

The first form of guidance bears all the characteristics of something universal that is related to human nature. This nature is capable of discovering and recognizing in individual acts those properties that render the act ethically obligatory and whose performance or omission makes the agent praiseworthy or blameworthy before he submits to any organized religion. The evidence comes from those passages of the Qur'an that speak about two forms of "straying away" (*ḍalāl*) from the moral path: the first form of "straying away" causes the *fiṭra* to become corrupted and lose its natural ability to know the right from the wrong by letting disbelief (*kufr*) and hypocrisy (*nifāq*) find their way into one's acts; the second form of "straying away" bolsters disbelief and hypocrisy in human character. This is alluded to in the verse "In their heart (the seat of human consciousness) is a disease and God increases their disease. A painful doom is theirs because they lie" (Q. 2:10). The first kind of disease that impacts human character is the result of human choice not to follow the guidance of one's infused moral aptitude; the second kind is imputed to God, who seals the heart of those who reject their natural ethical capacity and lose the capability of acquiring moral knowledge (Q. 61:5).

The spiritual guidance is related to the particular religion that is given to the prophets, the bearers of divinely inspired messages, to guide all human beings. The guidance through revealed scriptures is subsequent to the moral guidance that is already implanted at birth. The unencumbered natural disposition, although fortified with ethical cognition and volition, perceives the need for detailed guidance that can be acquired outside itself. Hence the revelatory guidance prepares the person to accept the existence of the one hidden from sensory perception, who is the originator of everything, in whom everything shall terminate and to whom everyone shall return (Q. 2:156). Just as God does not neglect even the minutest detail that is needed in the creation, so does God not neglect to provide all that would save humanity from damaging their deeds and morals. According to the revelation, there is no compulsion in the matter of religion; what is known as conceding willingly (*idh'ān*) to the belief in the oneness of God, the need for prophets, and the Day of Reckoning forms part of the rationally acquired fundamentals of religion (*uṣūl al-dīn*). Apparently, by accepting the moral challenge of conceding voluntarily to God's particular guidance through the revelation, human beings are able to maintain their universal moral guidance in an unimpaired state. The volition to perform moral action is owing to the human station being situated between the two forms of God's guidance: the prior (*sābiqa*) universal and the subsequent (*lāḥiqa*) specific guidance—the prior being related to the human capability to know right from wrong; the subsequent being derived from faith in the truthfulness of the revelation. In addition, faith in religion and commitment to moral action are located between the divinely conferred natural disposition and the revelation—the two forms of guidance that are correlated to bring about human prosperity in this and the next world. That which verifies that the subsequent religious guidance is derived from the prior natural constitution is the verse that speaks about God's providence: "God confirms those who believe with the firm judgment, in the present life and in the world to come, and God leads wrongdoers astray. And God does what God wills" (Q. 14:27). In other words, both spiritual and moral guidance is from God, as the Qur'an declares: "And whomsoever it is God's will to guide, God expands his bosom unto submission (*islām*)" (Q. 6:125).[9] Even more poignant is this reminder to the Prophet: "You will not be able to guide whom you like. Indeed, it is God who guides whom God wills. And God is aware of those who are guided" (Q. 28:56).

Hence, God's guidance is well-established in both its forms in the sense of showing the path, and when the Qur'an speaks about God denying guidance to those who do not believe, this denial applies only to the purpose of guidance, and not to the actual endowment of guidance, which is universal and not denied to anyone. In other words, God's denial of guidance pertains to the attainment of perfection through that guidance, and not to the actual bestowal of the mind and the power of deliberate action to perform moral obligation. The law of nature causes a person to pursue and discover the desired goal for which he is created. This is God's unchanging order (*sunnat allāh*). The divine order naturally confers the knowledge of ethical principles as absolute universals along with other rational principles, which is underscored in the verse cited earlier (Q. 6:125). Moreover, the immutable divine order warns those who reject the universal moral guidance connected with their natural constitution which is innately bestowed through creation:

> And whoever it is God's will to guide, God expands his bosom unto submission (*al-islām*),[10] and whomsoever it is God's will to send astray, God makes his bosom close and narrow as if he is engaged in sheer ascent. Thus God lays ignominy upon those who do not believe. (Q. 6:125)

Human Moral Agency

How does a human being surrender his will to God and yet maintain autonomous moral agency? Human moral agency is established by divinely implanted moral principles known to all intelligent human beings. Thus, for instance, reasonable people know that one ought to avoid what is harmful (*daf' al-ḍarar*) to one's own being (*nafs*) and to seek its good by engaging in attaining what is most beneficial. The *fiṭra* makes it conceivable to understand that human actions merit reward or punishment. This is the point when the question about the authority that can institute rewards and punishments both in this world and the next arises. The knowledge about that omnipotent and omniscient Creator functions as the fundamental source of the primary obligation to acquire the experience of moral and factual elements of life, which lead toward the perfection of intuitive reason (*ikmāl al-ʿaql*) and comprehension of the evidences supplied in creation. To put it differently, God provides the basis on which a person may acquire a natural knowledge about God's existence and God's endless gifts to humanity for which humans must show gratitude and to whom they must turn to worship. Furthermore, this intuitive knowledge serves as a basic condition for one's ultimate well-being that is firmly grounded in natural reason. The obligation imposed in intelligence (*al-takilīf al-ʿaqlī*) is given naturally to attain the final reward promised in the revelation.

God's benevolence (*luṭf*) continues to fortify natural reason by providing further incentive to do what is ethically praiseworthy by commissioning prophets to inform humanity about what is advantageous for their ultimate salvation. This is the basis for *islām* (submission) of a person in relation to God. Surrendering one's will to God indicates acceptance and compliance with God's authority in all those matters that go to form the order of creation (*ḥukm takwīnī*), which includes all the matters that are decreed by God, or the matters that go to form the order of divinely promulgated revealed law (*ḥukm tashrīʿī*), which include the command and decree that are part of the revelation. In view of that, submission to God is graded in accord with what is attainable by means of it. Thus, for instance, the first level of submission is acceptance of God's command and decree which is ontologically grounded in an entity extrinsic to the act of submission by reciting the formula of faith verbally, regardless of whether or not the mind agrees with it (Q. 49:14). From this sense of *islām* follows the first level of faith (*īmān*), which is the voluntary conceding (*al-idhʿān al-qalbī*) to the necessity of putting into action most of the religiously required practices—the orthopraxy. The second level of submission is conscientious compliance so as to advance in true belief in detail and in performing the good deeds that follow those beliefs, although it is possible to fall short in some instances. "[These are the ones] who believed Our signs (revelations) and were self-surrendered (*muslimīn*)" (Q. 43:69).

As a consequence, the distinction between these two forms of submission is qualitative, in the sense that the second form ensues from the detailed comprehension of faith in religious truth (Q. 49:15, 61:10–11) and compliance with the requirements of it, whereas the first level of submission is simply being guided to discover the latter. This qualitative submission leads to the third level, when the soul becomes fortified with the virtues and gains mastery over the beastly appetites. It is also at this level that a person begins to "worship God as if she sees God, and if she does not see God, then God certainly sees her." Nothing in human character at this third level is found wanting in terms of compliance with God's commands and prohibitions. It is a state of total submission to God's decree and God's order of creation (Q. 4:65). The corresponding level of faith prepares the believer for the world to come. All acts of personal piety are part of this level of faith (Q. 23:1–5). The person who has undergone transformation in the previous levels of submission has gained inner strength by remaining steadfast in the fulfillment of his duties the way these had to be performed. At this station of absolute submission divine providence enwraps him with God's bounties which God dispenses universally and perpetually, without restriction and disinterestedly, over which human will has no control (Q. 2:127–128). This state is captured in God's command to Abraham: "Surrender!" Abraham said, "I have surrendered to the Lord of the Beings" (Q. 2:131). The apparent sense of the command is based on *lex gratiae* and not *lex naturae*, for Abraham surrendered to God voluntarily, responding to his Lord's call and fulfilling God's command. Accordingly, these commands are directed toward him in the beginning of his spiritual and moral journey. Abraham's prayer at the end of his life with his son Ishmael, to make them surrender (*muslim*) to God and show them the ways of worship (Q. 2:127–128), is a prayer for something beyond his will. Thus, the submission requested in this prayer is in the meaning of faith at the highest level, that is, at the level when one wants to hold to this state of "active surrender" under all circumstances (Q. 10:62–63).[11]

Rereading of the Qur'anic passages that speak about infused morality and ingrained human ability to acquire moral knowledge demonstrates that, based on the idea of inherent human nobility in the Qur'an (Q. 16:70), it is not difficult to establish human moral agency and equality. Besides infused moral nature there is another fundamental Qur'anic concept that leads to establishing the notion that God's natural guidance is available to all human beings without exception because such guidance springs from God's special endowment of the *qalb salīm*, signifying "sound mind, moral disposition, the recesses of the mind (*dākhil al-khāṭir*), the seat of consciousness, thoughts, volitions and feelings, the reason" conferred upon humanity.[12] It is a faculty by means of which a human being distinguishes truth from falsehood, good from evil, beneficial from harmful. It confers on humanity meaning in life without which life becomes just physical presence.[13] Hence, to deduce a moral foundation for inherent human dignity based on religious premises, Muslim deliberations about equality and ingrained moral agency of all human beings need to reexamine Qur'anic doctrines that speak about human conscience and its freedom from any coercion.

The basic impulse of the Qur'an is dynamic and action oriented and seeks to create a perfect society on earth without turning moral inspiration into institutional power. Coercion in the matters of faith is contradictory to the moral quality of human interaction because it destroys a sincere motivation and defeats a spirit of tolerance within certain agreed upon individual and collective limits.

Interpersonal dealings in society need to be gauged in the contexts that define a person's relation to others, because it is in these contexts that he accepts (or rejects) moral values and authority and determines what kind of mutually agreed upon limits make life with others possible. Action that is informed by one's moral commitment and that carries the element of personal choice must be weighed in the moral scale so that an action's consequences for the development of human conscience become clear to the moral agent. Since the moral agent is endowed with conscience he has a duty to follow unfailingly the judgment of conscience in human action. At the same time, he also has a duty to conform to the commonly accepted standards of conscientiousness in arriving at the judgment without compulsion. It is important that each person in conflict situations regarding the dictates of conscience must determine his "sphere of duty" without any external pressure.[14]

The Qur'an also introduces a new morally oriented metaphor of *nafs* (soul) to supplement the function of "heart" (mind) as the seat of human consciousness to underscore an ontological reference to morally good or bad acts. The human ability to distinguish between blameworthy and praiseworthy in one's own actions is naturally given through God's act of creation.[15] The intuitive reason that distinguishes right from wrong, according to the Qur'an, is situated in human personhood that directs human life on earth according to a moral pattern (Q. 91:7–8). Human beings need to develop a perceptive conscience and unambiguous reason by continually working on overcoming the weaknesses of their personhood so that reverential fear of God (*taqwā*) leads them to pursue righteous conduct based on justice and honesty. The Qur'an speaks about the source of human responsibility—the element of personal choice which is never wholly absent but is a variable that determines human action (or inaction). However, it is the perceptive conscience and divinely conferred moral intuition that guard individuals from deciding to commit acts of disobedience by explaining to them or suggesting to them that the ontological reference of evil is God's prohibitions and that they should fear evil and preserve themselves from committing it. This is the Qur'anic notion of conscientious action based on reverential fear of God (Q. 97:19).

God's primary guidance, as noted earlier, is universal and given to all human beings in the form of spiritual and moral consciousness. This form of guidance is located in the inherent capacity of human beings to discover the unchanging laws of nature. Spiritual and moral awareness leads to righteous conduct, which actually precedes the guidance that comes through one's acceptance of a particular faith. Before calling humanity to faith, God confers on it an innate attribute that covers all the levels of potential response to the calling of faith, as outlined earlier. The highest level of human responsiveness to faith in God is reached when that faith turns into continual moral life. The subsequent guidance that God confers is after a person has attained moral and spiritual awareness through the naturally endowed attribute of seeking to understand the moral reasoning behind certain actions. This latter guidance prepares a person to respond to the faculty of knowing God, i.e., the *fiṭra,* by declaring faith and by providing him with the ability to gain confidence and a sense of inner security (*īmān*) and remain unshakable when encountering unbelievers or hypocrites. In this way, the primary guidance takes place in the state of the natural constitution (*fiṭra*), and the subsequent form of guidance occurs when the natural disposition becomes fortified with moral sensibilities and righteous conduct.

The Divine Order (*Fiṭrat Allāh*)

The prophetic statement that every child is created in a state of conformity to the natural constitution before he adopts a religion through parental guidance must be understood in the context of natural and scriptural guidance connected with creation. The primary form of guidance is part of the law of nature, which is immutable and eternal in the sense in which the Qur'an speaks about God's purpose for people: "God does not change what is in a people, until they change what is in themselves" (Q. 13:11). God's purposive creation does not change its course in guiding the people who might choose to corrupt the state of nature in which God creates them and, accordingly, face the consequences of depriving themselves of God's universal moral guidance available to unaided reason. What is critical for the Qur'anic notion of ethical necessity based on human natural constitution is to point out that although human beings are free to negotiate their spiritual destiny by accepting or rejecting submission to God's will, revealed through a specific scripture, they can neither deny the fact about their inherent capacity to discover moral law, nor can they escape the moral consequences of their actions in all spheres of human interaction. By leaving people free to respond to the second form of guidance based on the revelation, the Qur'an affirms that universal morality does not depend on the revelation, even when there is a correlation between reason and revelation, and even when revelation does not contradict the law of nature. In fact, the Qur'anic reference to the divine nature or the order of nature (*fiṭrat allāh*) upon which God has created the universe implies that nature is entirely godlike. Consequently, reason and revelation—the two interrelated manifestations of the divine—are not only compatible; they are essentially partnering in guiding the entire nature, including human life, to a purposeful existence.

In principle, the rationalist commentators of the Qur'anic notion of universal guidance (*al-hudā*) provide a synopsis of the thesis that the Qur'an describes itself as "the Guidance" (*huda*), meaning that it is a means to the desired goal. This is so despite the fact that the Qur'an consists of both clear and explicit (*muḥkamāt*) and ambiguous and implicit (*mutashābihāt*) verses. More profoundly, the latter verses cannot be explained without the assistance of reason, although it remains unstated that, based on the overall thesis about universal guidance, discussed earlier, the explanation of the latter verses does not depend on being necessarily "rightly guided [on the scriptural path]," as some commentators have contended. The reason is that guidance to the understanding of the meaning of revelation is possible even without "being rightly guided." Had it not been for the divine guidance afforded by human reason (*al-ʿaql*), it would have been impossible to distinguish between the clear and obscure message of the revelation. Consequently, the guidance that the Qur'an speaks about is in actuality universal rational guidance (*al-dalālāt al-ʿaqliyya*) and not a specific scriptural one, which is vulnerable to all kinds of interpretations by interested parties. In contrast and opposed to this rational understanding, the traditionalist Ashʿarite commentators reject this emphasis on the role of reason in comprehending religious guidance. Some traditionalists have in fact argued that scriptural guidance necessitates being "rightly guided to Islam," and it is essentially Islamic revelation, the Qur'an, that is the main source of that guidance, although reason has a subsidiary role in discovering the intent of the revelation for the desired goal of "submission to God's will" (*al-islām*).[16]

Since the Qur'an makes reason a separate source of moral guidance, not in contradiction but rather in correlation to the revelation, it is possible to speak about universal morality based on religious premises. Hence, religious premises provide the foundation for an ideal public order that furthers the acknowledgment of human moral agency as well as inherent human dignity as part of God's natural endowment through equal creation of all humans as human. Such a concept of morality is akin to a secular view of universal morality that undergirds, for instance, the UN's Universal Declaration of Human Rights. It is in this context that I speak of two universalisms that share a common understanding of what it means to be an autonomous moral agent endowed with inherent dignity to claim inalienable human rights as humans: a universalism based on a comprehensive moral outlook derived from public reason with its roots in a social contract and a universalism founded upon a comprehensive religious doctrine that calls upon humanity to build a just public order founded upon equality of all humans as humans. The challenge of secularly proclaimed ethical norms to the Muslim community, who also share universal moral norms with contemporary nation-states, cannot be ignored anymore, because ultimately it is faith in revelation that has the power to influence the acts of the faith community by demonstrating the compatibility between the two self-proclaimed universal systems of moral values. The secular challenge to Islamic juridical theology is to sharpen its universal self-understanding in order to contribute constructively to the protection of the norms that are imprinted on the clean slate of human nature (*fiṭrat salīma*).

Theoretically, without first fully expounding the thesis about natural law in Islamic philosophical theology, contemporary interpretive jurisprudence cannot expound an egalitarian concept of citizenship based on equality of all humans as human. The traditionalist juridical theology rejects the rationally inferred principle of inherent human equality in creation, which, in turn, leads to looking at the world only in terms of belief and disbelief. The natural law ethics, as pointed out earlier, could actually determine the course of investigation to revisit and revise the traditional disqualifications for inclusive membership of all human beings on the basis of divinely endowed human moral nature. Without acknowledging the sufficiency of the ethical principle that is ontologically grounded in human ethical knowledge that inherently knows the right from the wrong, it is impossible to gear the future direction of interpretive jurisprudence that would be responsive to contemporary issues in human interaction.

Scriptural Ethics

There is a recurring command in the Qur'an to "enjoin the good and forbid the evil" (*al-'amr bi-l-ma'rūf* and *nahy 'ani-l-munkar*). This command is prescriptive guidance to uphold moral values in society and to create institutions that promote these values. These moral values, however, are not presented as arbitrary in relation to a commonly recognizable moral good (*al-khayr, al-ma'rūf*). They are revealed in the Qur'an against the background of tribal society in Arabia, and, as such, the moral exhortations to "establish justice" (Q. 4:135) and to "judge with justice" (Q. 4:58) become comprehensible within the context provided by common usage before Islamic revelation defined the scale of divine justice. The Qur'an introduces the prescription to establish justice as an objective moral value, on the basis of which one can affirm it to be a universal and natural mode of guidance to which humankind in general can be called upon to respond. Moreover, justice follows from the precepts of natural law which is disclosed to a common human nature and is regarded as independent of particular spiritual beliefs. This observation regarding the objective nature of justice is important to bear in mind because the Qur'anic notion is built upon a universal standard that could become intelligible through some reference to an objective state of affairs.

In another place, the Qur'an recognizes the universality and objective nature of moral attributes, for example "goodness," which transcends different religions and religious communities, admonishes human beings "to be forward in good work (*khayrāt*)," and holds them accountable for their deeds regardless of their religious differences (Q. 5:48). This passage provides a clear assumption that certain basic moral requirements, like "being just" or being "forward in good work," are self-sufficient and apply to all human beings, regardless of differences in religious beliefs. The ideal human being, then, is the one who combines moral virtue with complete religious submission (Q. 2:12). Nonetheless, it seems that there is a basis for distinction between religious and moral action-guides in the Qur'an, where moral actions are intrinsically other-regarding, whereas religious actions are related to God. However, as discussed in relation to the religious act of submission (*islām*), moral actions are ontologically grounded on rational evidence supplied in creation on the basis of which reason may acquire natural knowledge about the existence of an omnipotent and omniscient God who has the power to justly reward and punish human beings in accordance with their actions. As a result, intuitive judgment is further strengthened by the religious act of submission to sacred authority.

It is in the realm of cognition of universal moral truth that human beings are treated equally and held equally responsible for responding to the ethical duty of being "forward in good work." Furthermore, it is this fundamental equality of all humanity at the level of moral responsibility that directs humankind to create an ethical order on earth and makes it plausible that the Qur'an manifests some kind of natural law accessible to all irrespective of a particular revelation. The concepts of divine command, wisdom, and guidance all point in the direction of a scripture-based natural ethics. Scriptural sources corroborate the fact that what is good and bad, obligatory or entirely wrong, is known intuitively and vindicated simply because God creates human beings with the indispensable cognition and volition to further their comprehension of the purpose for which they are created and to accomplish it by using their naturally acquired knowledge of right and wrong. In spite of this, the Qur'an also speaks about basic human weaknesses: "Surely human being was created fretful, when evil visits him, impatient, when good visits him, grudging" (Q. 70:19–20). This weakness reveals a basic tension in the scripture-based ethics that must be resolved by further acts of revealed guidance by God. The prophets and scriptures are revealed to show human beings how to change their character and bring it into conformity with the divine plan for human conduct. The prophets, in their mission, become the source of authoritative paradigms for the perfection of human societies. Their moral conduct becomes a foundation of emulation for their followers. In this way the scripture and the prophet complement each other in rendering religious guidance obeyed.

Traditionalist Divine Command Ethics

Rationalist ethics, with its doctrine of autonomous morality infused in human beings at the time of creation (Q. 91:6–7), was meticulously extricated from the Sunni Muʿtazilite and Shīʿite ethical epistemology based on the specific hermeneutics of religious texts. As a matter of fact, the scriptural evidence provided by the rationalists' interpretation was abundant and incontrovertible. The scriptural emphasis on the establishment of justice was by itself sufficient to prevail over the traditionalist thesis that rejected any substantive role for intuitive reason in deciphering the realization of justice connoted in the doctrine of *taqwā* (moral-spiritual awareness) that precedes *īmān* (faith) in moral guidance of the revelation. Yet, court-sponsored traditionalist theologians, who were instrumental in legitimizing authoritative and unjust politics of their rulers, questioned the most essential rational-objective underpinnings of the revelation. To be sure, human moral worth and autonomous moral agency were construed in excess of the scriptural notions of inherent human dignity as well as human capability to know the right from the wrong intuitively as part of divinely ordained nature. Early history of the community in the Meccan period (610–622) provided the context for judicial decisions that could not overlook the problem of disbelief and its potential to inflict harm upon Islamic public order. However, the critical question was whether it was ethically or theologically justifiable to extend the Qur'anic designation of "unbelievers" and their prescribed treatment to all unbelievers throughout human history.

The traditionalist theological debates on the status of unbelievers were shaped by their doctrine about God's foreordainment of human destiny and whether human beings possessed free will to negotiate this destiny at all. There was no ambiguity in the Qur'an that human beings exercised freedom to negotiate their spiritual destiny. However, human responsibility in this and other human acts and the final day of reckoning was built upon the moral worth of the human person with power to deliberate. Since human beings are capable of pain, of pleasure, and of grief, receiving benefit and suffering harm, they possess a normal maturity of intuitive reason to have the knowledge and understand all that is common to all reasonable persons to perform their obligations freely and deliberately. As long as that factual aspect of the intuitive sense of ethical principles was overlooked there was little chance for universal morality to emerge as part of the Qur'an's emphasis on the indiscriminate dignity for all Children of Adam. Indeed, the Ash'arite denial of human moral agency meant a radical change in the approach to morality as it applied to humans as human. The vindication of the absolute divine will over the intellect capable of cognizing good and evil led to the rejection of the notion that ethical values could be discerned by unaided reason. The concept of God as an unlimited and arbitrary power implied the reduction of all moral laws to inscrutable manifestations of God's omnipotence.

Such a doctrine meant a serious setback for self-sufficient morality as part of human natural constitution. According to the Ash'arite theologians, there was no natural constitution endowed with an innate moral capability to function as the basis of ethics that directed human purposive existence. Contrary to the

Qur'an, which emphasized God's unchanging order of nature, the traditionalist position affords no indication of the existence of an eternal and immutable order. It no longer constitutes a measure of a human being's dignity and of his capacity to participate in that order. The ontological reference of good or bad is not a human intuitive judgment given to all rational creatures. An action is not good because of its suitability to the intuitive nature with which God created humanity; rather it is so because God so wills by making it obligatory. God's will could also have willed and decreed the precise opposite, which would then possess the same binding force as that which has validity as long as God's absolute will so determines.[17]

This traditionalist rejection of moral law as an expression of God's will had ramifications for the juridical ethics whose scope was defined in terms of application of moral principles like "fairness" based on the Qur'an, which states, "God does not impose a moral-religious duty (*taklīf*) beyond one's capacity to perform it" (Q. 2:286). The Qur'anic notion about the essential humanity of all—believers and unbelievers—endowed with the same level of moral cognition and volition and accruing responsibility to obey religious moral duties required juridical ethics to promulgate laws that were ruled in accord with the principle of "fairness." For these jurists the matter of "disbelief" was relative, since the Qur'an approached the matter of guidance in religion without coercion, leaving it to human self-understanding to respond to the calling. The incongruity of generalizing the word *kuffār* (plural of *kāfir,* meaning "unbeliever") as it appears in the Qur'an was obvious, because if the verse that reads "As for the unbelievers, alike it is whether you have warned them or not, they will not believe" (Q. 2:6) were to be taken as God's foreordaining the unchangeable status of unbelievers, generalized and applied to all unbelievers at all times, it would lead to the closing of the gates of guidance on them forever. Such an interpretation was against the spirit of the Qur'an, which had come to guide humanity regardless of their acceptance or rejection of that divine guidance.[18]

It is significant to note that the Qur'an uses "disbelief" (*kufr*) in at least three senses: (1) in the sense of "denial" that signifies "rejecting" what God had commanded to be performed; (2) in the sense of "denial" of God's Lordship, which signifies "disavowal" of God's authority and rejection of God's blessing in such utterances as "There is no Lord, no Paradise, no Hell!"; and (3) in the sense of "rejection" of truth, when knowing the truth as self-evident a person chooses to reject it. In none of these usages does the Qur'an indicate that such a denial was foreordained or that the person committing such an act was not responsible for the choice and was immune from facing the consequences of his willful act. In other words, there is nothing in the Qur'an to suggest that unbelievers suffer permanently from lack of ethical knowledge or moral worth.

The political context of these early debates also involved the determination of responsibility for the sinful behavior of those who were in power. After all, people suffered at the hands of these rulers, and religious leaders were keen to hold them responsible for their bad behavior and to require them to compensate the victims. The fundamental question that was raised by the theologian-jurisprudents was: Did the people act as God's free agents or were their acts predetermined by God's overpowering will? The Qur'an proffered a complex view about God's will as it interacted with human acts. There are verses that speak about God "sealing their hearts" or "When they swerved, God caused their hearts to swerve; and God guides never the people of ungodly" (Q. 61:5). These were taken to imply that God foreordains everything for good or bad. Other verses imputed the responsibility of being misguided to the people, thereby making it possible to speak about human free will. To be sure, the Qur'an presented a multifaceted correlation between divine predetermination and human responsibility.

Muʿtazilite theologians, who were also known as those who upheld the doctrine of divine justice, demonstrated with much textual evidence that their rational conclusion about God's judgment of human action being ontologically grounded in human ability to act freely was critical to their understanding that it was ludicrous to maintain that humans could be held accountable for their acts without the capacity to will and execute them. As a matter of historical relevance, the rationalists also elaborated on their idea of obedience to rulers, pointing out explicitly that there is no obligation to obey them if they command things that are unjust. In other words, human responsibility was commensurate with freedom to exercise choice of action.

Inasmuch as human beings are free agents, they can reject God's guidance, although, because of their innate disposition (*fiṭra*) prompting or even urging them subtly to believe in God, they cannot find any valid excuse for this rejection. Even then, their rejection pertains to the procuring of what is desirable, and not to the act of apprehending in the first place what is desirable and praiseworthy. However, when human beings choose to reject this guidance, God denies further guidance to them: "Those that believe not in the signs of God, God will not guide them" (Q. 16:104). This denial of guidance clearly pertains to the guidance that would lead to the procurement of the desirable end of acquiring knowledge of the ontological basis of truth of ethical predicates, not to the initial moral guidance that is infused in the hearts of all human beings, in the form of an innate disposition, to guide them toward the good end.

To reiterate, the fundamental Muʿtazilite doctrine is that human beings, being endowed with an innate capacity to know right and wrong and with free will, are responsible for their actions before a just God. Furthermore, as per their epistemology, good and evil are self-sufficient rational categories that can be known by intuitive reason, independent of revelation. God created human intellect in such a way that, if unhindered by social traditions and conventions, it is capable of perceiving good and evil objectively. Moral law is the expression of God's will in creation. This is a corollary of another fundamental Muʿtazilite doctrine, that

God's justice cannot be fulfilled without providing objective knowledge of good and evil, as determined by intuitive reason, whether the revelation decrees it so or not. Without such objective ethical knowledge, and in the absence of any contact with a prophet or sacred scriptures, no human being can be held accountable for his deeds.[19] In this way the Mu'tazilites emphasized complete human responsibility in responding to the call of universal moral guidance through autonomous reason, which was further expounded by the guidance through revelation.

The Ash'arites essentially rejected both the idea of natural reason as an autonomous source of moral guidance and moral law as an expression of the divine will. They maintained that an action is not good because human intuitive reason says so, but because God so wills it. As such, ontological reference of good and bad is God's permission and prohibition, respectively. It is presumptuous to judge God's action restricted by God's justice. Divine acts cannot be judged on the basis of categories that God has actually provided in the scripture for directing and judging human performance. There is no way, within the bounds of ordinary logic, to explain the relationship of God's power to human actions. God's absolute will provides validity to human action, regardless of whether human reason judges it as good or otherwise. Based on observed fact, there is no universal agreement among intelligent people regarding these values of acts (good or bad, just or unjust) that the rationalists claim are grounded in the attributes of actions; they are actually derived from scriptural prescriptions as a result of God's commands and prohibitions. Hence, human action is the result of God's pure will without any foundation in reality, without any foundation in the essential nature of things.

Both these theological standpoints were based on the interpretation of Qur'anic passages, which undoubtedly contain a complex view of human responsibility in procuring divine justice on earth, as mentioned earlier. On the one hand, the Qur'an contains passages that would support the Mu'tazilite position, which emphasized complete responsibility in responding to the call of both natural guidance and guidance through revelation. On the other hand, it has passages that could support the Ash'arite viewpoint, which upheld the omnipotence of God and hence denied humans any role in responding to divine guidance. Nevertheless, it allows for both human volition and divine will in the matter of accepting or rejecting faith that entailed the responsibility for procuring justice on earth.[20]

Interpretive Jurisprudence as the Nucleus of Islamic Ethics

The responsibility of procuring justice puts an enormous burden on traditionalist theology because its rejection of natural endowment of innate moral capacity in humanity has led to a detrimental neglect of the ethical presuppositions of the normative juridical tradition. According to the Ash'arite ethical theory, an action is not good because it correlates with the essential nature of human being; it is so because God so wills. What if God wills and decrees the precise opposite of that good? Does it still have the same binding force as that which is now valid because God's absolute will so determines? Ironically, in their opposition to the rationalist ethical theory, Muslim traditionalist theologians were inclined to afford validity only to those acts that had the sanction of the divine will in the form of revelation. They ruled out any moral restriction—in fact any restriction at all—on God's sovereignty and absolute discretionary authority to manage human affairs. As a consequence, both the universal moral significance of Qur'anic idiom and its implications for the enunciation of Islamic natural law theory were discarded.

The primacy of the divine will over intuitive reason led to the denial that good and evil can have any other ontological reference than the will of God that expressed itself in providing the blueprint for human activity in the Sharī'a. The scales of justice that were to be implemented in the Islamic public order were not available to human reason except through the mediation of supernatural revelation. In other words, the Sharī'a is the embodiment of God's will for humanity without any foundation in reality, without foundation in the essential nature of things—it is eternal and hence immutable. God's pure will was the pivot of Sunni theology and ethics which impacted the development of normative juridical ethics in the methodology related to interpretive jurisprudence.

The ethics related to interpretive jurisprudence seeks to address, accommodate, and reconcile the demands of justice and public good in normative sources. For instance, in dealing with immediate questions about the rights of minorities and religious communities living in the Muslim world, Muslim jurists draw on legal doctrines and rules in addition to analogical reasoning based on paradigm cases in the classical tradition. The practical judgments reflect the insights of a jurist who has been able to connect contemporary situations to an appropriate set of linguistic and rational principles and rules that can provide a basis for a valid conclusion of a given case. A cursory treatment of the substance covered in these practical decisions shows that it deals with an elaborate system of duties. The conceptions of justice or public good in these practical judgments, even when they appear to have universal application, created institutions and practices that establish duties, not rights. The universal Qur'anic notion of human dignity (*karāmat al-insān*) was evoked quite often without any emphasis on equal and inalienable rights held by all human beings because of the way God had honored all of humanity. The tradition limited full legal rights to free adult Muslims. It failed to develop the idea of the moral worth of all human beings through divinely conferred intuitive reason and dignity—the two notions that would have led to the affirmation of the equality of human beings as human. Consequently, the universal morality founded upon essential nature of human beings and their human moral worth remained unexplored among jurists until recently. As pointed out in the beginning of the chapter, the challenge to rethink Muslim ethics in order to elaborate legal principles in the light of new concepts like equal citizenship and democratic governance remains unanswered.

The epistemic problem that confronts Muslim jurists can be traced back to the historically severed connection between juridical theology based on the moral worth of each human person and prevalent text-based Islamic jurisprudence. Take the case of a Muslim man deciding to take a second wife by divorcing his first wife of many years. Although, according to the Sharīʿa rulings, taking a second wife is not illicit, how can a juridical ruling permit this person to divorce his longtime wife because she happens to be old without considering the morality of such a decision? Even if the ruling is textually and legally correct, how can it be morally justified? Interpretive jurisprudence has yet to reassert the essentially moral nature of human being and confirm that moral law is an expression of the divine will. Unless the doctrinal and ethical presuppositions of the early juridical tradition are investigated and expounded afresh, the epistemic problem will continue to produce intellectually impoverished and ethically insensitive legal decisions.

The enunciation of underlying ethical principles and rules that govern practical ethical decisions is crucial for making any religious perspective an intellectually insightful voice in the contemporary debate about a morally defensible cross-cultural defense of human dignity and moral agency. All communities share certain moral principles (compassion, honesty, justice, and so on); all require rules like fairness and just restoration as essential elements in regulating responsible interpersonal relations; yet major global controversies persist on issues such as cultural relativism that hampers the implementation of universal human rights cross-culturally. What kind of ethical resources do different traditions possess that might lead to a common ethical discourse about, and perhaps even a resolution of, global controversies in the matter of freely enjoining implementation of the human capacities of ethical decision-making?[21]

Traditional Muslim scholarship, as a rule, has avoided critical assessment of the normative resources that might actually contribute to a resolution of contemporary ethical-legal issues like the treatment of apostates. One of the most controversial rulings in interpretive jurisprudence is the death penalty for an apostate. The Qur'an deals not only with individual religious freedom but also with the creation of a just social order. Under certain conditions the Qur'an gives the state, as the representative of society, the power to control "discord on earth," a general state of lawlessness created by taking up arms against the established Islamic order.[22] The eradication of corruption on earth, taken in the light of the Qur'anic principle of instituting good and preventing evil, is a basic moral duty to protect the well-being of the community. In the Islamic polity, where religion is not divorced from the public agenda, leaving adherents of competing doctrines free to pursue their beliefs engenders an inherent tension between religious communities that has to be resolved through state regulation.

The "millet system" in the Muslim world provided the premodern paradigm of a religiously pluralistic society by granting each religious community an official status and a substantial measure of self-government. The system, based on the millet, meaning a "religiously defined people,"[23] was a "group rights model"[24] that was defined in terms of a communitarian identity and hence did not recognize any principle of individual autonomy in matters of religion. And this communitarian identity was not restricted to identifying non-Muslim *dhimmis*[25]; the millet's self-governing status allowed it to base its sovereignty on the orthodox creed officially instituted by the millet leadership. Under the Ottoman administration, this group status entailed some degree of state control over religious identification, overseen by the administrative officer responsible to the state for the religious community. In addition, the system allowed the enforcement of religious orthodoxy under state patronage, leaving no scope for individual dissent, political or religious. Every episode of the individual exercise of freedom of conscience was seen as a deviation from the accepted orthodoxy maintained and enforced by the socioreligious order.

The uncritical approach to the normative sources has deep roots in the juridical theology of revelation in Islam. There are two major trends concerning the meaning and relevance of the revelation for Muslims. According to one, Islamic revelation in its present form was "created" in time and space and, as such, reflects the historical circumstances of that original divine command. According to the other, the revelation was "uncreated," and hence its current form is not conditioned by place and time. Most traditionalist scholars reject any hints that the revelation's interpretation is a cultural or historical variable. Quantitative and qualitative changes in the modern Muslim world have raised questions about the relevance of traditional readings of the revelation to contemporary ethical and social exigencies.

The Core of Juridical Ethics on Human Dignity and Justice

The title of Chapter 5 indicates conceptual and historical problems because the discussion about natural law, inherent human dignity, and human moral agency are part of the modern political and human rights discourse with deep secular roots that can be traced back to Enlightenment ways of thinking about universal morality. In contrast, Islamic juridical ethics expresses religious-moral commitments grounded in revelation-based reasons that are particularistic and, therefore, incongruent with the global purport of the concepts under consideration. [26] Since secular public reason denies the effectiveness of argument based on particularistic religious reason in matters with political implications (lest it destabilize public order through its intolerant exclusivist doctrines), the task of this chapter was to focus on ethics related to juridical methodology in order to provide Islamic perspectives that could speak in a universal idiom to all human beings.

This process of universalization of religious idiom had to unavoidably rely on two hermeneutical moves applied to normative Islamic sources like the Qur'an and the Tradition in order to bring the relevant materials in conversation with modern secular ethical discourse. Secular ethical discourse claims to provide a language of universal morality that speaks to all persons and communities across state boundaries. Hence, in order to be inclusive, Islamic discourse on human dignity and related concepts had to at least give voice to peoples across religious and cultural boundaries. The first hermeneutical move of necessity involved deconstructing the contextual aspects of the classical juridical heritage of Muslims by looking at the way religion and politics in Islam interacted. This fundamental move misrepresented the original universal intent of the relevant texts for exclusivist political and religious reasons. The second hermeneutical move, as expected, involved providing a fresh commentary that is consistent with the inclusive intent of the religious discourse and relevant to the modern discourse on human dignity and justice. However, both these epistemic moves can be criticized for lack of indisputable historical information in determining when such hermeneutical distortions in the original intent of the texts were introduced. Moreover, it is not epistemically feasible to indicate with certainty a relationship between the history of moral discourse and the history of legal-religious formulations of Islamic orthopraxy. Obviously, fresh interpretations of classical usage now, made to resonate with the secular purport of modern ethical language, bear the approval of original universal and inclusive denotations of Islamic revelation without access to a history of judicial precedents. Here an ahistorical approach of interpretive jurisprudence is in serious competition for legitimacy with a secular liberal political discourse. Public reason, free from religious premises, has convincingly argued for the dignity and fair treatment and justice for all humans as human.

Technically, the search for Islamic moral perspectives on human dignity and justice is faced with both conceptual and historical challenges. Conceptual challenges connected with human dignity arise with the claims by liberal secularists that it was not until secular public reason began to look at individual freedoms within the context of modern religiously and politically pluralistic societies that a universal source of specific capacities and freedom of choice was identified as inherent attributes based on a belief in the innate propensities of human nature. Similar conceptual reservations are noticeable in the ways in which modern liberal political thinkers have used the term "justice" to argue for a "free-standing political conception" that can hopefully generate necessary overlapping consensus among intelligent persons in a pluralistic world for social cooperation. Historical problems in dealing with the contextual aspects of Islamic normative texts go beyond the usual historical inquiry that seeks to determine the origins of these concepts—whether they go back to classical sources, which include religious reasons, or whether they simply go back to the European domination of Muslim peoples when Enlightenment thought, with its distinctive claim of locating universal morality outside religion, was in vogue. The idea of inalienable human rights as universal is a distinctive creation of Western culture, which emerged at some specific, identifiable period in postwar European history. The view about the principle of inherence was its most persuasive tool to argue that the idea was common to all societies. Whatever the account of the origin and early development of the idea among Muslims, my objective in this chapter was to underscore the difficulty of reading modern discourse in the classical sources, especially when this modern discourse dismisses religious reason as "unreasonable" or "irrational."

The Ashʿarite theological doctrine that the will of God is the ultimate source of morality played a prominent role in defining human worth in juridical theology—the tradition that is under severe criticism for perpetuating discriminatory attitude toward women and non-Muslim minorities. In addition, there was a problem with the extreme Ashʿarite view of the absolute sovereignty of God and its political abuse to further moral numbness among people to meet the dangerous challenge of the absolutist rule of the caliphs and the sultans. Although they did not speak directly about natural law, Muʿtazilite theology was devised to challenge the view that Islamic Sharīʿa was not merely an expression of the divine will; it was also an expression of the divine morality that was conferred on humanity through the very creation of human nature (*fiṭra*). This Muʿtazilite doctrine is truly universal, and being firmly rooted in the Qur'an itself, it is eternal and immutable. If the traditionalist Muslim scholars can accept the centrality of natural law theory in Islamic juridical methodology, then the need to treat all humans as capable of understanding and of free choice in the Muslim world can be based on this foundational doctrine, which treats human equality as its first and essential tenet. More important, if it can be shown that the Qur'an neither contradicts the law of nature nor rejects the evidence of reason as unreliable and, hence, incompatible with the goals of revelation, then one can admit the thesis that the law of nature is embodied in the Qur'an. Natural law goes back to God in the sense that its precepts derive their authority from the fact they are confirmed and implemented by the revelation as the "eternal, immutable tradition of God (*sunnat allāh*)."

6
The Ethics of Interpretive Jurisprudence

From its inception, when it came to guide the practice of religion, Islam presented morality as the primary and autonomous source for religious action-guides. In fact, based on different passages of the Qur'an, it is plausible to maintain that the ontological basis of the truth of ethical predicates is morally aware spirituality (*taqwā*) that precedes the declaration of faith (*īmān*). Additionally, the legislative will of God, the Sacred Lawgiver (*al-shāriʿ al-muqaddas*) that lays down the guidelines for orthopraxy, promotes the moral ideal (*tazakkī*) for human behavior. In that sense, religious-moral action-guides (*aḥkām sharʿīya*) in Islamic revealed law are rooted in ethical concerns and considerations for the betterment of humanity. In the revelation, God simply causes things to happen in their usual sequence by creating what is advantageous (*manfaʿa*) to occur after a certain act. Additionally, God causes things to happen in their regular sequence in order to create what is disadvantageous (*maḍarra*) to occur after a certain act. God's commandment or prohibition does not negate or render redundant reason-based informal analysis of the act. Reason in this context is employed informally to underscore the ontological basis of permission or proscription. Religious obligations and prohibitions, although stemming from God's legislative will for the well-being of humanity, are essentially compatible with morality, as upheld by the rationalists. In other words, the revelation-based Sharīʿa is correlated to rationally determined moral action-guides.

Although the language of Islamic revelation has substantively corroborated the universality of human existence, affording it a meaningful way of relating peoples of different religions and cultures in a single human community (*umma wāḥida*), paradoxically today it is the traditionalist text-based system of contention that imparts moral disagreements by manipulating hermeneutic tools to divide people and to disseminate a relativistic and culturally inflexible approach to determine the rights and responsibilities of, for instance, women and minorities. It is not an overstatement to suggest that, in large measure, it is the emphasis on particularity of the traditionalist text-based discourse connected with women's position in Muslim societies that has stifled the promotion of women's inherent dignity and equality in all social and political arenas that are faced with modernity's cultural and morally relativist challenge.

The implications of the paradox of universal morality and the interpretive politics of textuality for the implementation of women's and minority rights in the

Islamic Ethics. Abdulaziz Sachedina, Oxford University Press. © Oxford University Press 2022.
DOI: 10.1093/oso/9780197581810.003.0006

Muslim world are for the most part evident in the evaluation of equal rights of all humans, regardless of their gender, race, or creed. In fact, one of the major impediments to the universal recognition of all humanity sharing equal dignity and rights has been claims about the absolutely binding nature of revelatory texts and the exclusive authenticity connected with the traditionalist chain of hermeneutics. Selective retrieval of the political jurisprudence that endorses legitimate use of force to combat injustices suffered by the people serves as a warning to contemporary Muslim leadership to heed the call for impending social and political reforms. Moreover, the failure of imported modern ideologies to implement political and social change in Muslim societies has inevitably led to radical support for confrontational jurisprudence that persuasively advocates the return to Islamic fundamentals as a counterpoise to secular modernity.[1] Assertions of cultural authenticity and integrity in the face of Western domination and modernization have ended up separating the all-inclusive relationship between revelation and reason, between divine commands and their ethical presuppositions, rendering the juridical decisions in respect of women's contributions repressive and unjust in major areas of human interaction in Muslim societies. Undeniably, one can trace these discriminatory legal-ethical decisions to the traditionalist rejection of rationalist-objectivist morality that developed a practical solution of adopting moral aspects of local cultural traditions and synthesize them in their religious-ethical interpretations of Islamic textual materials. The traditionalist jurists maintained a negative view of rationalist ethics that advocated autonomous moral agency firmly based on the rational ability to negotiate one's morally upright decisions. They criticized naturalist-rationalist ethics by pointing out that it was mainly concerned with worldly goals, separated from the ultimate ends connected with life in the hereafter that the Sharīʿa intended. More specifically, as they asserted, rationalist ethics was incapable of representing the comprehensive objective of human salvation. Hence, in spite of the doctrinal basis for maintaining that God is not subject to any limitations or constraints in providing what is most beneficial to human beings, it was declared that God was not bound to do the most expedient for humanity. God's commands are beyond rational scrutiny. Nothing can be obligatory prior to the revelation of the religious law—the Sharīʿa. The mainstream juridical project was conceived as the text-based investigation (*al-ijtihad al-naqlī*) that determined the textually derived objectives (*maqaṣid*) of the law. Accordingly, the traditional juridical project stressed and guaranteed control over knowledge of the authenticated orthopraxy that promised believers comprehensive prosperity (*falāḥīya*) in this and the next world.

Against this growing emphasis on authoritative text hermeneutics to render the validity of a legal-ethical ruling, rationalist theologians—the Muʿtazilites and the Shīʿites—firmly asserted that God's commandments cannot contravene the rationally comprehended ethically right or wrong. The moral agency of a human being means that the act that is performed belongs to her, and it is attributed to her as her act by virtue of its correlation to capability to act which God creates in her when she decides to perform the act. Accordingly, actions that are obligatory in Sharīʿa are undeniably good, and actions that are forbidden in the Sharīʿa are inevitably bad. Islamic tradition shows that ethics paves the way for the divinely ordained Sharīʿa. There is no way to comprehend the divinely ordained purposes (*maqāṣid*) (including five indispensable objects: religion, life, reason, lineage, and property) without first determining the parameters of moral philosophy that must govern the interpretive jurisprudence. The ethical foundation of interpretive jurisprudence is in reality inferred from the religious epistemology connected with the infused morality of human nature.

It is important to note that the appeal to the morally infused nature of humanity has been the source of Qur'anic bafflement at human arrogance and disbelief in this clear moral epistemology in the Qur'an (Q. 91:6–7). From the point of overall moral directives of the revelation, if the essential relationship between religion and ethics cannot be severed in the Qur'an, then in the study of interpretive jurisprudence we cannot dismiss the basic moral philosophy of the entire juridical project. In fact, interpretive jurisprudence needs to engage in critical review of its judicial decisions (*fatāwā*) to determine their cognitive validity by analyzing and correlating them to their moral consequences.

The text-based investigation in interpretive jurisprudence essentially discovers normative values preserved in primary religious texts to apply and correlate revelatory and rational justifications in deducing authoritative decisions. As a matter of fact, the validity of the inferred judicial decisions depends upon critical evaluation of the moral ramifications of a case. The evaluative process reveals the modus operandi that is in place to determine the interaction between the factual elements and the moral values to reach the concluding judicial decision. Whether implicitly or explicitly, these evaluative judgments were based on rational analysis of moral values and, hence, were treated as conjectural (*ẓannī*) opinions. The reason was that in the earlier initial formulations ethical arguments were open to further reflection and refinement when they were reexamined in the context of historical narratives preserved in the scriptural sources like *ḥadīth*-reports. The interim nature of a judicial decision was obvious. Thus, for instance, in recognizing certain rights over one's personhood (*ḥaqq ādamī*), including one's body, there was a serious problem in extending that right to include donation of one's organ, a kidney, for example, for transplant without weighing the probable detriment that could come to the donor when the incision was made to remove the kidney.

In Chapter 4 I underscored the importance of exploring ethical presuppositions of the juridical inquiry that have been utilized to formulate the responsa issued by Muslim jurists in the past. Both theological doctrines with practical implications and normative status of ethical values derived from the scriptural sources have been major resources for formulating the orthopraxy. The ethical principle of "public interest" (*maṣlaḥa*) was textually and rationally extricated from the doctrine that God does what is most salutary (*aṣlaḥ*) for people to advance spiritually and morally. In addition, critical study of traditional materials provided reliable textual information to establish the cognitive validity of judicial decisions. In two areas of Islamic scholarship, namely, philosophical theology (*kalām*) and juridical methodology based on the study of authoritative principles (*uṣūl al-fiqh*) of jurisprudence, ethics has guided juridical research to discover universal principles that constitute a major part of justificatory reasoning for the derivation of fresh rulings. Obviously, fresh rulings in orthopraxy depend upon the revelatory as well as rational underpinnings to extract the sources of normativity. A contextual history of interpretive jurisprudence indicates that in view of insufficient textual materials to cover future contingencies, no contemporary judicial decision in social or scientific advancement would have been conceivable without evaluating the moral thinking behind the juridical investigation.

Traditional text-based jurisprudence (*al-ijtihād al-shar'ī*) has steadfastly resisted any suggestion that it needs to strike up a partnership with and be guided by the secularity of modern interpretive jurisprudence (*al-ijtihad al-'aqlī*) to infer morally unassailable and universally applicable ethical and religious opinions. One of the morally and religiously critical issues pertains to the question of sanctity of life: Is saving life a religious commandment or a moral duty? Could one consider the sanctity-of-life principle without critically evaluating contemporary moral utterances regarding ownership of the human body? Is moral argument in support of an absolute individual right to determine the end-of-life decision a consensual agreement based on recognition of relational ethics affecting immediate family members? If modernity is understood as a period that largely displaced religious ethics by challenging traditionalist comprehension of the human-God relationship, and by questioning the authority of religiously inspired moral tradition in providing the sole criteria of judging an act's moral validity, then one should reckon with a crisis of epistemology in contemporary traditional interpretive jurisprudence (*'ulum shar'īya*).

Undoubtedly, the major source of contention between tradition and modernity is related to the determination of the source of human moral behavior, whether it originates in revelation or reason. Modernity is ostensibly nurtured by modern secular ethics that rejects supernatural sources for justificatory moral reasoning. In other words, it is the prioritization of secular public reason over the claims of supernatural religious reason rooted in its metaphysical foundation in revelation that has created the debate over the role of religious tradition in determining the social and political standards in the development of a nation-state.

Whereas traditional jurisprudence continues to discuss the absolute rights of God (*ḥaqq allāh*) and the relative, not natural, rights of humans (*ḥaqq ādamī*), modernity with its firm belief in social change and individualism has moved toward total emancipation of individual from community and ethics from tradition, leading to the thorough secularization of public space and equality of all human beings.

The modernity that was adopted in the Muslim world did not seriously consider the secular presuppositions of the sources of normativity in the secular project of superseding religion and supplanting it with materialism. At the same time, the inherent secularity of Islamic tradition, as discussed at several points in this study, was totally ignored under the hegemony of traditionalist orthodoxy based on divine command ethics that had impacted Sunni text-based legal methodology. It was this text-based attitude that refused to appraise the moral epistemology and the ontology of human action that was founded upon belief in the objectivity of moral values, the ability of infused morality written into human nature, and the organically inbuilt theory of natural law that regarded human beings as in possession of autonomous moral agency. By submerging ethics into religion, Muslim jurists insisted on the text-based logic and methodology that guaranteed the absolute status of the revelation as the only source for future ethical decisions. For instance, in the ethical-religious disputes about end-of-life decisions, some Muslim jurists have been guided by textual evidence that remains to be investigated in its historical and social contexts. These textual proofs have acquired absolutely authoritative status through the juridical interpretation that rules out understanding the family and social-economic burdens that extraordinary medical intervention is imposing by prolonging life when there is little benefit accruing to the patient or her family. Ethical analysis informed by religious beliefs can actually determine a better outcome for all the parties involved in such cases. There are times when extraordinary medical intervention in the case of a terminally ill patient has harmed the well-being of the patient and her family going through their economic crisis to continue with the expensive services in healthcare.

Certainly, instead of asserting the moral foundation of interpretive jurisprudence to deduce practical decisions for a changing community, traditionalists emphasized absolute obedience to the Tradition (*sunna*), rejecting the notion of natural rights and freedom of choice based on divinely decreed common human nature. For them, it was the interpretive jurisprudence that defined the parameters of God's absolute rights and the contours of limited rights of human beings. The ethical presuppositions of religious practice were totally disregarded in order to maintain the absolute authority of the traditional interpretive approach that determined the validity of contemporary social practice regulated by the revelatory texts. Consequently, it is plausible to maintain that modern social-cultural institutions in the Muslim world were constructed to perpetrate traditionalist orthopraxy without any concern for suitability or relevance of their rulings to the changing social circumstances and their deeply moral ramifications. Contemporary youth in the Muslim world are alienated from both the identity-generating dogmatist religious authority (the *mujtahid* or *mufti*, *'ulamā'*) and the autocratic political authority that do not believe in the human rights or fundamental freedoms demanded by modernly educated men and women.

The Spiritual-Moral Culture of the Revelation

The thrust of the religious culture of the revelation is founded upon sincere faith in God, which, as a rule, is accompanied by a call to act morally (*ṣāliḥāt*). As part of personal development toward higher spiritual stations, the Qur'an makes spirituality dependent upon good behavior—hence the centrality of morality in revelation. Such a connection between faith (*īmān*) and practice (*'amal*) nurtures the attainment of exalted stations in religiosity by encouraging a person to demonstrate the truthfulness of spirituality through moral behavior. Islamic traditions, like those of other Abrahamic religions, maintain nearness to God as the main criterion of assessing whether spirituality is naturally tied to morality. In connecting faith and action as the main criterion for moving on a path to spiritual perfection leading to the love of God, the Qur'an enjoins believers to follow the example of the Prophet: "Say (oh Muḥammad), 'If you love God, follow me, and God will love you, and forgive your sins; God is All-forgiving and All-compassionate' " (Q. 3:31). Historically, following in the footsteps of the Prophet also defined the spirituality that was founded upon the paradigm of the exemplary associates of the Prophet. Spirituality was dependent on devotion and love of the Prophet through obedience to his religious and moral authority, which is preserved in the Sharī'a.

The major contribution of this study is to demonstrate the main thesis of Islamic ethics, that, according to the Islamic revelation, humanity has been created with the single objective of furthering the moral vision of God's purposes for human society. In the Abrahamic spiritual-moral legacy, a monotheistic worldview is founded upon the moral challenge of developing faith independent of racialist presuppositions which would have compromised the equality of all human persons solely based on their inherent dignity and innate ability to live a morally upright life. What mattered to the Compassionate God, as the Qur'an asserts, was how one adopted an outsider to become part of one's community, sharing equality in creation.[2] The Qur'an presented a divinely decreed opportunity to build a just social order that demanded a personal devotion to apply its universal moral teachings to inhabit the earth in a newly formed community under the divinely appointed exemplar, the prophet (Q. 38:26, 5:48, 49:13).

From its inauguration, revelation regarded human rationality as a secure guide to undertake submission to the Compassionate Being "who taught [the] human the use of [the] pen, taught [the] human what he did not know" (Q. 96:5). More than anything, humans needed to know how to live and to cooperate with one another, and therefore the revelation emphasized the oneness of humanity (*ummatan wāḥida*) (Q. 2:213) committed to live a moral life that would show a serious commitment to care for the needy and the destitute. However, compassion for the downtrodden and opposition to the corrupt behavior of those in powerful positions were not possible without first engaging in self-purification (*tazakkī*)[3] through righteousness and moral excellence in one's own life. Moreover, the prophetic example (*uswa*) provided the incentive to pursue personal as well as collective reforms to manifest the challenge of the Qur'an to create a just polity as the natural consequence and perspective of the faith commitment that the revelation required. The Abrahamic emphasis on justice and the biblical confidence in ordinary humans' ability to uphold justice were part of the Qur'anic moral worldview. Indeed, the infused moral guidance presented the first Muslim community with a blueprint of a morally upright society that must be established as an objectification of personal moral purification (*zakā*). This was the social-political context of the belief that the divinely taught moral values—the *sharīʿa*, in its essential meaning of "the open way that leads to the source of life (lit. water)"—are part of the divinely ordained proposal for human conduct (Q. 45:13), which is subject to the interpretation of the practicing community. The Qur'an saw a morally-spiritually committed individual (*muttaqī*) as the product of familial and social expectations. It was not sufficient for one person to choose the path of reform; rather, in the Qur'anic collective moral view of society, society collectively has to move toward moral excellence on which depended the ethics of interpersonal justice. Obedience to the Prophet as the champion of moral life (*khuluq ʿaẓīm*) was a path for everyone, not just the believers. All humans were expected to respond to the universal moral challenge to build an ideal society.

The historical development of the Sharīʿa demonstrates that it is not simply a code of Muslim practice; rather, and critically so, its moral foundation is a comprehensive and universal ethical system that necessarily deals with every aspect of human personal and social practice that touches upon the function of morally infused conscience to live in justice and peace with one another. Accordingly, as the divinely ordained value system, the Sharīʿa envisions that infused morality will be able to determine the ethical consequences of interpersonal and human-divine relations for every act performed as part of one's individual and collective responsibility to uphold justice. For instance, what was the obligation of the eldest son when his old parents, because of their age and other disabilities, were not able to provide for their livelihood? The case was not simply a matter of establishing legal responsibility of the eldest son for the disabled parents; rather, the underpinning of the juridical decision imputing that duty to the son was thoroughly based on the ethics of the child-parent relationship. After all, wasn't it the father or the mother who cared for the child when he was growing up? More important, the rationally derived principle of "gratitude to benefactor" (*shukr mun'im*) has been emphasized in the rationalist-objectivist juridical theology as a universal moral response to the awareness that one has been the beneficiary of another person's moral actions and, accordingly, should behave kindly toward the benefactor in the future. The social factors that are associated with gratitude are also consistent with a conceptualization of gratitude as an affect that is relevant to people's cognitions and behaviors in the moral domain. More important, expressions of gratitude are based on verifiable experiences of elements that touch human beings in all cultures.

As a further illustration, take the case of spousal dispute in matters of child custody when divorce takes place: What recourse does the mother have against the father's claim to sole custody afforded by traditional jurisprudence? The nuclear family—man, wife, and children—was emphasized as a self-reliant unit. The position of husband was strengthened by making him responsible for the maintenance of his wife and children. In this way the husband retained wide authority over the wife, to the exclusion of both his family and hers. The children were to be the husband's. In Islam, part of the male prerogative as provider for the family was the right of divorce. And yet in interpretive jurisprudence, the jurists put restrictions on the husband's presumed freedom in matters of divorce. The marital rules encouraged individual responsibility by strengthening the nuclear family. For a woman to divorce a man would mean she unsettled her husband's economic investment. According to all schools of religious practice, a husband could divorce a wife almost at will, but a wife who wished to leave her husband had to show good reason. The main legal restraint upon the man in divorce was essentially financial and a matter of a legally and morally binding contract between equal parties. It became customary that only a part of the bridal gift (*mahr*, *ṣidāq*), which the man settled upon his wife, was paid at the time of marriage; if he divorced her without special reason, he had to pay her the rest of the bridal gift. But if she obtained a divorce from him, she forfeited whatever part of the bridal gift he had paid. Since the law gave the children to the husband, the entire question of custody, unfortunately, was restricted to the already established legality of the claim of the father over the counterclaim of the mother. In contemporary interpretive jurisprudence, as soon as the case of child custody is brought to the moral and psychological planes of human relations, it becomes obvious that the right of the mother trumps the right of the father, since the complicated relationship of the child to the biological and psychological connection of the mother is decisive in assessing the validity of the father's claim to sole custody of the offspring.

Intuitively Extracted Ethical Principles in Interpretive Jurisprudence

To understand practical aspects of Islamic ethics as it pertains to jurisprudence, we need to dwell on the prevalent processes in interpretive jurisprudence that cover all the actions humans perform. The first and foremost ethical principles are to be sought in the revelation. The textual resources function as a repository of narratives about legal-ethical cases that enable the jurist to extricate operative moral reasoning used to infer a ruling. Clearly, the linguistic and lexicographical investigation of the scriptural sources grew out of the immediate interest to situate the empirical narrative in its social and cultural contexts. The Qur'anic Arabic brought to light expressions of moral attitudes and factual elements of the selected precedents to lay down their gradual transformation and adoption as the moral idiom under Islam. The religious language of morality passed through an inevitable change of meaning to reflect universal moral values that directed the justificatory reasoning to become a technical term for future reference. In theory, the linguistic and ethical research served the long-term goal of developing juridical moral language to provide the solution to the pressing issues that could serve as paradigmatic cases (*uṣūl*) aimed at teaching righteousness as a principle to cultivate moral excellence.

Moral juridical terminology founded upon meticulous analysis of primary texts becomes indispensable for understanding the authority invested in the jurists. The jurists undertake to integrate the moral and legal in their claim to sole discretionary control (*taṣarruf*) over properties and persons in traditional jurisprudence. This control was logically discussed in chapters dealing with financial transactions (*amwāl*) as well as administration of justice (*qaḍā*) and legal penalties (*ḥudūd*). However, the jurists needed to establish criteria to determine the qualifications and moral probity of a person who, in his role of a guardian (*walī*) and superintendent (*nāẓir*), could be authorized to handle the goods in trust that belonged, for instance, to an orphan. In this evaluation the jurists were guided by relational ethics that determined whether an orphan's welfare could be entrusted to a jurist to assume administration of the inherited estate. The jurists introduced a number of rules as part of their strategy of extrapolating judicial rulings that protected and supervised an orphan's estate. One of the rules was about determining the ordinary usage of the terms employed by the people in the context of their social relationships and responsibilities for an incompetent person (in this case a minor) to take over the management of his inheritance. The linguistic analysis constituted some of these questions: Do people express any moral qualms and discomfort in handling the goods that belong to orphans? How do they express that discomfort? Do they simply employ the religious categories of "permissible" (*jā'iz*) or "illicit" (*ḥarām*) to express their concern when treating their moral responsibility toward a minor? Do they engage in expressing their evaluative moral attitude or feeling by any rational analysis? Or do they simply use moral terms like "good" (*ḥasan*) or "corrupt" (*fāsid* or *qabīḥ*) to express their overall inability to treat the matter legally in fairness and honesty?

Literary analyses of Arabic usage and syntax assumed a critical part of juridical inquiry to understand the complexity of the textual resources and the interrelationship of different parts of the juridical corpus from the sections on the "Book of Trade" (*kitab al-tijāra* or *al-makāsib*) to the discussions about the "Book of Guardianship" (*kitab al-wilāya*) for derivation of authoritative decisions in the general area of ethics of managing the goods of minors. Social conventions became an inseparable part of evaluative judgments that determined the moral character of the religious discourse. In a way, the principle provided a breakthrough in resolving a number of ethical issues related to the supervision of the goods belonging to orphans. The moral discourse working through legitimate legal expressions created categories that captured the sense of "praiseworthy" (= prudentially necessary [*wujūb iḥtiyāṭ*]) and "blameworthy" (= commonsensically to be avoided [*tark al-awlā*]) aspects of an act leading to a judicial ruling that declared the conduct licit or illicit depending upon its ethical ramifications. Gradually, the ethical and legal became integrated in the meaning of "obedience" to divinely ordained rulings of orthopraxy (*al-aḥkām al-shar'īya*).

In the realm of human-God relations moral self-purification that came from practicing righteousness was associated with physical purification, with its evident connection to spiritual and moral improvement. Taking the example of the commandments to give alms and observe ritual purity, both these acts were directly connected to righteousness aiming to generate moral purity. Deep in the revelation was the idea of working toward moral excellence by engaging in spiritual devotions. Two essential areas of human life define its scope: (1) acts, both public and private, connected with the pillars of faith to cultivate spirituality and (2) acts of public order to improve interpersonal justice. The first category of actions, undertaken with the intention of seeking God's pleasure, is collectively known as "worship" of God. This includes all the pillars of faith in the Muslim creed, including daily worship, fasting during the month of Ramadan, almsgiving, and so on. The second category of actions, undertaken to maintain social order, are known as "social transactions" (literally "social intercourse"). The religious calibration of these two categories depended upon the meticulous division of jurisdiction (*niṭāq sulṭa*). In Islam all actions should be performed to secure divine approval, but human agency and institutions have jurisdiction only over the social transactions. The acts of worship are exclusively within God's jurisdiction—God alone reserves the right of judging their final merit and reward. Human courts, however, are empowered to enforce the laws that govern interpersonal relations in society. Remarkably, from the early days of Islam, the Sharīʿa recognized the secularity of human institutions without presuming to meddle in the God-human relationship. This distinction between the two areas of jurisdiction allowed Muslims to adopt local cultures and institutions to enhance the administration of newly conquered regions of the world. It also secured a better understanding of the Qur'anic principle of coexistence among diverse communities. This latter principle was firmly founded upon the separate jurisdictions for human-God and interhuman relations.

The authoritative aspect of the revelation as the critical source of documentation, for both the traditionalist and the rationalist jurists, cannot be overstated. There was a persistent requirement to uncover paradigm cases and dependable principles from the religious texts that, on the one hand, established the validity of the judicial decision and, on the other hand, served as trustworthy precedents for solutions to future similar instances involving justice in human relations. For example, the Qur'anic insistence on written agreements in matters of financial obligations engendered a tradition of written contracts in all those matters that involve two parties. It has further inspired the requirement that all transactions involving any social or financial obligation must be properly attested by qualified witnesses so that human relations are conducted in fairness and justice. In both civil and criminal cases, the Qur'an laid down an ethical standard of conduct from which jurists extracted legal rulings in the sphere of all human interaction.

Evidently, in order to create such a comprehensive legal-ethical system, Muslim scholars had to look beyond the Qur'an. The Qur'an saw the Prophet as a leader whose actions were normative and worthy of emulation. In fact, the Qur'an insisted that obedience to God meant obedience to the Prophet, the noblest exemplar (*uswa ḥasana*) for all those making a commitment of faith. Clearly, for the Qur'an there can be no community without the Prophet. Hence, the Prophet's life became an ethical touchstone for what Muslims call the Sunna, the Tradition. The early community used the word *sunna* to mean a legal-ethical precedent from which jurists could generate further laws for the growing needs of the community. Gradually, the term was extended to include the entire tradition that traced all aspects of Muslim life back to the Prophet, his family, and his early associates. The intellectual activity surrounding the interpretation of God's will expressed in the Qur'an and the evaluation of the *ḥadīth*-reports that were ascribed to the Prophet became the major religious-academic activity among

Muslims, laying the foundation for subsequent juridical deliberations—what became known as *fiqh* ("understanding"), or interpretive jurisprudence.

Interpretive jurisprudence was, then, developed as an application of the norms of moral-legal conduct detailed in the Sharīʿa. Islamic legal methodology and moral philosophy, as it was developed in the 9th and 10th centuries, recognized four sources on the basis of which ethical-legal decisions could be deduced: the Qur'an, the Tradition, the consensus (*ijmāʿ*) of the early community of Muslim scholars, and analogical deduction (*qiyās*) based on established cases that functioned as paradigmatic precedents. Muslim jurists developed a number of rational methodological strategies to extrapolate fresh rules from the Qur'an and the Tradition to resolve new cases. The predominant consideration in this interpretive enterprise was the innate human ability to discover the moral teachings of the Qur'an. The practical guidance of the Qur'an that underscored its intuitively construed moral foundation was employed to develop an elaborate system of juridical ethics that helped jurists to provide rational and textual justifications for their rulings. For instance, when was it appropriate to risk one's life to save another? Through a moral analysis of the virtue of sacrifice without endangering one's own well-being, the jurists permitted not only donation but also sale of a needed body part or an organ to save another person's life. Moreover, after a careful risk-benefit analysis, further rulings were deduced that justified risking one's life for one's loved one, under critical conditions. The operative principle that undergirded the ethical aspects of the case and its solution was to determine the suitability (*munāsaba*) of the ruling by investigating that it promotes that which is beneficial (*manfaʿa*) to all persons and avoids that which is deemed harmful (*mafsada*) to all. Certainly, one of the primary objectives of the Sharīʿa is dependable and incessant promotion of benefit and exclusion of harm. Accordingly, vital organs like eyes that one needed for living a normal life were exempt in this ruling because deforming one's countenance was morally and religiously wrong. To be sure, Muslim jurists were charged with deciding whether an obligatory act warranted enforcement by secular authorities or by God's judgment in the hereafter. In some cases of blasphemy, for example—especially those that might threaten the social order—the ruler might be empowered to institute the appropriate penalty (*ta'zir*) even if the religious transgression ultimately lay outside the jurisdiction of human judiciary.

All schools of Islamic legal thought, although granting males a privileged role in the social hierarchy, presupposed a considerable social role for women. The Qur'anic injunctions concerning propriety were stretched by means of the Tradition to impose seclusion. The veil (*ḥijāb*) was presented as a tool of personal modesty, and the female apartment was viewed as an enhancement of family privacy. These measures were not intended to become a form of social distinction, as it did with upper-class women living in rigorous segregation. It became a mark of a woman of a quality that she was secluded from all men but those in her own family.

As interpretive jurisprudence became a highly technical process, disputes about method and judicial opinions crystallized into schools of orthopraxy that bore the names of prominent jurists who founded them. The rite that followed the Iraqi tradition was called "Ḥanafī," after Abū Ḥanīfa (d. 767), the *imām* (teacher) in Iraq. Those who adhered to the rulings of Mālik b. Anas (d. 795), in Arabia and elsewhere, were known as "Mālikis." Al-Shāfi'ī founded a legal rite in Egypt whose influence spread widely to other regions of the Muslim world. Another rite was associated with Aḥmad b. Ḥanbal (d. 855), who compiled a work on *ḥadīth*-reports that became the source for juridical decisions of those who followed him. Shī'ites developed their own legal rite and methodology, known as the Ja'farī school, whose leading authority was Imam Ja'far al-Ṣādiq (d. 748). Normally, Muslims accepted the rite prevalent in their region. Most of the Sunnites follow Hanafi or Shafi'ī; Shī'ites follow the Ja'farī school. In the absence of an organized church and ordained clergy in Islam, determination of valid religious practice was left to the qualified scholar of religious law. Hence, there emerged a living tradition, with different interpretations of the Qur'anic laws and prophetic traditions, giving rise to different schools of the orthopraxy.

Islamic Ethics in Interpretive Jurisprudence: Revelatory or Rational?

Muslim scholars have customarily regarded morality as a derivative of religion. Even among the rationalist theologians who regarded reason and conscience as internal channels to ethics, the predominant view regarding the ethics connected with interpretive jurisprudence was integral to the original wording of the Qur'an and the Tradition. Accordingly, juridical methodology remained text-based jurisprudence that approached infused morality as a reliable source of ethical decision-making.[4] In other words, rationally inferred moral values were integral to the divinely ordained rulings in the Sharī'a, which correlated the findings of revelation and reason to deduce reliable judicial decisions. The prevalent methodology in Islamic jurisprudence, as analyzed in the previous section, does not reveal the entire process to detect the moral philosophy behind a specific ruling. Nevertheless, the critical analysis of linguistic aspects (*baḥth al-alfāẓ*) of original Arabic religious texts to establish the meaning of a particular text as well as its relation to other texts that clarify the text under consideration reveals the profound relation of these deduced rulings to deontic or consequential ethics. For obvious reasons, interpretive jurisprudence, without formally acknowledging it, depended upon ethical appraisal of the case to discover and verify the purposes of divine guidance in both its forms: through reason and through revelation.

It is important to concede that the contemporary project of determining the epistemic sources of Islamic interpretive jurisprudence affirms only religious texts like the Qur'an, the Tradition, and the scholarly consensus (*ijmāʿ*), to the exclusion of the epistemic valuation of naturally endowed infused morality. In other words, there is no role assigned to external moral reasoning to infer fresh rulings in the area of, for instance, social ethics. In an important way, the thesis of this study is to reinstate the centrality of the Qur'anic moral epistemology that originates in human nature as a reliable primary source for ethical deliberations generated by modern living in Muslim communities around the world. In the absence of any additional religious text-based repository for interpreting the divine will for humanity, it is imperative that Muslim jurisprudence reestablishes the epistemic agency of infused morality. Historically, rational moral norms like the "public good" (*maṣlaḥa*) and "No harm, no harassment" (*lā ḍarar*) interacted with textual sources to produce practical guidance in large sectors of mundane affairs in Muslim regions. The critical role of such moral principles was to provide rational criteria to verify that the jurist's intellectual endeavors in deducing further rulings did not end up issuing a ruling that contradicted the objectives of the Sharīʿa. Consequently, there was no hesitation in admitting the external sources of legal reasoning as long as there was a possibility of drawing analogical deductions (*qiyās*), however far-fetched, from authoritative textual sources.

With the growth of in vitro fertilization (IVF) reproductive technology and the so-called surplus embryos readily available for experimentation, the Muslim conception of the integrity and the life of the early human embryo is in serious danger. Stem-cell research is promising critical therapeutic benefits, and it is hard to imagine that Muslim scientists are not interested in harvesting stem cells from human embryos and fetuses in the hope of treating hitherto incurable diseases. Whether created for reproduction purposes or research, there is no legal or moral basis to deny the dignity of the so-called spare embryos. The loosely applied principle of public good (*maṣlaḥa*) seems to have provided an easy justification for any procedure that actually requires more scrupulous ethical analysis because it is a potential life that is involved. A more relevant principle in this case states, "Averting corruption has preponderance over advancing public good." Nevertheless, in the juridical tradition, on the basis of the penalties prescribed for feticide, there is an agreement that the fetus before ensoulment cannot be accorded the status of a full person. Also, no funeral rites are to be performed for a fetus before the first trimester.[5]

Advancements in biomedical technology have led to a reconsideration of some classical formulations about abortion. A number of juristic principles, including the "contrariety between two harms" (*taʿāruḍ al-ḍararayn*) and "protection against distress and constriction" (*'usr wa ḥaraj*), have been invoked to rule in favor of the priority of saving the mother's life on whose well-being the life of the fetus depends. Also, in the case of rape or incest, the psychological damage suffered by a woman has been duly recognized as a justification for abortion (*ijhaḍ janīn al-ightiṣāb*).

Such a devaluation of pre-implanted human embryos in the IVF clinics can lead to their exploitation for therapeutic purposes or even commercial undertakings that seek to profit from their research potential. Muslim jurists have not considered all the negative facets of their ill-conceived countenancing of both unregulated IVF and the discarding of the unused embryos, as if potential human life could be treated like a commodity. The problem is rooted in traditional Islamic jurisprudence, which ignores any ethical analysis of such cases and simply bases its rulings on legal principles that imply but do not expressly articulate an ethical code. If Muslim jurists had paid due attention to Islamic ethics, wherein the objective nature of human action is analyzed in terms of good and evil and which informs many of the legal doctrines and much of the methodology of Islamic jurisprudence, then they would have considered the moral status of the embryo meticulously, a task rendered all the more urgent by advancements in medical technology.

The major problem, as I see it, pertains to the denial of the moral status of a fetus outside the mother's womb. There is little doubt that the progressive development and viability of the embryo indicate and express a moral and legal progression of rights and dignity. Even if full personhood and ensuing complete rights are achieved only after birth, the Sharī'a takes into account the various stages of biological development to assess the level of damage done to the fetus, thus reaffirming a progressively growing respect for the dignity and rights of the fetus. At no point does the tradition differentiate between pre-implanted embryos and those that are already implanted in the uterus. All the laws in criminology speak only of the in-uterus embryo.

Nonetheless, in interpretive jurisprudence, the matter of ensoulment is of critical importance because of the need to demarcate the beginning of legally recognized personhood that would render abortion a crime unless the mother's life is at stake. This view of abortion is also supported by modern Arabic usage, in which the word *ijhāḍ* denotes a fetus that is aborted from the womb before the first trimester, that is, before ensoulment; the word *isqāṭ* denotes a fetus that is miscarried between the fourth and the seventh months. However, in popular understanding, only this later stage of fetal development gives rise to personhood, in which case the abortion of pre-ensouled fetuses would be permissible.

The legal-moral status of an entity is described in terms of obligations and relationships that it shares with other moral agents. If fetal tissue is treated as an organic nonhuman life form, then it might be permissible to treat it as an organ in a woman's uterus and, when aborted, lawful material for research, especially the socially redeeming medical quest to foster human health and longevity. On the other hand, if human embryonic cells are considered human entities, then our moral relationship and obligation toward them shifts sharply. The fetus is guaranteed legal rights by the Sharīʿa, and the evidence for this view is abundant in many works of Islamic jurisprudence. If the moral status of the fetus is conceded from the moment of conception, then it puts constraints on medical research that wishes to use the "spare" IVF embryos to derive stem cells, because of our obligation to another entity that is not capable of protecting itself and consenting to its use for research.

Abortion is permitted in some circumstances and is required in others, especially when the mother's life is in grave danger. Islamic sources have recognized threat to mother's life as grounds for abortion, but they have not given the same consideration to the condition of the fetus because until recently it was not possible to know anything about the genetic or medical makeup of the fetus before birth. Any consideration regarding the fetus's health raises serious questions as to what constitutes a sufficient defect to warrant abortion. It certainly represents a novelty in Islamic jurisprudence which requires jurists to be extremely cautious in providing rulings that might be abused in inferring a general permission to abort a defective fetus. In fact, the Islamic Juridical Council that meets regularly to deliberate and decide on such matters has already approved clinical abortion of embryos that have been genetically screened as suffering from Down syndrome. Now it is true that the principle of "No harm, no harassment" has provided some jurists justification for abortion in severe cases, like those in which the fetus has minimal brain tissue or a degenerative disease like Tay-Sachs that will lead to the infant's death within a few years of birth, at most. But overall there are too many unknowns as far as their impact on the future of human society goes. Are we moving toward eugenics, which tends to define qualifications for a genetically superior race that leads to depreciation of disabled people?

Islamic jurisprudence requires unequivocal evidence to support any ruling that might have an adverse impact upon the future of human society. The advances of modern genetics have given rise to fundamental ethical problems in dealing with what constitutes a defect in justifying abortion. Some Muslim jurists have strictly forbidden abortion under any circumstances before or after the ensoulment has occurred. Actually, contrary to some Muslim physicians-cum-interpreters of Islamic medical ethics who seem to maintain unquestioning legitimacy of abortion during the first trimester, at the end of which, according to a majority of jurists, ensoulment occurs, the Sharīʿa views the process of gestation developmentally from the time the embryo attaches itself to the uterus. This occurs around the tenth or eleventh day after conception. However, after the first trimester, that is, 120 days, the Sharīʿa equates clinically induced abortion to murder and imposes penalties in proportion to the age of the fetus. The reason is that the Sharīʿa accords the fetus the same sanctity that the mother as a person enjoys. Both deserve the same respect, and as such neither has preponderance over the other.[6]

The question connected with the moral standing of embryonic and fetal life remains unresolved in interpretive jurisprudence because of the lack of a precise definition of life and of the beginning of life that involves religious, ethical, legal, and social considerations. Although jurists do not dispute the biological fact of life and the sanctity the fetus enjoys because of that, they differ as to the stage of fetal development at which the fetus has absolute inviolability (*dhimma ṣāliḥa*) and possesses full rights as an independent person.[7] Hence, there are disagreements about the moment of conception and the time when the ensoulment—the infusion of the soul into the body of the fetus, thus conferring moral status on the fetus—occurs, and whether the viability of the fetus is marked when it is capable of living as a newborn outside the womb. In juridical terminology, the fetus is defined as an entity that in one sense does not acquire personhood (*nafs*) directly so as to benefit from rights.[8] Furthermore, in Islamic jurisprudence abortion rulings are not framed in terms of a resolution to a conflict of rights between the pregnant woman and her fetus. According to some Sunni jurists, for instance, as long as the fetus remains in utero it does not have independent and absolute inviolability because it is regarded as a part of the mother's body. However, as soon as it becomes separated from the uterus, with the capability of surviving outside the womb, then it is regarded as a person (*nafs*) possessing inviolability and rights like inheritance, proper lineage and so on.[9]

As such, the fetus in the womb has a relative claim for life and for rights based upon its eventual personhood in that it is a potential human being while in utero. The closer to birth the fetus is, the closer to personhood it can be considered and the greater justification it has to be accorded rights.[10] Such an estimation of the personhood of the fetus is behind the contemporary liberal juridical opinions among Sunni jurists who do not regard abortion as forbidden if the mother's life is in danger at any stage of gestation, including the last days before the child is born.[11] This conditional permission linked to the impending danger to mother's life is often overlooked when clinical abortions are readily performed in the Muslim world with no impunity. To add to this religiously and morally problematic attitude to the pre-ensoulment embryo, there are juridical rulings that permit abortion for the reason of poverty.[12] These rulings actually lead to abortion as a method of population control. Certainly, by the ethical standards provided by the Qur'an, it is unacceptable to allow abortion to function as a method of population control.[13]

To sum up, both revelation and reason are involved in directing human action in achieving the overall religiously and morally charged objectives of Islam.

Obviously, the revelation depends upon reason for its interpretation and application. In deriving the ethical norms found in the revelatory texts, it is reason that undertakes to investigate the texts' ethical presuppositions to advance problem resolution in all areas of human interaction. In other words, textual hermeneutics is dependent upon the rational capacity of its interpreter, who sits in dialogue with the revelation to extract its appropriate meaning for application in specific contexts. The entire project of exploring the practical implications of the textual primary sources calls for meticulous methodological investigation to deduce religious, moral, and legal action-guides on the basis of Sharīʿa norms that cover a wide range of topics relevant to everyday life. More pertinent to the objectives of the religious law is the precondition that regards the fulfillment of moral-religious duty (*taklīf*) of the Sharīʿa obligatory upon a person with the innate capacity to understand the moral goal of orthopraxy. In view of that precondition, interpretive jurisprudence has fixed the age of biological maturity by taking into consideration a child's ability to understand the reason behind the need to show gratitude to the benefactor.[14] The litmus test to determine rational maturity that the jurisprudence uses remains intuitive reason and its ability to know the right from the wrong.

The Role of Traditional Epistemology in Interpretive Jurisprudence

As discussed earlier in this study, the traditionalist thesis of human moral knowledge was built around the exclusive role revelation played in informing humanity about good and evil. Muslim theologians, whether traditionalist or rationalist, took up questions such as the objective or subjective nature of good and evil and whether moral responsibility is divinely or rationally determined. Muslim philosophical theology, as discussed earlier, has yielded a lively diversity of views about human ethical knowledge. Some of the questions raised in this connection include: What part does divinely endowed human nature (*fiṭra*) play in ethical epistemology? Is this nature totally dependent upon an external source like God's revelation to inform it about the good or evil aspects of an act? What is the ontological reference to intuitive reason in the divine order of things? Is a human being capable of knowing those characteristics that render an act obligatory or good or bad freely and deliberately? These questions bear directly on the subject of this study because they undergird the religious thought that informs the ethical and legal deliberations in the juridical tradition of Islam.

The rationalist ethical epistemology and its accessibility to human reason were not acceptable to those Muslim thinkers who saw rationalist-natural theology as a threat to the supremacy of revelation as the main source of ethical values. For the majority of the people in the community the ontological reference to good and bad was God's command and decree. Moreover, they believed that the basic tenets of Islam were self-evident and therefore required no intellectual defense. The purpose of God's revelation, according to these Muslims, was to obey God's commandments unquestioningly. The champions of this notion of unquestioning faith in God's commandments were the traditionalists.

The traditionalists, understandably, limited philosophical theology to a defense of the doctrines communicated in the *ḥadīth*-reports, which were regarded as more reliable than abstract reason in construing individual principles. They emphasized the absolute will and power of God and denied nature and humankind any decisive role in deciphering the moral law. What humans perceive as causation, they believed, is actually God's habitual behavior. They countered the rationalist view of the objective nature of good and evil and insisted on the omnipotence and benevolence of God by maintaining that good and evil are what God decrees them to be. God transcends the order of nature; hence, the notion of free will is incompatible with a divine omnipotence that governs all earthly activity.

The logic of this thinking among the traditionalist jurists can be uncovered in their treatment of ethics as a separate discipline. As a rule, the moral dimension of a case is subsumed under interpretive jurisprudence, more specifically, under its methodology that brings moral principles to bear upon the ultimate formulation of a judicial ruling. Consequently, epistemologically and ontologically moral analysis of human action has remained underdeveloped in legal theory. The normal procedure that engages in retrieving authentic texts to formulate a ruling ignores a critical methodological prerequisite, namely, to apply the rationally analyzed ethical norms to scrutinize the contextual aspects of the case (e.g., religiously spurred and justified militancy) before issuing the judicial rulings. In that sense, the rulings of interpretive jurisprudence lack the necessary universal moral consideration to engage in conversation with other religious or nonreligious ethics. In terms of cognitive validity, when compared with revelation-based authoritative religious rulings, the traditionalist jurists regard moral valuation based on rational analysis merely conjectural (*ẓannī*), even if the former ruling is essentially inferred on the basis of a particular textual hermeneutics. It is safe to assume that, according to the traditionalist view of divine command ethics, orthopraxy had to build itself upon a scriptural foundation provided by the Qur'an and the Tradition (the only dependable way of deriving religious action-guides) to the exclusion of rational-objectivist ethics built upon the Qur'anic notion of infused morality in human disposition. The traditionalist response to modernity and its conscience-based rationalist ethics was to deny the role objectivist ethics, independent of revelation, plays in the derivation of orthopraxy.

What does this rupture between interpretive jurisprudence and ethics mean to the future of the belief among large sectors of Muslims that it is the revival and reapplication of the classical Sharīʿa that will usher in the ideal reform of Muslim societies? Thus far, Muslim thinkers have suggested broadening the application of the principles (*uṣūl*) in methodology to accommodate contemporary issues in all areas of science and its relation to society.[15] Take, for instance, justice, a core value in human relations: as a moral virtue it must provide the parameters of its application at all levels of interpersonal relations; however, as a duty in jurisprudence, it should be undertaken to determine its level of obligatoriness or otherwise for application. Different contexts in social relations demand different applications of justice as a principle of fairness or of equitable distribution of limited resources. The change of context in the contemporary allocation of limited resources in poor countries has often led to miscarriages of distributive justice. In those specific circumstances, can the ethical-religious responsibility of alleviating poverty be sidestepped because the judicial opinion based on the principle of "averting probable harm" (*dafʿ ḍarar muḥtamal*) can be evoked to provide dispensation to the well-to-do to shun their moral responsibility toward the downtrodden simply because such generosity might cause greater harm by making the poor dependent on the rich? Interpretive jurisprudence is equipped to bypass ethics, for instance, in gray areas when one has recourse to legal stratagems (*ḥīla*, plural *ḥiyal*) to support illegitimate personal interests and greed. These stratagems provided legal means by which some jurists helped their clients to avoid obligatory acts or to render permissible what was ethically and religiously forbidden. The Sharīʿa was the repository of immutable moral values for the purpose of promoting the best interests of all human beings. Its objectives were universal and provided clear guidelines to jurists to enact moral and religious action-guides for future generations. How could traditionalist jurisprudence ignore its intimate relationship to ethics for the future application of these universal norms?

This problem of strict adherence to the juridical opinions of one's preferred jurist—a kind of blind following of a religious authority (*taqlīd*)—that has become the benchmark of modern religious-juridical hegemony among Muslims has deep roots in the self-serving ends of the religious establishment. In a wider public sphere the situation raises a critical question that can be heard all over modern Muslim societies: Has interpretive jurisprudence (*fiqh*), with its emphasis on licit-illicit (*ḥalāl* and *ḥarām*) acts, replaced ethics, with its primary concern with the rightness (*ḥusn*) or wrongness (*qubḥ*) of human acts? Even more serious is raising the consequential aspects of the neglect that exists in matters of crucial importance in ethics of controversial practices like "honor killings" in some parts of the Muslim world. The problem arises from the differing definitions of core coordinates of social life and the ways one can mediate between the rights of women and the rights of the family as part of relational ethics. Women's rights in the context of family relations are contested and differently defined across Muslim world. To put it differently, instead of paying serious attention to the moral values embedded in the Sharī'a ordinances, the emphasis has shifted on the legality of orthopraxy.

Epistemological Shift from Ethics to Jurisprudence

In order to understand the epistemological shift that casts a long shadow of doubt on the ability of human reason to discover the moral presuppositions of religious praxis, we need to evaluate the intellectual investment that was made by the traditionalists in the preservation of the prophetic heritage. It is plausible to maintain that by the 10th century, usually labeled the Classical Age in Islamic studies, when the interpretations of the Qur'an and the *hadīth* collections became available to jurists, in order to determine authoritative practice interpretive jurisprudence began to prioritize text (*naql*) over reason (*'aql*). The early reliance on Arabic tribal practice and prevailing practical ethics (*al-ma'ruf* = known customary practice) in the social and cultural milieu of 7th-century Arabia became less weighty in providing fresh rulings in social ethics. The victory of rationalist theologians over the traditionalists in the 9th and 10th centuries and the impending compilation of the traditional resources (*ḥadīth*-reports and the Qur'anic commentaries) set the stage for the ultimate takeover by the text-based traditionalist's juridical methodology, necessitating a permanent rupture between reason-based and revelation-based independent inquiry in religious practice. In Islamic sciences there began a long process in which interpretive jurisprudence in its investigation of new social conditions began to doubt the reliability of human reason to discover authentic religious practice. The juridical rulings requiring unquestionable obedience, although being deontic in the sense that they were deduced on the basis of moral principles and rules in the revelation, became less concerned with understanding the ethical principles set in the divine commands in the revelation.

Contemporary Muslim jurists, who maintain that the study of religious law and ethics is intertwined in philosophical theology as well as juridical methodology, contend that their interpretive methodology and expected outcome of their investigation to discover authentic praxis in both disciplines are not that different. In reality, according to these jurists, the judicial ruling and ethical solution converge in developing a moral analysis to elaborate fundamental concerns of reason and revelation for inferring moral-religious justifications. Consequently, the jurist is committed not only to discovering the correlation between legal and ethical decision but also to discovering a ruling that would guarantee one's salvation in the hereafter. In other words, both jurisprudence and ethics are geared toward solving the practical problems encountered by people in their everyday life. Undoubtedly, Muslim jurists, having been trained primarily as religious scholars, concentrate on issues of obedience and disobedience to God in their search for appropriate rulings in applied jurisprudence. Their text-based investigation, on the one hand, takes them on a different path of research that determines the permissibility or impermissibility of a certain act from the Divine Lawgiver's point of view; on the other hand, the ethical approach is employed to understand the reliability of rationally derived knowledge about the good and bad aspects of the act. This latter procedure enables them to distinguish praiseworthy from blameworthy human conduct in order to extrapolate a moral recommendation.

In the context of the present debate about the intimate relation between religious law and ethics in Islam, Muslim scholars elaborate on the reason to integrate ethics in the Sharī'a studies by differentiating between the concept of ethics and the discipline of ethics—*al-akhlāq* (a plural form of *khulq*) and *'ilm al-akhlāq*. I have, more or less, explained the concept of ethics among Muslim scholars in the early parts of this study. To reiterate here, the discipline of ethics, according to some, deals with discernible human conduct from the point of its sources, motives, and objectives. The subject, moreover, defines values and practical rules that need to be observed in one's conduct in order to determine different aspects of the attitude or its form, just as one deals with the instruments that persuade one to a sense of duty to do the right and to avoid the bad behavior.

An additional feature of ethics that is identified by Muslim scholars is its instrumentality in restoring the spiritual and moral well-being of the people afflicted by corrupt and undesirable human conduct. If human conduct becomes distorted, ethics, as exemplary conduct, attempts to transform human conduct and restore it to its healthy state. Most Muslim thinkers agree that vices must be treated as psychological disorders that require therapy. According to these thinkers, the discipline of ethics (*'ilm al-akhlāq*) resembles medicine because, based on this therapeutic feature, ethics treats the spiritual ailments of human dispositions. In view of that, ethics teaches techniques of treating psychological disorders and maintaining sound mental health. Indeed, the ultimate goal of ethics, according to Islamic philosophical ethics, is the attainment of happiness (*al-sa'āda*).[16]

To sum up, the epistemological shift from ethics to jurisprudence in Islamic sciences can be traced back to the growing influence of the rationalistic approach to the search for practical solutions to the expanding social and political role of religion in the public arena. The Qur'an in its overall guidance of the community's spiritual and moral well-being remained the major source for practical guidelines. However, adhering to the letter and spirit of the Qur'an needed the perpetual presence of the Prophet's elaboration of the precise meaning of its prescriptions, posthumously compiled under the Sunna (the Tradition). Since such a possibility was ruled out by the Qur'an in asserting the mortality of the Prophet (Q. 3:144), it is correct to assert that without the Prophet's personal prestige it was not possible to acknowledge the validity of the extra-Qur'anic source for the moral-ethical objectives of the revelation. Consequently, the religious status of prophetic guidance in the form of *ḥadīth*-reports was elevated to become part of the revelation and was acknowledged as an indispensable resource to provide the necessary documentation for determining authentic and developing orthopraxy.

The Qur'anic notion of divinely endowed intuitive reason, capable of distinguishing the good from the bad (Q. 91:8), was almost forgotten; additionally, the innate capacity of human nature to know moral truth was rejected without any hesitation. The consequence of denying intuitive reason's metaphysical grounding in the revelation for discovering moral truth ended up undoing the intrinsic connection between reason and revelation—the two authoritative sources of orthopraxy—in comprehending the universal moral values of the Qur'an and their application in specific instances. This disjunction manifested in the overbearing prominence given to text-based juridical inquiry (*al-ijtihād al-shar'ī*) over teleological estimation and consequences of human acts. Retrospectively, the study of philosophical theology to understand the doctrinal positions adopted by rationalist-objectivist and traditionalist-subjectivist ethicists leads a researcher in Islamic ethics to justifiably conclude that the negative consequence of traditionalists' success in suffocating the rationalist tendency in ethics led to the helplessness of the Qur'anic moral epistemology to guide orthopraxy permanently. Ironically, in spite of the revelatory confidence in the workings of infused morality to guide all believers to perform all those acts that are morally obligatory while abstaining from performing those that are blameworthy, the intentional damaging of the reputation of inspired moral epistemology to guide human progression led to the demise of rationalist-objectivist deontic ethics among Muslim traditionalist jurists, who are, with hindsight, actually struggling to estimate the cost of uncritically submitting to modernity by promoting outdated traditionalist textual hermeneutics.

Modernity remains absolutely committed to discrediting revelation-based ethics and replacing it with reason-based moral deliberations with changing moral values and relativized moral solutions. Contemporary Muslim jurisprudence is hostage to a traditionalist worldview that believes in uncritical and ahistorical interpretation of the Qur'anic norms in the context of the Tradition. More critically, the traditionalists contended that the rationalist confidence in the ability of reason to determine the quality of human acts, independent of revelation, was at the most tenuous. Then again, the normative divine command ethics functions as the sole trustworthy supplier of judicial decisions to guide the community's orthopraxy in the modern world. The classical legal doctrine that no judicial decision can become binding unless it is based upon validated revelatory text—the Qur'an and the Tradition—gradually became a lead legal doctrine that imposed textual restrictions upon independent inquiry about the moral ramifications of the case. Henceforth, intuitive reason that studied a practical case by taking into consideration social and psychological contexts to determine its ethical-legal outcome became restricted to reasoning based on authoritative texts (*al-naql*). The jurists did not trust independent reasoning (*ijtihād*) that was preoccupied in preserving personal interests and hegemonic ambitions of the jurists rather than in analyzing and applying ethical values governing human conduct in the wider society.

Revelatory Reason versus Human Reason in Islamic Ethics

To assess the consequences of negating the inherent connection between the universal moral values of the revelatory texts and their application in Islamic jurisprudence, we need to revisit the profound relationship between revelation and reason in directing the moral life of the community. That connection between religious and public reason was severed when public reason, as the reliable arbiter on issues not regulated by the authenticated text, was epistemically invalidated. The advocates of rational inquiry (*al-ijtihād al-ʿaqlī*), who upheld the ability of intuitive reason to determine good and evil, were discredited as undependable promoters of orthopraxy.

At this point it is reasonable to raise a question about the traditionalist belief in the authenticity of transmitted scriptural sources, without engaging in establishing their congruency for their admission as documentation to formulate a solution, namely: How should we appraise the accuracy of the scripture-based ruling when the only legitimate approach to assert its authenticity is dependent upon the agent's subjective faith in the authoritativeness of the text? The argument to prove the divine origin of all scriptural sources in order to establish their veracity (*ḥujjiya*) is susceptible to circularity, since in the absence of sensory observation or application of logic based on rational analysis, the supernatural origin is impossible to authenticate. Moreover, nonempirical argument is also incapable of deliberating on questions that regulate the ethics of human acts by investigating their situational aspects based on the observable facts. The traditional epistemic claim regarding supernatural logic is faith-based doctrine about God's perfection and the infallibility of God's legislative will. Compared to the divine perfect reason, human reason and logic are regarded as fallible and prone to serve the interests of the investigator. In contrast, the revelation-based juridical ordinances, as the traditionalists contend, compensate human intellectual deficiencies to discover legitimate human entitlements and responsibilities. To be sure, according to the traditionalist and rationalist jurists, the scope of Islamic jurisprudence is to reliably infer and expound rulings that are in the best interests of the community. Hence, the emphasis on scripture-based juridical review renders additional ethical inquiry regarding human acts redundant and justifies dispensing with independent rational inquiry about the ethical aspects of a case to determine a cognitively valid ruling.

Devaluation of human reason as a reliable source for understanding the moral law became the main argument against approving the epistemic validity of rationally inferred rulings and the ultimate prominence attached to *al-ijtihād al-sharʿī*—text-based inquiry in Islamic jurisprudence. Even as the epistemological apprehension of discursive knowledge based on public reason became the main source of limiting juridical inquiry to scriptural sources, the resolution required a meticulous analysis of ethical aspects of a case under review. This indispensable analysis depended upon two varieties of fundamentally changed circumstantial factual elements that confronted the jurists before a relatively reliable judgment could be obtained:

1. Substantial transformation of circumstances: For the alignment of circumstances between a well-established ruling and the new case a researcher needs to investigate the contextual aspects of a case to determine the cognitive validity of admitting the rule of "resemblance" (*tashābuh*) between the old and the new case. In the context of ethics, which evaluates the permissibility of a resembling aspect or lack of it in an act, sometimes the social or cultural situation changes so radically that it no longer bears any resemblance to previous circumstances that permitted that act in the first place. This kind of considerable change is known as "transformation" or "transmutation" (*istiḥāla* or *qalb*) in jurisprudence. Such a transformation leads to a change in the ruling. Take, for instance, the Muslim–non-Muslim composition of citizenry in modern Muslim states. Whereas the classical rulings of the juridical corpus retained the distinction in its treatment of non-Muslim protected peoples (*ahl al-dhimma*) as second-class citizens, today these rulings would be correctly construed as a violation of the equality of all citizens in a modern nation-state. Hence, any discriminatory policy based on the classical rulings would be incompatible with the ethical principle of justice, as maintained by reason and revelation in Islam.
2. Functional transformation: Sometimes the circumstantial aspects do not show change in their external, conventional form; rather this change is indicated in their social function. By "social function" I mean the modes of their utilization in society. Circumstantial transformation of social

> function occurs when the past function becomes inapplicable and is either replaced by a new social function or generates new functions alongside the old ones. Here the example of prevalent gender discrimination in the historical jurisprudence on the basis of functional difference between the roles of a man and a woman as breadwinner indicates explicitly the change in the social function of a woman as earner and her responsibilities and entitlements along with a man in furthering the family's good (*maṣlaḥa*) in all its dimensions.

Another example of the intricate relationship between ethics and tradition is provided by traditional Islamic jurisprudence's interdiction regarding the buying and selling of blood. Many jurists have based this prohibition on the idea that blood is ritually unclean (*najis*) and has no beneficial or rationally recognized use. This view conforms to that which prevails in a number of traditions that clearly prohibit the buying and selling of ritually unclean materials. Such a view is understandable given the inability to use blood for transfusion in the early days of Islam. Blood in the pre-Islamic Arabian culture was used to treat certain kinds of ailments or was consumed as a food in folk medicine to treat some diseases. Islam, however, emphasized the harm that resulted from these procedures and banned the sale of blood.

Today blood is known to have beneficial, even life-saving uses in transfusions. Hence the buying and selling of blood—even giving it as a gift—has been deemed permissible by Muslim jurists. Today blood can be preserved in most sterilized conditions and can be transported where needed without causing any harm to the recipient of a transfusion. In other words, with changes and developments in society and culture, substances that were once regarded as harmful or useless are now regarded as critical and indispensable to human life. Hence past juridical rulings have been changed to accommodate these functional transformations.[17]

The traditionalist project of delimiting religion and of ontologically connecting ethics to religion created a dilemma for those who were searching for solutions facing the community by extending the denotation of textual evidence without giving voice to conscience or reason to accommodate the changes in modern familial and societal relations. There are many instances in juridical sources where deduction of every juristic guideline inferred from any rational proof was set aside or ignored because of epistemological hurdles in its validity as a source of authoritative knowledge. The impact of situational change on doctrinal tradition had to be appraised through a meticulous intellectual analysis so that it could expound on unresolved existing moral cases. Indeed, the promise of inherited tradition was to overcome perplexed practicality by searching for another precept, though rational, to clarify justifiable precaution or clearance from obligation by ignoring the doubt. The traditionalist jurists had to accommodate human moral agency if the transformations in the rulings of the Sharīʿa had to reveal the precept of practicality (*al-aṣl al-ʿamalī*) that have been spurred by social and cultural change. For example, it is now permissible to transplant organs retrieved from a dead person or through donation. It is worth keeping in mind that there are those jurists who oppose these rulings, and, in most cases, their prohibition is based on a lack of relevant technical information about the method of organ retrieval.

My research is prompted by the need to undertake a careful analysis of the juridical-ethical literature to unearth the kind of reasoning, whether legal or moral, that has gone into formulating opinions in the field of ethics among both Sunni and Shīʿite Muslims. I have attempted to explore the situational transformations in important areas of social interaction in order to delineate a set of rules and principles to guide Muslim ethical deliberations and responses.

Epilogue

This study is in many ways a pioneer effort in defining and constructing Islamic ethics, in general, and ethical underpinnings of interpretive jurisprudence, in particular, that informs the entire field of orthopraxy among Muslims. I have very little to stand on in terms of primary sources in the field of juridical ethics founded upon principles derived from the revelation and reason, except classical studies on Islamic jurisprudence that deal with methodology in which principles and rules are identified and applied to discover denotation of the textual resources to establish authoritative religious and moral action-guides in the area of human-God and interhuman relations. The presumption of obligation, prohibition, or recommendation of any act is dependent upon the jurist's exertion of intellectual tools to verify the admission of textual or rational proof that can establish the correct practice. Hence, in concluding this study, the following points are important to keep in mind:

1. There are very few sources in Arabic or Persian devoted to specifically Islamic ethics embedded in the issues dealing with uncovering action-guides, either from the classical or the modern period. The field of ethics connected with interpretive jurisprudence is the unique approach of this study to bring to light the configurations of revelation- and reason-based ethics of the Sharīʿa. Hence, the research has many rough edges that will, I hope, prompt other ethicists to pursue further research in Islamic ethics.
2. The present work opens a new window into Islamic jurisprudence. It is an attempt to lay the foundation of Islamic ethics beyond philosophy and traditional jurisprudence in order to prompt future scholars of Islamic jurisprudence and ethics to refine the detonation of the primary religious and intellectual sources of Islamic juridical theory and practice and Islamic philosophical theology, with serious consideration in the field of legal-ethical methodology and practical applications.
3. This book does not claim to be an ethical prescription that can be applied to various aspects of life in acquiring moral personhood. Hence, it avoids a discussion of the rulings in interpretive jurisprudence per se. I have tried to underscore the reasoning that underlay the juridical investigation to improvise a missing dimension in modern Islamic juridical studies, namely, ethics. Accordingly, even when it specifies rulings on specific issues, the

Islamic Ethics. Abdulaziz Sachedina, Oxford University Press. © Oxford University Press 2022.
DOI: 10.1093/oso/9780197581810.003.0007

study is a kind of independent exploration of what lies beyond traditional jurisprudence in Islamic studies. A newly published multivolume study on the ethics of jurisprudence, *Mā warā' al-fiqh* (Beyond Interpretive Jurisprudence),[1] captures the essence of my research—independent of the published book, especially in my ethical approach to methodology that is open to varying interpretations and judgments. I have simply advocated a different reading of Islamic juridical tradition as a fundamental source for the study of Islamic ethics.

The Future of Islamic Ethics at the Core of Interpretive Jurisprudence

My research interest in jurisprudence and ethics was undertaken with the limited objective of locating Islamic ethics outside philosophy and theology. My main aim was to steer Islamic ethics away from its traditional location in Greek philosophy. This historical connection with Hellenistic moral thought occurred much later, following the translations of Greek heritage into Arabic. Where was Islamic moral thought before that period? If the Qur'anic worldview could be encapsulated in one word, then unhesitatingly, based on the numerous references to the idea of "reverential piety," one could mention ethics, with a clear scope of nurturing and maintaining the central idea of *taqwā*—spiritual-moral awareness as an essential element of human conduct. A long-held idea about Islam's essential characterization as "orthopraxy" made it imperative to uncover ethics in the heart of the Qur'an and the prophetic heritage. How else could one explain the pre-Islamic idea of *jāhilīya* as the backdrop for social reform that the Prophet was seeking? If *tawḥīd*—affirmation of the oneness of God—ushered in a new center for moral accountability, then moral law had to be expounded from day one of the new religious movement in Arabia.

The intention of bringing up the early history of the Muslim community is simply to assert that religious practice in all its forms—orthopraxy—was an inseparable part of the new Muslim identification, clearly instituted to combat prevalent hypocrisy in the commercial culture of tribal life that claimed superiority on the basis of kinship. New scales of justice were part of the orthopraxy. The Qur'an, through its severe critique of the economic imbalances and utter degradation of human dignity in Arab society of the 7th century, offered a faith that had to work toward improving the appalling treatment of orphans, the needy, and widows. Islam provided the key element of human moral responsibility by setting forth the thesis of human creation with an infused scale of moral judgment (*fiṭra*). It laid down the universal objectives (*maqāṣid*) that were to be implemented in the community, in its intra- and intercommunal relations. It is significant to note that the divinely ordained infused morality became the core source for the formulation of the orthopraxy that not only dealt with the rituals and regulations about worship; it also laid down the guiding principles of just interaction in all areas of interpersonal relationships.

If such a development in a profound relationship between history and moral appeal could be corroborated with absolutely reliable evidence to be derived from the Qur'an and the Tradition, then it is academically possible to set the origins of Islamic ethics from the time the Qur'an emphasized the need to establish prayers and moral conduct. This takes me to the main contribution of this study: that orthopraxy must have originated in the early days of moral-religious inquiries in the community. At this point I am reaching out to my colleagues in Islamic legal and philosophical-theological studies to go beyond the Orientalist project of analyzing classical Arabic and Persian sources for what they offer to construct a historical development of Islamic thought and practice in the classical age. A missing dimension in the Orientalist scholarship has always been a lack of interest in factual experience with Islamic thought as it is practiced in the Muslim world and in their centers of higher religious learning. If I can criticize Muslim religious thought as having ignored and avoided any serious discussion of the application of the Qur'anic notion of personal moral purification (*zakā*) to reveal in clear contours the purposes of revelations and commissioning of the prophets to become spiritual and moral guides to humanity, then I can extend a fair evaluation of the Orientalist-Western scholarship, which has continued to ignore or sidestep what Islam is offering religiously to millions in the world and in their centers of legal-religious studies. This fact is observable in the so-called detached (call it "objective," if you will) scholarship that is being produced in many prestigious institutions of higher learning in Europe and North America. I call this scholarship the "traditional" Western erudition of the "sources and evolution" of Islam as a culture and civilization. The religious legitimacy of Islam (including the Qur'an) was always questioned by the latter scholarship since there was hardly any "originality" in what Muḥammad taught. Wasn't he taught by Jewish and Christian teachers? Wasn't he heir to the followers of other monotheistic traditions who acted as his informants?

The story is long, and time is of the essence for me. There is no need to engage in counterpolemics and apologetics to "save" Islam from such an unfair treatment, whose days are, fortunately, numbered. The time has come to avoid the "logocentrism" of Orientalist-Western scholarship and allow Islamic studies to converse with the global community "beyond Orientalism" (*mā warā' al-istishrāq*). Like other Abrahamic and non-Abrahamic traditions, and unlike the claims put forward by militant Muslims in their dream to dominate the world, Islam wants to see a real development of ethics of concern and empathy for all human beings. The Qur'an, like all other scriptures, indicates that the prophetic mission receives increase and the blessings of God by enabling a prophet to guide human beings by purifying them (*tuzakkīhim* and *tuṭahhiruhum*) through the practice of sharing their possessions (Q. 9:104) in the form of almsgiving (*zakāt*). The performance of a moral act of sharing one's possessions (*māl*), according to the Qur'an, purifies the performer (*nafsahu*) and occasions an increase of the rest of the assets. More pertinent, in view of the emphasis upon purification of wealth through charity, the Qur'an makes it abundantly clear that in principle self-purification (*ṣafwat nafs*) leads the person to perform goodness (*zakkaytuhu*) or righteousness (*al-ʿamal al-ṣāliḥ*) toward all God's creatures to attain a higher level of piety.[2]

The future of Islamic ethics is with interpretive jurisprudence for the simple reason that as long as Islamic piety as a force of spiritual and moral development remains part of the orthopraxy, moral discourse will be needed to perform the most important epistemological as well as ontological evaluation of the divinely ordained Sharīʿa through its divinely endowed infused morality to discover the universal from the moral analysis of its particularly religious action-guides. Interpretive jurisprudence needs trustworthy partnership with rational inquiry (*al-ijtihād al-ʿaqlī*), including nonreligious comprehension of the divine purposes, if it is ever going to be a relevant source of guidance in interpersonal just relationships built on the twin inherent principles: human moral agency and human dignity, regardless of membership in any faith community.

Notes

Acknowledgments

1. The present study undertakes to synthesize my thought in theology and jurisprudence from the following works authored by me in chronological order to bring the juridical theology and ethics in conversation: *Human Rights and the Conflict of Cultures: Western and Islamic Perspectives on Religious Religion Liberty*, co-authored with D. Little and J. E. Kelsay (Columbia: University of South Carolina Press,1988); *The Just Ruler in Twelver Shi'ism: The Comprehensive Authority of the Jurist in Imamite Jurisprudence* (New York: Oxford University Press, 1988); *Islamic Roots of Democratic Pluralism* (New York: Oxford University Press, 2001); *Islamic Biomedical Ethics: Principles and Application* (New York: Oxford University Press, 2009); *Islam and the Challenge of Human Rights* (New York: Oxford University Press, 2009).
2. Colleagues in the Middle East have often inquired about the main characterization of the project: Is it *fiqh*? Is it *kalām*? Is it Aristotelian ethics in Islamic garb? On confessing that the study is dealing with ethics and its intimate relationship with the Sharīʿa, I have been told, "Actually, Sharīʿa is ethics!" Correct, but how exactly? When pointing out the dearth of moral analysis in the contemporary deduced rulings (*aḥkām*), they have admitted the need for *akhlāq fiqh*. "Ethicization" of jurisprudence, then, has been endorsed as an appropriate appellation for the scholarly endeavor of this study.
3. Richard M. Frank, *Classical Islamic Theology: The Ashʿarites* (New York: Routledge, 2008), p. 38.

Chapter 1

1. Among Western scholars of Islamic law and theology, Kevin Reinhart has raised the intellectual placement of Islamic ethics in Islamic studies. In his several articles he has argued about ethics being part of the Islamic juridical tradition. In "Islamic Law as Islamic Ethics," *Journal of Religious Ethics* 11.2 (1983): 186–203 he clearly states that "Islamic law is the central domain of Islamic ethical thought, both for Islamic studies and for comparative religious ethical studies." According to this view, the jurists were engaged in elaborating religious practice firmly founded upon revelatory sources and juridical methodology that appraised the ontological and epistemological estimation of moral-religious obligations (*taklīf*) as part of the orthopraxy. Contrary to Wael Hallaq's opinion in *A History of Islamic Legal Theories* (Cambridge: Cambridge University Press, 1997), where he maintains that Islamic law owes its development to the legal contents of the Qur'an, their elaboration in the Tradition (*sunna*), and the continuation of some pre-Islamic Arab practice, Reinhart maintains that the

classical age of Islamic law reveals the integration of the two disciplines—jurisprudence and ethics—to formulate the religious practice that impacted the development of different schools of legal rites. However, the formation of legal rites followed a long period of ferment in religious thought and sectarianism. We are still left with an important question: How does one account for the early period of the formation of the community and its adherence to religious-moral practice? Was that period of almost two centuries devoid of ethical reflection? Were there no ethical dilemmas connected with resolving legal issues and defining the true identity of a Muslim or the formulation of correct social and political practice? As this research will demonstrate, there is a need to go beyond the juridical tradition to uncover the continuous role ethics has played in developing the sense of obligation to the Creator and becoming an inseparable part of any deliberation about orthopraxy. Technically, Islam emerged to organize a religious world community that needed both law and ethics.

2. *Mithāq al-madīna* simply means a "contract between [Muḥammad and the Jewish tribes] in Madīna" and has been translated as "constitution" by W. Montgomery Watt in his monumental study of the early history of Muslim community, *Muhammad at Medina* (Oxford: Clarendon Press, 1956). Watt discusses the Constitution of Medina, its sources, objectives, and reliability, in Chapter VII, pp. 221ff.
3. The Qur'an, 91:7–10, speaks about "inspired" (*alhama*) knowledge of good and evil when being created. "Inspired" in the Qur'an suggests "innate" or "inherent" moral knowledge. Among ethicists this "inspired" moral knowledge is identified as "infused" in human nature through the very act of creation (Arabic *FṬR* derives the noun form *fiṭra* = infused [while being] created). Hence, throughout this study "infused" signifies "innately endowed in human nature through creation."
4. See Muḥammad b. Muḥammad al-Ghazālī, *Iḥyā' 'ulūm al-dīn* (Jedda: Dār al-Minhāj li-al-Nashr wa al-Tawzī', 1432/2013), Volume 1, *kitāb al-'ilm*, pp. 221ff. The entire section is a comparison between those scholars whose knowledge about exoteric aspects of religion is the source for their material gains in the world and those scholars whose knowledge of the esoteric dimension is the source for their ultimate salvation in the hereafter. It is a rich commentary on the classification of Islamic knowledge and the authorities (the Prophet, Moses, Jesus, and a number of Sufi teachers) that Ghazālī cites in support of his criticism of the power-hungry worldly jurists.
5. See Wael B. Hallaq, *Authority, Continuity and Change in Islamic Law* (Cambridge: Cambridge University Press, 2001); Muḥammad Taqī al-Ḥakīm, *al-Uṣūl al-'amma li al-fiqh al-muqarin* (Beirut, Dār al-Andalus, 1983).
6. Reference to "modernity" in this study is used to indicate social change and its effect on human experience that questioned the absolute nature of religious truth and sought to develop a new identity that was secular and that encouraged a sense of self, of subjectivity and individuality. This is a fundamental aspect of modernity that distinguishes the modern from the traditional. Islamic "modernity" has not come to grips with the bases of critical change that has occurred in human understanding of the relationship between the natural and the supernatural, changes in the modalities of interaction between individuals and groups. The term "modernity" allows me to move between historical Islam and modern Muslims struggling to understand their

roles in producing the necessities of life and responding to moral dilemmas as global citizens. Modern Muslims have been uprooted from the moral bedrock of their tradition and have been captured by the conservative spirit of their tradition. The search is for stability in orthopraxy that appears to be less relevant today than at any other time.

7. In his paperback edition of *A History of Islamic Legal Theories* (New York: Cambridge University Press, 1999), Wael Hallaq has responded to the criticisms of those who challenged his stance on the centrality of the Qur'an as essentially a legal text. In the context of these criticisms he further elaborated the development of the Islamic legal theories without even casually exploring the ethical sources of moral reflections in the elaboration of the orthopraxy that comprehensively included human-God and human-human relations. The treatment of the Qur'an as the major source of legal precepts and practice necessarily begs the question of the document's soteriological objectives. According to Hallaq, "While it is true that the Qur'an is primarily a book of religious and moral prescriptions, there is no doubt that it encompasses piece[s] of legislation, strictly speaking" (NY: Cambridge University Press, 1997, p. 3). Further, he claims that based on the Prophet's "pragmatic" awareness, the need for legal injunctions overshadowed the moral and spiritual aspects of the "repetitive" Islamic revelation. Accordingly, he asserts that there are some 500 verses that deal with legal matters. I am not sure about the source of this information. Well-established Orientalist scholarship had for a long time upheld the thesis about the political ambitions of the Prophet and downplayed the moral-spiritual facets of the Qur'an. My own studies in the jurisprudence related to the Qur'anic text lead me to assert that Suyūṭī's *al-Itqān fī 'ulūm al-qur'ān* maintained that of the total of 6,236 verses there were some 305 verses dealing with legal matters, of which 104 verses specifically deal with devotional matters; 70 deal with family law; 30 with penal law; 30 with justice, equity, and rules of consultation. Hence, in principle, as maintained by Muslim legal scholars, the Qur'an's essential objective was to lead humanity to explore their naturally endowed sense of right and wrong and to follow the revelatory guidance to attain moral excellence (*taqwā, zakā*) by observing the ethics of human relationships. The overall objective pursued by the revelation is the improvement of the human society in which justice and fairness would serve as critical values. Islamic legal theory could not be rendered religiously legitimate activity without evaluating the "religious" aspects of the Sharī'a and their impact on the moral-legal articulations of the orthopraxy (*al-takālīf al-shar'īya*). If the religious action-guide (*ḥukm*) was ontologically grounded in the divine command ethics, then any *shar'ī* decision had to demonstrate its moral foundation. Without the ethical analysis of God's commandment there was no objective way to ascertain the cognitive validity of the new judicial decision.

8. The translation of *'ilm al-kalām* has been rendered in various ways. I have adopted "philosophical theology" in line with the scope of the subject matter among a number of rationalist theologians among the Mu'tazilites and Shī'ites like Qāḍī 'Abd al-Jabbār al-Asadabādī and Naṣīr al-Dīn al-Ṭusī. For detailed development of this science among Sunni religious thinkers, see Frank, *Classical Islamic Theology*, pp. 7–37.

9. *Al-islām huwa al-ḥall* has remained the slogan adopted by a majority of the traditionalist reformers since the 1970s. These reformers have formed a common front

to challenge the secular reformers who have undermined confidence in Islam as the essential and authentic tool of progress in modern times. However, as Armando Salvatore has demonstrated in *Islam and the Political Discourse of Modernity* (Reading, Berkshire: Ithaca, 1997), the slogan remained an empty political tool rather than a thorough reinvestigation of Islam as a source of scriptural and rational hermeneutics in the context of modernity.

10. In all Muslim countries Muslim jurists have engaged in resolving the ethical quandaries faced by people in their everyday interactions as modernly educated men and women. Hence, a number of issues related to modern banking and medical treatment have engaged the minds of traditional jurists. Since these modern issues cannot be resolved simply on the basis of textual information in the classical juridical heritage, rationally independent investigation has produced a growing number of studies titled *Mustaḥdathāt al-masā'il* (New Issues). The textual or rational approach to problem-solving is present in these publications.
11. See Dimitri Gutas, review of Majid Fakhry, *Ethical Theories in Islam*, *Journal of the American Oriental Society* 117.1 (January–March 1997): 171–175.
12. George F. Hourani, *Islamic Rationalism: The Ethics of ʻAbd al-Jabbār* (Oxford: Clarendon Press, 1971).

Chapter 2

1. *Taqwā* and its verbal noun form, *mutaqqī*, mean "the one who has reverential fear about the consequences of one's behavior." The context of the verse, with reference to the "unseen," suggests the presence of a hidden power that is watchful of human conduct. Hence, the translation that I have adopted (spiritual and moral awareness) in all my studies dealing with ethics in the Qur'an. Fazlur Rahman in his classic study *Major Themes of the Qur'an* (Minneapolis, MN: Bibiliotheca Islamica, Inc.1994) has adopted this translation for *taqwā*.
2. W. Montgomery Watt, *Muhammad at Mecca* (Oxford: Clarendon Press, 1953), pp. 165–169; W. Montgomery Watt, *Bell's Introduction to the Qur'an* (Edinburgh: Edinburgh University Press, 1970).
3. In the following pages I will discuss the development of the concept of *akhlāq* in the meaning of "morality" as well as "ethics." Muslims, whether scholars or not, hardly use the term "ethics" when speaking about the *fatwā* of Muslim jurisprudence. Although recently some Muslim physicians aspire to differentiate between "morality" and "ethics" when reading English articles, even for them Islamic rulings are concerned with the religious law (the Sharīʻa) and not ethics per se.
4. Ibn Manzūr, *Lisān al-ʻArab* (Beirut: Dār al-Ṣādir, 1991), 14:358. The idea of *zakā* is similar to the Greek idea of eudaimonia—a state of having a good indwelling spirit—that engages in self-purification in order to love and surrender to God by increasingly cultivating personal piety by doing the right actions (*ṣāliḥāt*) taught by the revelation.

5. See Abū Ḥāmid Muḥammad b. Muḥammad al-Ghazālī, *Shifā' al-ghalīl fī bayān al-shabah wa al-mukhīl wa masālik al-t'līl*, ed. Hamad al-Kubaysī (Baghdad: Maṭba'at al-Irshād, 1971), p. 160 for the objectives of the divine lawgiver. I have used "orthopraxy" throughout this study in place of the commonly used "legal rite" (*madhhab*). Islam is inherently a religion that prescribes the acts of worship and interpersonal relations in what is popularly known as Sharī'a. Since this study deals with the sources of religious practice (*usūl al-fiqh*) and interpretive jurisprudence (*al-fiqh*), I have chosen the major source of religious identity of Muslims, namely, orthopraxy (*al-aḥkām*), in dealing with Islamic ethics.
6. George Hourani, *Islamic Rationalism: The Ethics of 'Abd al-Jabbār* (Oxford: Clarendon Press, 1971) and a number of important articles on the subject of ethics by him have inspired my work in ethics; in addition, Majid Fakhry, *Ethical Theories in Islam* (Leiden: E. J. Brill, 1994) has served as a corrective study for this book in that I have consciously avoided the approach adopted by Fakhry. In some important ways Richard Frank's approach to ethics and moral reasoning in jurisprudence in his *Classical Islamic Theology: The Ash'arites* is a major contribution in Sunni approach to *kalām*-oriented moral reflection and discussion about classification of human acts in that theology. It is rare to see such thoughtful and meticulous analysis of juridical heritage through ethics in Frank's detailed elaboration of moral obligation in the predominant Sunni-Ash'arite traditionalism and its comparison with Sunni-Mu'tazilite rationalism.
7. See Aḥmad al-Sharbāṣī, *Mawsū'a akhlāq al-qur'ān*, 6 vols. (Beirut: Dār al-Rā'id al-'Arabi, 1987).
8. Ibrāhim b. Mūsā al-Lakhmī al-Gharnāṭī al-Mālikī, al-Shāṭibī, *al-Muwāfiqāt fī uṣūl al-sharī'a*, 4 vols. (Beirut: Dār al-Ma'rifa, 1975), 4:210.
9. In this study I have capitalized "Tradition" in the translation of this technical term *sunna*, which refers to all that is reported having been said, done, and silently confirmed by the Prophet. The translation of *ḥadīth* is rendered either lowercase "tradition" or simply *ḥadīth*-report.
10. Abū Ḥāmid Muḥammad b. Muḥammad al-Ghazāli, *al-Iqtiṣād fī al-I'tiqād*, ed. 'Ādil al-'Awwā (Beirut: Dār al-Amāna, 1969), p. 170.
11. Ibn Manẓūr, *Lisān al-'Arab*, 10:86–87.
12. Ibn Miskawayh, *Tahdhīb al-akhlāq* (Cairo: Maktaba Ṣabīḥ, 1959), p. 21.
13. Ghazālī, *Iḥyā' 'ulūm al-dīn*, 5:189.
14. Ghazālī, *Iḥyā' 'ulūm al-dīn*, 5:190.
15. Ghazālī, *Iḥyā' 'ulūm al-dīn*, 5:190.
16. Abū Ḥāmid Muḥammad b. Muḥammad al-Ghazālī, *Mīzān al-'Amal*, ed. M. S. al-Kurdī (Cairo: Matba'a al-'Arabīya, 1923), pp. 47ff.
17. Ghazālī, *Iḥyā' 'ulūm al-dīn*, 5:190–191.
18. Ghazālī, *Iḥyā' 'ulūm al-dīn*, 5:190.
19. See Abdulaziz Sachedina, *The Islamic Roots of Democratic Pluralism* (New York: Oxford University Press, 2001), Chapter 5, pp. 135ff. undertakes to discuss the Qur'anic genesis story with its specific message of human spiritual and moral education for developing an excellent personality based on the human desire of obtaining sacred power. The act of penitence and purification was preparatory to attain connection with divine powers.

20. Muḥammad b. ʿUmar b. al-Ḥusayn al-Rāzī, *al-Tafsīr al-kabīr* (Cairo: al-Maṭbaʿa al Baḥiyya al-Miṣriyya, 1938), 30:81.
21. Ghazālī, *Mīzān al-ʿamal*, pp. 254–255.
22. Rāzī, *Tafsīr al-Kabīr*, 30:81.
23. In Muḥammad ibn Abī Bakr Ibn al-Qayyim al-Jawzīya, *Madārij al-Sālikīn bayn manāzil 'iyyāka naʿbudu wa iyyāka nastaʿīn*, 3 vols. (Beirut: Dār al-Fikr li-al-Ṭibāʿa wa al-Nashr wa al-Tawzīʿ, 1988), Volume 1 discusses the integration of ethics in religion at several points while introducing his commentary on the specific aspects of faith and practice in the first chapter of the Qur'an, Al-Fātiḥa.
24. I have adopted "action-guide" from David Little and Sumner B. Twiss, *Comparative Religious Ethics: A New Method* (New York: Harper and Row, 1978), pp. 24ff. In their discussion of methodology, they introduce the phrase "action-guide" as a certain kind of moral, religious, or legal evaluation of actions performed by human beings that characteristically express and are often based on notions like intentions, attitudes, motives, practices, and dispositions. The authors also introduce the expression "action-guide institution" to convey that evaluation of action always points to the action's justifiability in practical terms that reflect in some ways "how human beings and groups think, feel, and act" (p. 27). Muslim notions of religiously and morally imposed obligations (*taklīf*), either rationally imposed (*al-ʿaqlī*) or scripturally required (*al-naqlī*), and their performance resemble the conceptual aspects connected with intention, attitude, and disposition necessary for the execution of one's duty. Muslim descriptions of the modality of performing orthopraxy brings me closer to the way "action-guide" is introduced in comparative ethics by Little and Twiss.
25. Frank, *Classical Islamic Theology*, pp. 211ff. cites several Ashʿari theologians, including al-Bāqillanī, Abū Isḥāq al-Isfarā'īnī et al., in his section on moral obligations in theology. Frank has done a great service to the scholarship on theological ethics by providing a nuanced discussion of the "objectivist-rationalist" and "subjectivist-traditionalist" Sunni ethics.
26. Sayyid Muḥammad al-Ṣadr, *Fiqh al-Akhlāq*, ed. al-Shaykh Kāẓim al-ʿIbādī al-Nāṣirī, 2 vols. (Najaf: Hay'at Turāth al-Sayyid al-Shahīd al-Ṣadr, 1438/2017).
27. Muslim philosophical ethics regarded values as objective. These values can be known entirely by the independent reason of wise people. Objective qualities of acts make them right. Muslim philosophers emphasized the inward and practical sides of acts, while drawing upon Aristotelian ethics. See George Hourani, *Reason and Tradition in Islamic Ethics* (Cambridge: Cambridge University Press, 1985) pp. 15ff.
28. Rāzī, *Tafsīr al-Kabīr*, 30:81.
29. The Muʿtazilites and the Ashʿarites expounded their orthopraxy on the basis of religious endorsement of subjective relativism in custom and culture in the derivation of their judicial rulings. See in the next chapter elaboration on this point.
30. See Hourani, *Reason and Tradition in Islamic Ethics*, chapter on Ghazālī.
31. I have adopted the phrase and its referent from Alan Gewirth, "Common Morality and the Community of Rights," in *Prospects for a Common Morality* (Princeton: Princeton University Press, 1993), pp. 30–31, where he defines a "common morality" as a positive concept of morality that consists of a "set of rules or directives for action that are upheld [as] categorically obligatory," in contrast with a normative concept which

"consists in the moral precepts or rules or principles that are valid and thus ought to be upheld as categorically obligatory."

32. Scholars of *uṣūl al-fiqh* do not deal with ethical issues separate from legal ones in the juristic application. In line with their theological positions, the role of human reasoning is estimated in understanding ethical principles, whether they are cognitively placed in the nature with which God creates human beings or are extracted from the commands and prohibitions in the revelation. For various theological opinions as they relate to the legal-ethical deliberations, see Abū Ḥāmid Muḥammad b. Muḥammad al-Ghazālī, *al-Mustaṣfā min ʿilm al-uṣūl* (Damascus: Mu'assasa al-Risāla, 2012), 1:67ff.
33. This is John Rawls's method of narrowing "the range of disagreement" in matters of securing democratic liberty and equality, in order to include "our considered convictions at all levels of generality," on due reflection, or "reflective equilibrium," without regarding any particular level of abstract principle or judgments in particular cases as "foundational." Rawls uses the example of the convictions about the desirability of, for instance, religious toleration and rejection of slavery, achieved through a process of "reflective equilibrium" to "organize the basic ideas and principles implicit in these convictions into a coherent political conception of justice," without giving the foundational voice to either the convictions or principles in determining the ultimate judgment. See his *Political Liberalism* (New York: Columbia University Press, 1993), p. 8.
34. In Muslim philosophical sciences the "unknown" is called *al-maṭlūb*, "that which is sought," and the known is called *muqaddima*, "premise"; in contrast, in the traditional sciences, which includes theology and ethics, the "unknown" is called *farʿ*, "branch" or "derivative," and the known is called *aṣl*, "root" or "paradigmatic precedent." I have used *maṭlūb* in its philosophical as well as lexical sense to indicate the analogical reasoning (*qiyās*) that depends on both the traditional sources as well as human reasoning to uncover new decisions in the area of social ethics. See Harry Austyn Wolfson, *The Philosophy of Kalām* (Cambridge, MA: Harvard University Press, 1976), pp. 6–7.
35. For details, see Hourani, *Islamic Rationalism*, pp. 103–104.
36. Ghazālī, *al-Iqtiṣād fī Iʿtiqād*, p. 214–215.

Chapter 3

1. By "scriptural" I mean not only that which is regarded by Muslims to have been revealed to Muḥammad, the Prophet, by God, but also the pattern of conduct of Muḥammad himself, usually known as the *sunna*. In other words, "scriptural" also denotes the normative in Islam. The Sunna (= the Tradition) in religious sciences is composed of major compilations of the *ḥadīth*-reports, which include the six officially recognized collections of the *ṣaḥīḥ* ("sound" traditions) among Sunni Muslims and the four *kutub* (books) among Shīʿites.
2. Ghazālī, *Mustaṣfā*, 2:470.

3. Sachedina, *The Islamic Roots of Democratic Pluralism*, Chapter 4, pp. 102ff. takes up the impact of skewed interpretation of sacred texts like the Qur'an and the Tradition that has led to intensification of interreligious violence through retaliation and retribution. Undoubtedly, the selective retrieval of these sources has cast Islam and its practitioners in a harsh and inhumane light. In order to meet this negative challenge, jurists need to take up rational analysis of intercommunal ethics based on the Qur'anic principles of peace with justice for all human beings.
4. A number of morally problematic events in the early history of the Muslim community revealed the intricacies of inferring true implications of particular judgments that highlighted moral and factual elements that challenged the religious orientation of early political society and religious leadership. A number of widely reported morally troubling episodes displayed theodicy: If all of the divine acts are just, how can one explain the wrongs committed against godly persons? Does God allow evil to triumph over good? Is the defeat of good and just acts preordained by God?
5. See Sachiko Murata, *Temporary Marriage in Islamic Law* (CreateSpace Independent Publishing Platform, London: 2015) discusses the evolution of the *mut'a* marriage, demonstrating how the legal schools handled the difficulty of this well-known type of contractual marriage for a specific period, requiring the paying of a bridal gift (*ṣidāq*). Obviously, the institution was abused even before Islam sanctioned it under the Prophet. The jurists were rightly suspicious of its moral provenance because there was no limit to the number of the women for which a person could contract a temporary right to conjugal relations for as short as one night or a few hours. The institution was blatantly abused by men at will. The juridical rulings in the postprophetic period prohibited these relationships, declaring them to be illicit and liable to severe penalties that were reserved for fornication.
6. Abdulaziz Sachedina, *Islamic Biomedical Ethics* (New York: Oxford University Press, 2009), Chapter 7 deals with autopsies in the classical juridical corpus and the way these have been used as precedents to resolve the contemporary question of medical research and education.
7. 'Abd al-Salām 'Abd al-Raḥīm al-Sakarī, *Naql wa zirā'a al-a'ḍā' al-ādamiyaa min al-manẓūr al-islāmī: Dirāsa al-muqārana* (Cairo: Dār al-Manār, 1988), p. 118.
8. Muḥammad b. al-Ḥasan al-Ḥurr al-'Āmilī, *Wasā'il al-shī'a ilā taḥṣīl masā'il al-sharī'a* (Beirut: Dār Iḥyā' al-Turāth al-'Arabī, 1391/1971), 2:675, Ḥadīth 1.
9. Muḥammad Mu'min, "al-Tashrīḥ fī al-ta'līm al-ṭibbī," *Fiqh ahl al-bayt* 1.1 (1416/1995): 81–109 undertakes to provide detailed documentation for the prohibition to perform autopsies on the dead and notes the exceptions to this general prohibition under the present technological advancement in medicine and biological sciences.
10. See the proceedings of the conference on biomedical ethics that took place under the auspices of the University of Medical Sciences of Mashhad in March 1990: *Majmū'-e maqālāt seminar-e dīdgāh-ha-ye Islām dar pizishkī*, ed. Sayyid Ḥusayn Fattāḥī Ma'ṣūm (Mashhad: Ferdowsi University Press, 1992), especially the last section (pp. 490ff.). In this section, the rulings of various prominent Shī'ite jurists on autopsy and related questions are recorded. A similar conference was held in Mecca in 1985 in which the Sunni jurists resolved the permissibility of retrieving organs from the deceased

under the guidelines provided by the Islamic Juridical Council. See *Qarārāt Majlis al-Majma' al-Fiqhī al-Islāmī*, eighth session, pp.146–149.

11. Muḥammad Sa'īd Ramaḍān al-Būṭī, *Qaḍāyā fiqhīya mu'āṣira* (Damascus: Maktabat al-Fārābī, 1414/1994), pp. 109–137 discusses issues related to derivation of benefits from human bodies, both while alive and after death. On pages 133ff. he takes up the issues that have arisen about the general right of utilizing the cadaver for forensic medicine and for medical education.
12. Abū Dāwūd Sulaymān b. al-Ash'ath al-Sijistānī al-Azdī, *Sunan* (Beirut: Dār al-Kutub al-'Ilmīya, n.d.), 3:212–213, Ḥadīth 3208.
13. Ghazālī, *al-Iqtiṣād fī al-I'tiqād*, pp. 168–176 provides the traditionalist interpretation of the ethical categories in the context of ethical-legal usage in juridical theology and interpretive jurisprudence.
14. See Muḥammad Riḍa Muẓaffar, *Uṣūl al-fiqh* (Najaf: Dār al-Nu'mān, 1966).
15. Richard Frank, *Philosophy, Theology and Mysticism in Medieval Islam*, ed. Dimitri Gutas (New York: Routledge, 2005), pp. 124–126 cites both the traditionalist and the rationalist theologians of Sunni *kalām* in his section "Reason and Revealed Law."
16. Hourani, *Islamic Rationalism*, Chapter 5 takes up Ghazālī's classification in his *al-Iqtiṣād*.
17. There is an overall dearth of ethical approaches to the morally troubling questions about embryonic inviolability as well as end-of-life decisions for patients suffering from irreversible coma. Various Muslim scholars have ventured to provide Islamic solutions in the context of growing consciousness about the need to meet the demands of ethical pluralism in multicultural societies. However, Islamic juridical analysis that depends on textual sources and their interpretation to provide reliable rulings thus far ignores daunting moral investigations to assess wider implications of medical practice.
18. Aḥmad b. Muḥammad b. Ḥanbal, *al-Musnad* (Cairo: Dār al-Mārif bi-Miṣr, 1957) 3:479.
19. A number of Muslim jurists, from both the Sunni and the Shī'ite orthopraxy, have endorsed the secular court's granting of divorce on the basis of the principle that states the "[p]romotion of public good (*istiṣlāḥ*), and prevention of corruption (*mafsada*)" is to be preferred in solving a marital problem. This is part of Qur'anic ethics. After all, as the supporting argument to endorse this nonreligious divorce goes, the secular courts exercise necessary investigation before deciding to grant a divorce. The author has consulted several such cases on ethical grounds with religious authorities in Iran when a Muslim man could withhold religious divorce simply to make it harder for a divorced woman to remarry. Furthermore, it is important to note that such decisions are made in alignment with *'umūr Ḥisbīya*, matters that fall under "guardianship," allowing the superintendent to take into consideration the best interests of the contesting parties.
20. In this work I will refer to this principle as the principle or the rule of "No harm, no harassment."
21. Ghazālī, *Mustaṣfā*, 1:286–287.

22. Shāṭibī, *al-Muwāfiqāt*, 2:4–5 believes that essentially legislating laws and promulgating religions have the welfare of humanity as their main purpose. Furthermore, he maintains that even when theologians have disputed this doctrine, pointing out, as the Ash`arite theologian Rāzī has done, that God's actions are not informed by any purpose, the same scholars in their discussions on legal theory have conceded to the notion, though in different terms, that divine injunctions are informed by God's purposes for humanity. Shāṭibī clearly indicates that inference of divine injunctions provides evidence about their being founded upon the doctrine of human welfare, to which Rāzī and other Ash'arites are not opposed.
23. Subkī, *al-Ibhāj fī sharḥ al-minhāj* (Beirut: Dār al-kutub al-'ilmīya, 1404/1419), 3:62.
24. Shāṭibī, *al-Muwāfiqāt*, 2:6.
25. Shāṭibī, *al-Muwāfiqāt*, 2 :20–24.
26. Shāṭibī, *al-Muwāfiqāt*, 2:24.
27. For instance, after explaining the good of this and the next world, Shāṭibī opens up a new section and states very clearly that, as for the public good and corruption, if they happen to be outside customary law, it requires further investigation before any ruling can be given. He provides examples of eating a dead body or other contaminated foods under certain circumstances out of necessity and cutting a limb that has been infected by an incurable disease, and so forth, on the basis of disagreement between the good or interest and potential corruption that might occur while adopting one or the other course of action. See *al-Muwāfiqāt*, 2:23–25.
28. Subkī, *al-ibhāj*, 3:178; Muḥammad b. Muḥammad Ibn Amīr Ḥāj, *al-Taqrīr wa al-taḥbīr* (Beirut: Dār al-Fikr, 1996), 3:201, 281 attributes the rejection of *maṣlaḥa* to Hanafites, most of the Shafi'ites, and later Hanbalites. Ibn Taymiyya, *Majmū'a al-rasā'il wa al-masā'il* (Beirut, Dār al-Kutub al-'Ilmīya, 2000) 5:22–23 defines the principle as one by means of which jurists must investigate whether a particular case will cause benefit and that there is nothing in the revelation that would negate it. He also mentions that some jurists have disputed its validity as a source of law, and others have equated it with *al-ra'y*, that is, a sound opinion; still others have regarded it being close to *istiḥsān* (choosing the better of the two or more decisions). Some others have claimed quite the opposite, holding that all legal schools among Sunnites have admitted the principle as a valid source for the derivation of fresh rulings. See, for instance, Muḥammad Sa'īd Ramaḍān al-Būṭī, *Ḍawābit al-maṣlaḥa fī al-sharī'at al-islāmiyya* (Beirut: Mu'assasa al-Risāla, 1410/1990, 1386/1966), pp. 278, 319–325.
29. Subkī, *al-Ibhāj*, 3:178; Ghazālī, *al-Mankhūl*, p. 354; Ibn Amīr Ḥāj, *al-Taqrīr wa al-taḥbīr*, 3:371; Muḥammad Sa'īd Ramaḍān al-Būṭī, *Ḍawābit al-maṣlaḥa fī al-sharī'at al-islāmiyya* (Beirut: Mu'assasa al-Risāla, 1410/1990, 1386/1966), p. 319 regards Mālik as the main propounder of the principle of public good.
30. Ibn Amīr Ḥāj, *al-Taqrīr wa al-taḥbīr*, 3:201. Ghazālī, *al-Mankhul*, p. 354 attributes two views to Shāfi'ī: one in which he regards only that *maṣlaḥa* as admissible where the documentation is derived from one of the well-established principle sources, such as the Qur'an or the Tradition; another in which he says that once admitted, it can be invoked in any relevant case.
31. Muḥammadī, Abū al-Ḥasan, *Mabāni-yi istinbāṭ-ī uqūq-i islāmī* (Teran: Intisārāt-i Dānisgā-i Tirān, 1373/1994), p. 227.

32. Madkūr, *Madkhal al-fiqh al-islāmī* (Cairo: Dār al-Naḥḍa al-'Arabīya, 1960), pp. 97–98; Zanjānī, Māmūd Abū al-Manāqib, *Takhrīj al-furū'' 'alā al-uṣūl* (Beirut :Al-Risāla Foundation, 1398/1977), p. 39.
33. Ibn Taymiyya, *Majmū 'a al-rasā'il*, 5:22–23; see also Subkī, *al-Ibhāj*, 3 :186–187.
34. Subkī, *al-Ibhāj*, 13 :187.
35. Muḥammad b. 'Umar b. al-Ḥusayn al-Rāzī, al-Maḥṣūl fī 'ilm al-uṣūl al-fiqh (Riyadh: Jāmi'at al-, 1400/1979), 6 :224.
36. Haythamī, Nū al-Dīn al-, *Majma' al-zawā'id*, (Beirut, Dār al-Minaj, 1989), 4:329.
37. Ibn Qayyim al-Jawzīya *I'lām al-muwaqq'īn* (Beirut: Da.r al-Kutub al-'Ilmīya, 1979), 3:10–11.
38. *Nahj al-balāgha*, Sermon 17.
39. Madkūr, *Madkhal al-fiqh al-islāmī*, pp. 102.
40. It is important to note that since the establishment of the Shī'ite ideological state in Iran, the question of public good has become an important source of legal thinking and problem-solving, similar to the Sunni states in the premodern as well as modern days. Under the leadership of Ayatollah Khomeini, Shī'ite jurisprudence has once again become research oriented. A number of conferences have been held since the revolution in 1978–1979 to discuss the role of time and place in shaping the rulings through independent reasoning. The proceedings have been published in several volumes under the title *Ijtihad va zamān va makān* (Qum: Nigār, 1374 Sh)

Chapter 4

1. Ghazālī, *al-Mustaṣfā*, 2:478.
2. Ghazālī, *al-Mustaṣfā*, 1:286–287.
3. Shāṭibī, *al-Muwāfiqāt*, 2:4–5 believes that essentially legislating laws and promulgating religions have the welfare of humanity as their main objective. Furthermore, he maintains that even when theologians have disputed this doctrine, pointing out, as the Ash'arite theologian Rāzī has done, that God's actions are not informed by any purpose, the same scholars in their discussions on legal theory have conceded to the notion, although in different terms, that divine injunctions are informed by God's purposes (*maqāṣid*) for humanity. Shāṭibī clearly indicates that deduction of divine injunctions provides evidence about their being founded upon the doctrine of human welfare, to which Rāzī and other Ash'arites are not opposed.
4. Subkī, *al-Ibhāj*, 3:62.
5. Ḥusayn Ṣābirī, "Istiṣlāḥ va pūyāyī-yi fiqh," *Majalla-yi Dānishkada-yi Ilāhiyāt Mashhad*, nos. 49–50 (1379 Sh): 235–286, gives an overview of the principle and its acceptance or rejection among the Sunni and Shī'ite jurists.
6. Shāṭibī, *al-Muwāfiqāt*, 2:6–7.
7. Ghazālī, *al-Iqtiṣād fī al-I'tiqād*, pp. 168 states clearly that God is not under any obligation to provide justifications for divine commandments, whether moral or legal, in the context of juridical theology and interpretive jurisprudence to establish objectively good and evil. In fact, Ghazālī asserts, the rulings are not inferred through reasoning; they are deduced through revelation.

8. Ghazālī, *al-Mustaṣfā*, 2:406 introduces rational proof and the principle of continuity (*istiṣḥāb*), pointing out in clear terms that revelation-based ordinances cannot be attained by intuitive reason (*al-ʿaql*). Common good is also introduced as a "presumed" (*mawhūm*) source for preserving the interests of the people.
9. Sachedina, *Islamic Biomedical Ethics*, pp. 45–73.
10. Ghazālī, *al-Mustaṣfā*, 1:286–287.
11. Ghazālī, *al-Mustaṣfā*, 2:481. However, he clarifies that the deriving of benefits and repelling of harms is only for the people and for their need to obtain their purposes, since God is free from needs or interests.
12. Among contemporary Muslim thinkers who have critically evaluated the problem of compatibility between Islamic juridical tradition and the search for universal moral values that can speak to all humans primarily as humans, one can mention Mohsen Kadivar, who, with his seminarian and university education, has provided one of the most profound analyses of the relativity of Islamic laws in the area of its penal system, and Khalid Abou El-Fadl, who has authored a number of fundamental studies about Sunni juridical tradition and its methodology in the area of Muslim politics and interpretive jurisprudence on numerous modern issues confronting Muslim societies.
13. Ayatollah Muḥammad Riḍā Kanī, *Nuqṭahā-yi āghāz dar Akhlāq-i ʿAmalī* (Qom, Iran: Daftar-i Nashr-i Farhang-i Islāmī, 1381/2003).
14. Abdulaziz Sachedina, *Islam and the Challenge of Human Rights* (New York: Oxford University Press, 2009), pp. 42–43.
15. Various articles in Terence Cuneo, ed., *Religion in the Liberal Polity* (Notre Dame, IN: University of Notre Dame Press, 2004) discuss some of the issues raised in this section. See, in particular, the introduction by Cuneo.
16. See Sachedina, *The Islamic Roots of Democratic Pluralism*.
17. Ghazālī, *al-Mustaṣfā*, 2:406 apparently regards rational proof and the principle of continuity (*istiṣḥāb*) to be based on intuitive reason (*al-ʿaql*). Hence, "common good" is also introduced as a "presumed" (*mawhūm*) source for preserving the interests of the people.
18. ʿAbd al-Fattāḥ ʿAhmad, al-Fāwī, *Al-Akhlāq: Dirāsat falsafīya dīnīya* (Cairo: Maṭbaʿa al-Jablāwī, 1990), p. 14.
19. A number of prominent Muslim modernists were interviewed by *Kayhān-i andīshe* (vol. 44) to seek their response to the question of the compatibility of democracy with the Islamic government in Iran. It is revealing to note that these interviews were published in full without any censorship. However, that has not led to constitutional democratic governance. The struggle to work toward religiously just politics still awaits realization.
20. Human rights violations suffered by thousands of civilians for being identified as Shīʿa, especially in Afghanistan under the Taliban and in Iraq under Saddam, went unnoticed until mass graves were discovered in those countries after the U.S. invasion of Iraq in 2003. The suffering of the Hazara and other Shīʿite tribes simply because they departed from the majoritarian theology remains to be written by conscientious observers of human rights violation. Minorities in general suffer everywhere unless the state institutes policies to protect their human rights. Religious minorities in the Muslim world are no exception to this overall discriminatory theology and inhuman treatment by the rulers.

21. Fahmī Jad'ān's "Al-ṭā'a wa al-ikhtilāf fī ḍaw' ḥuqūq al-insān fī al-islām," in *Ḥuqūq al-insān fī al-fikr al-'arabī*. Ed. Salmā Kaḍrā Jayyūsī(Beirut: Markaz Dirāsat al-Waḥdat al-'Arabīya, 2003), pp. 201–220, makes the case for the revival of the Mu'tazilite rationalist theology to support fundamental freedoms like freedom of religion and conscience. See also Naṣr Ḥāmid Abū Zayd, *Al-ittijāh al-'aqlī fī al-tafsīr: Dirāsa fī qaḍīya al-majāz fī al-qur'ān 'inda al-mu'tazila* (Beirut: Dār al-Tanwīr, 1982), a study of al-Qāḍī 'Abd al-Jabbār al-Mu'tazilī's take on intellectual exegesis of the Qur'an in his magnum opus. *Al-Mughnī*.
22. In a number of articles in the volume on human rights in Arabic thought, some modernist authors have taken up theological ethics and its implication for human rights. See, for instance, Fahmī Jad'ān's "Al-Ṭa'a wa al-ikhtilāf fī ḍaw' ḥuqūq al-insān fī al-islām," in *Ḥuqūq al-insān fī al-fikr al-'arabī*. Ed. Salmā Kaḍrā Jayyūsī (Beirut: Markaz Dirāsat al-Waḥdat al-'Arabīya, 2003), pp. 201–220; Muḥammad 'Ābid al-Jābirī's "Mafāhīm al-ḥuqūq wa al-'adl fī nuṣūṣ al-'arabīya al-islāmīya," in *Ḥuqūq al-insān fī al-fikr al-'arabī*. Ed. Salmā Kaḍrā Jayyūsī (Beirut: Markaz Dirāsat al-Waḥdat al-'Arabīya, 2003), pp. 25–76.
23. See various passages (Q. 8:172, 33:72) that relate the divine covenant and signify the bidimensional aspects of human personhood.
24. Ghazālī, *al-Iqtiṣād fī al-I'tiqād*, pp. 168–170.
25. Kent Greenawalt, *Religious Convictions and Political Choice* (New York: Oxford University Press, 1988), p. 68.
26. See Sachedina, *Islam and the Challenge of Human Rights*, Chapter 3.
27. The tradition that says "God created human being in His image (*taṣwīrihi*)" has been recorded in one of the most authentic compilations of the Sunni traditions, *Ṣaḥīḥ al-Bukhārī*. However, the interpretation has less to do with the theological justifications about human rights and more with the nobility conferred on human beings by God's act of creation.
28. Schacht, *Introduction to Islamic Law* (Oxford: Clarendon Press, 1950), pp. 175–176.
29. The instructions given to the governor are widely reported in all major historical works written by Muslim historians. The important principle of equality in creation is part of the following text (emphasis added):

    Infuse your heart with mercy, love and kindness for your subjects. Be not in [the] face of them a voracious animal, counting them as easy prey, for they are of two kinds: *either they are your brothers in religion or your equals in creation*. Error catches them unaware, deficiencies overcome them, (evil deeds) are committed by them intentionally and by mistake. So grant them your pardon and your forgiveness to the same extent that you hope God will grant you His pardon and forgiveness. For you are above them, and he who appointed you is above you, and God is above him who appointed you.

Chapter 5

1. Ghazālī, *al-Iqtiṣād fī al-I'tiqād*, pp. 214–215.

2. Muḥammad al-Ashmāwī, the Egyptian modernist jurist, has written several critical works on historical Islamic legal tradition and its inability to deal with political and social development.
3. Frank, *Classical Islamic Theology*, pp. 111 cites Ash'ari theologian Abū Isḥāq al-Isfarā'īnī (d. 418/1027), as an author of the common doctrine of the Sunni approach to *kalām*-oriented moral reflection.
4. Marshall G. S. Hodgson, *Venture of Islam: Conscience and History in a World Civilization* (Chicago: University of Chicago Press, 1974), 3:166.
5. Sayyid Quṭb, *Fī ẓilāl al-qur'ān* (Beirut: Dār al-Surūq, 1973), 1:26.
6. Ṭabāṭabā'ī, Sayyid Muḥammad Ḥusayn al-: *al-Mīzān fī tafsīr al-Qur'ān* (Cairo: Dār al-Ma'ārif, 1332/1954), 1:43ff.
7. Edward William Lane, *An Arabic-English Lexicon*, off-print edition (Beirut: Librairie du Liban, 1968), part 6, p. 2416.
8. Rāzī, *al-Tafsīr al-kabīr*, 1:9.
9. Ṭabāṭabā'ī, *al-Mīzān*, 1:43–52.
10. Most of the exegetes of the Qur'an take *al-islām* as the proper noun, meaning the religion that was preached by the Prophet of Islam in the 7th century. However, the contextual aspect of the verse Q. 6:125 evidently introduces *al-islām* as signifying the "act of submission" as the desired spiritual and moral purpose of God's creation. It is in this sense that all humans and all of nature are inclined to be *muslim*, that is, those who have "submitted" to the will of God.
11. This section captures the main line of thinking in the Mu'tazilite-Shī'ite position in Ṭabāṭabā'ī, *al-Mīzān*, 1:302–303, which explains the submission of the entire order of nature to God's will and the gradual submission of humanity and the resulting levels of faith in God's absolute will without compromising human moral agency and freedom of religion.
12. Lane, *Arabic-English Lexicon*, part 7, p. 2554.
13. Ṭabāṭabā'ī, *al-Mīzān*, 26:356.
14. David Little, "Duties of Station vs. Duties of Conscience: Are There Two Moralities?," in *Private and Public Ethics: Tensions Between Conscience and Institutional Responsibility*. Ed. Donald G. Jones, (New York: Edwin Mellen Press, 1978) p. 135.
15. The story of Joseph in the Qur'an introduces the metaphor "the soul that incites to evil" (*al-nafs al-'ammara*), the soul that can correct its shortcomings through self-discipline and through God's mercy and forgiveness. See Q 12:53–54. The reflective function of the soul here is the function of conscience which allows humans to reflect upon their own nature and approve and disapprove its performance in accord with the standard laid down in the "heart"—the mind that sits in judgment.
16. Rāzī, *al-Tafsīr al-kabīr*, 2:19–22.
17. Major works on dialectical theology written by al-Ash'arī and other prominent theologians in this school emphasize God's sovereignty based on God's absolute will without foundation in the essential nature of things, rejecting moral law as an expression of the divine will. See Frank, *Clasical Islamic Theology*, pp. 204ff., where he cites Baqillānī and other traditionalists. For the overview of this theology, see Ghazālī, *al-Iqtiṣād fi al-I'tiqād*, pp. 214–215.

recommended (*irshādī*); required ought to (*mawlawī*), 11
in traditionalist and rationalist ethics, 69–70
orientalist scholarship on ethics, 182
orthodoxy, 10
orthopraxy, 1, 3, 11
blue print for community, to preserve *maqāṣid*, 22
connected with social ethics, 3
deontic, 37
epistemology of, 5
moral obligation to promote good, 85
moral principles part of, 84–87
obligatory in, 67–68
Sharī'a-oriented practice, 52
source of Muslim identity, 10
traditionalist have ignored ethics, 132
overlapping consensus, 47–48, 122–123

paradigmatic authority, obedience to, 4
political culture, translation of, 3
political language, universality of secular, 3
political society, combines public and private, 42
political theology, 7
endorses moral agency, 113
goal of establishing just order, 7
integrative, 120–121
Islamic, 48
prophets, their mission, 16
public good = common good, 11
authoritativeness, of, 53
biomedical issues resolved by, 59
collective or individual welfare, 71
contested principle, 59
defined, 48–49
Ghazālī's definition, 49–50
inductive principle, 50
Rāzī's definition, 48
safeguarding lawgiver's purposes, 55
Shāṭibī's view, 51, 83–85, 91–92

Qur'an:
allows religious pluralism, 119–120
basic impulse of, 137–138
challenge for, 46
choice of spiritual path, 2
concept of justice in, 39
disbelief, treatment of, 13, 144
dual responsibility for justice, 118
endorsement of intuitive reason, 2
idea of justice, 2
ideal society, 113–114
incentive of, 19
inclusive moral language, 107
jāhilīya based on kinship, 39
Meccan sections morally transformative, 39
moral foundation, 2
moral purity requires power of faith, 116
moral worldview, 19
notion of universal guidance, 139–140
Prophet, embodiment of, 35
recognizes objective-universal moral virtues, 40
responsive to infused morality, 93
universal idiom, 2
universalism, spiritual, 47

reason and revelation, correlation, 1
correlation between secular and religious, 48, 51–52, 97, 101
interdependence of spiritual and secular, 48
involved in directing human acts, 170
natural reason, 60
public reason, 98, 176
purpose of revelation, 123, 171
reason, religious, 48, 97ff.
revelatory v/s human reason, 176–179
sources of values and systems, 124
Reinhart, Kevin, 185n1
religion:
advances God-human relations, 40
absolute necessity of secular order, 48
no compulsion in, 110–111
overlap between religion and secular, 41ff.
religion and ethics, 1, 31, 57
ethics leads to practical capacity, 31
religion leads to theoretical propensity, 31
religious message, core of, 100
coexistence and cooperation, 100–101
religious and secular, 16
religious convictions, 103–104
religious governance, 103
religious life, 105–106
religious meaning, relative, 102–103
religious reasons inaccessible to outsiders, 113
religiously generated quest for moral purity, 115–116
research question, 2
revelation, source of guidance, 39, 53, 58
absolute authority of, 5
deontic normative, 5
dependent upon Prophet, 5
founded upon moral-religious idiom, 3
spiritual-moral culture of, 158
"uncreated" doctrine, 149
world-embracing tradition, 45

scriptural authority, 1
scriptural and rational moral values, 7
scriptural, definition of, 191n1
scripture based reasoning, (*al-ijtihād al-shar'ī*), 20

secular:
necessity of, 48
secularity, functional, 111
Semitic culture, 105, 122
Sharīʿa:
abortion, 166–170
apostasy, 117
autopsy, 63–64
cadavers 65
categories of action, 21
changes of laws, 60–61, 64
child custody, 160–161
community-oriented, 13
correlation (*mulāzama*), 45–46
culture, variable in law, 63
custom (*ʿurf*), 63–64, 70
death and dying, 65–66
death penalty, 148
deontic characterization, 21
deontological ethics of, 51
divorce, permissible, 96, 160
endorses "no harm, no harassment," 71, 74
ethics and law in orthopraxy, 71–72
five purposes of, 55–56
flexibility in rulings, 53
functional secularity, in, 5
guarantees sanctity of fetal life, 139
ḥadīth -reports = paradigm cases, 40
human dimensions, 43–44
human-God relations, 43
human reasoning, role of, 31
integral part of ethics, 25
intellectual sources of, 46
intoxicants, prohibition of, 93
IVF, 166–167
jawāz = permissible = good = praiseworthy, 8–9
juristic preference (*istiḥsān*), principle of, 46
justice and equity, 45
language of obligation, 46
maṣlaḥa = public good, 50–51
millet system, 149
moral analysis, 65–66
normative essentialism, 10
normative practice, in, 6
obligation, religious-moral, in, 32
organ retrieval, 66–67
penal system, 56
practice of community, 44
preponderance, principle of, 74
primary ordinances, 57
public good, 123
reason, limitations of, 36–37
religious authority, 31
repository of immutable moral values, 172
revealed law, 30
"ritual duties" (*ʿibādāt*), 5
Shāṭibī's three universal goals, in, 55–6
situational aspects, of, 5
social and cultural change, 20
suicide in, 64
taḥrīm = forbidden = evil = blameworthy, 8
teleological/deontological, 32
temporary marriage, 62
theological justification, 32
Shīʿites, moral empowerment, 37
authority, credible, 53
ongoing revelatory authority of Imams, 53
rationalist-objectivist, 61–62
thesis about moral values, 72

takhalluq = to feign morality, 31
taklīf
al-ʿaqlī = rational; *al-samʿī* (text-based), 51
moral-religious action guide, 51
must be carried out, 115
taqwā = spiritual-moral awareness 25, 38
= reverential fear of God, 138
ontological reference, 138
thesis of the book, x
"tradition" = *sunna*, 4
tradition, the (Sunna):
four compilations of Shīʿite, 6
major compilations, of, 6
require absolute obedience, 157
six compilations of Sunni, 6
source of ethical reflection, 45

ulema = jurist-theologians
favored authoritarianism, 199
function of, 16, 29, 32
juridical authority of, 58–59
universal morality, foundationless, 4
universalism, language of, 4
universalization of religious idiom, 150

values:
ontological status of, 19

wajib = obligatory = command of God, 38

zakā
in the meaning of righteousness 24
personal moral purification, 17–18
tazakkī = purification through morality, 18n2, 25, 37, 134
tazkīya self-regulating morality, 43
tuzakkīhim purify them morally, 183
zakkaytu = perform goodness, 20